A NATIONAL JAUNT

Footster's Guide to Washington, D.C.

. . . .

From the National Mall to the National Nearby

Ken Wilcox

Tired Dogs Press

2016

A National Jaunt

Footster's Guide to Washington, D.C.
From the National Mall to the National Nearby

Ken Wilcox

Tired Dogs Press
© 2016 Ken Wilcox
All rights reserved.

Library of Congress PCN: 2016914265
ISBN: 9780996225908

Designed and published by Tired Dogs Press, Alexandria VA. Photography by the author, except page 55 by Josh Fitzgerald, and pages 61 and 127 by Kris Wilcox. Maps by Creative Force Maps and the author. Printed in Canada on FSC-certified, 10% PCW, chlorine-free paper.

Front cover: Freedom Plaza, Pennsylvania Avenue, Old Post Office and U.S. Capitol

MIX
Paper from responsible sources
FSC® C016245
FSC
www.fsc.org

Comments, kudos and corrections are welcome. Please visit:
www.anationaljaunt.com

• •

Disclaimer

Dedicated to:

The National Park Service staff of the National Capital Region for looking after this fabulous place.

And to Mrs. Michelle Obama, for reminding us to ~m~o~v~e~

CONTENTS

Acknowledgements

I NEED TO EXPRESS a few thank-yous first to the friends, associates and total strangers who provided insight and bits of information necessary to fill in the gaps, correct my errors and help shape this guide into what I hope is a useful resource for footsters. Thanks to my loving wife, Kris, for fixing my imperfections and tolerating endless detours to collect notes and photos when we were supposed to be headed elsewhere.

Big bear hugs to fellow Northwesterner and long-time mountain buddy, Bud Hardwick, for traveling thousands of miles to D.C. to jaunt the Jaunt, manuscript in one hand, red pen a-blazin' in the other. His keen insight and contributions were substantial. Any remaining errors, of course, are entirely Bud's (except any after page 1). Thanks, too, to my office pal and travel-advisor extraordinaire, Lee Emery, for routinely popping by with the latest scoop on a new place to visit, a new experience to be had, outdoors or in, and not to be missed. Appreciation also to Rod Burton for the huge help with cover design.

I also want to acknowledge the good work of the park rangers, interpreters and maintenance staff of the National Park Service, celebrating in 2016 the agency's 100th birthday. It's so easy to take their work for granted, yet D.C. would be in a complete shambles without them. Let's also thank the museum staff and volunteers of the Smithsonian Institution. They do amazing work and are always generous in pointing the way and sharing information.

For all the anonymous conversations that revealed or confirmed a factoid or historical nugget, and for all the fine coffee shops with Wi-Fi and a comfy stool by the window, I'm grateful.

A National Jaunt	Miles	Hours	Kids/ADA*	Page
The Complete Circuit	12.0	6 - 12	✿✿/✿✿	38
Jaunt Section 1	1.3	1 - 1.5	✿✿/✿✿	38
Jaunt Section 2	2.0	1 - 1.5	✿✿/✿✿	46
Jaunt Section 3	1.8	1.5 - 2	✿✿/✿✿	56
Jaunt Section 4	2.0	1.5 - 2	✿✿/✿✿	64
Jaunt Section 5	1.3	1 - 1.5	✿✿/✿✿	72
Jaunt Section 6	1.9	1.5 - 2	✿✿/✿✿	80
Jaunt Section 7	1.7	1 - 1.5	✿✿/✿✿	86
West-Central Loop	4.6	2 - 3	✿✿/✿✿	95
West Loop	4.1	2 - 3	✿✿/✿✿	97
East Loop	2.2	1.5 - 2	✿✿/✿✿	99
East-Central Loop	3.8	2 - 3	✿✿/✿✿	101
Other Jaunts	Miles	Hours	Kids/ADA*	Page
River Loop & T. Roosevelt Island	2.0 - 6.5	1 - 4	✿✿/✿	105
Georgetown Loop	1.6 - 3.8	1 - 2.5	✿/✿	113
Embassy Row	1.3 - 2.7	1 - 2	✿✿/✿✿	118
Dupont Circle to Adams Morgan	2.2	1.5 - 2	✿	123
Rock Creek Hiker-Biker Trail	2.7	1.5 - 2	✿/✿	126
Peirce Mill–Boulder Bridge Loop	4.0 - 6.0	2 - 4	✿✿	127
Rapids–Rolling Meadow Loop	2.2 - 4.2	1.5 - 2.5	✿✿	130
National Zoo to Dupont Circle	3.3 - 4.4	1.5 - 2.5	✿✿	133
Chinatown to Dupont Circle	1.7	1 - 1.5	✿/✿✿	137
Old Downtown–Chinatown Loop	2.0	1 - 2	✿/✿✿	140
Capitol Hill–Eastern Market Loop	2.8	1.5 - 2	✿/✿✿	145
Anacostia Riverwalk	2.7 - 3.5	1.5 - 2.5	✿✿/✿✿	148
Potomac Heritage Trail	3.6 - 9.0	2 - 6	✿✿	152
Four Mile–Bluemont–Lubber Run	3.7 - 5.5	1.5 - 3.5	✿✿/✿	156
New Town/Old Town Loop	2.5	1.5 - 2	✿/✿✿	160
Old Town Lower Loop	1.4	1 - 1.5	✿✿/✿	164
MVT: Memorial Bridge–Old Town	3.3 - 6.7	1.5 - 3.5	✿/✿	169
MVT: Old Town–Dyke Marsh	2.8 - 7.8	1.5 - 4	✿✿/✿✿	172

*Good/very good (✿/✿✿) for kids. Good/very good (✿/✿✿) for wheelchairs and strollers.

RECOMMENDED WALKS

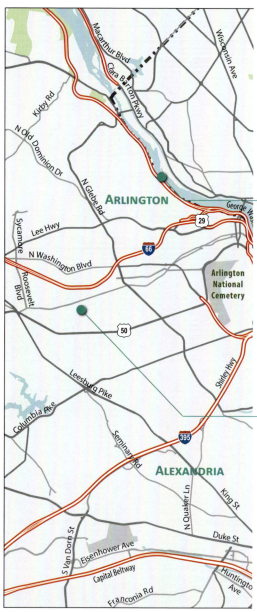

Rapids Bridge-Rolling
Meadow Bridge

Peirce Mill-
Boulder Bridge

Rock Creek
Hiker-Biker Trail

Dupont Circle to
Adams Morgan

National Zoo to
Dupont Circle

Potomac Heritage
Trail

Georgetown Loop

Embassy Row

River Loop & T.
Roosevelt Island

Chinatown to
Dupont Circle

A NATIONAL JAUNT
& 4 Loops

Old Downtown-
Chinatown Loop

Four Mile-Bluemont-
Lubber Run

MVT: Memorial-
Bridge-Old Town

Capitol Hill-
Eastern Market

Anacostia Riverwalk

Old Town Lower Loop

New Town/
Old Town Loop

MVT: Old Town-
Dyke Marsh

ARLINGTON

George Wash

29

66

Arlington
National
Cemetery

50

ALEXANDRIA

395

Macarthur Blvd

Clara Barton Pkwy

Wisconsin Ave

Kirby Rd

N Old Dominion Dr

N Glebe Rd

Sycamore

Lee Hwy

N Washington Blvd

Roosevelt
Blvd

Leesburg Pike

Columbia Ave

Seminary Rd

Shirley Hwy

N Quaker Ln

King St

Duke St

S Van Dorn St

Eisenhower Ave

Capital Beltway

Franconia Rd

Huntington
Ave

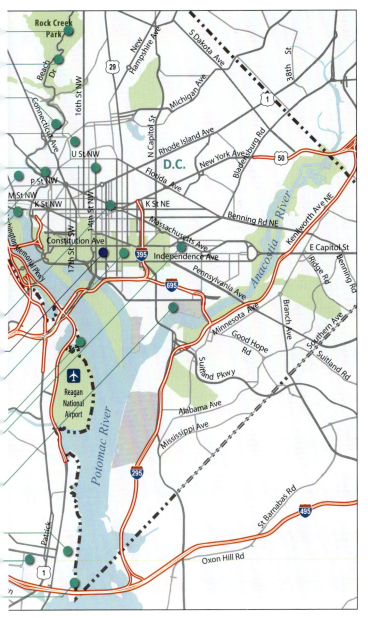

Freedom Plaza, on the first leg of the Jaunt.

Introduction

This guide is for people who go giddy outside. As someone who loves to hike like there's no tomorrow, whether it's backpacking in America's most awesome national parks and wilderness areas, or exploring the civilized streets, greenspace and historic core of some far-flung city, I find there's invariably as much to enjoy in the journey, that is, in the walking, as there is in the destination. The nation's capital is no exception. In fact, when it comes to America's urban outdoors, I can think of no better place for itchy feet than Washington's big outside.

It's no mystery that the nation's capital is a city of stunning architecture, expansive parks, outstanding museums, iconic memorials and monuments, and vignettes of American history seemingly hidden or commemorated under every rock and tree. Somewhat less conspicuous are the countless connections to the people and cultural traditions from around the globe that have contributed immensely to the American story. Thus a stroll around the National Mall,

Street vendor at Eastern Market, Capitol Hill.

from one amazing landmark to the next, is truly a world-class experience.

But the good stuff doesn't stop there. Areas that loosely surround the Mall, like Capitol Hill, Chinatown, Dupont Circle, Embassy Row, Rock Creek Park, Georgetown, the Potomac and Anacostia Rivers and beyond—areas I like to think of as the "National Nearby"—are also rich with sights and surprises that offer easy, fulfilling additions to any footster's itinerary.

Together, the **National Mall** and **National Nearby** form the core of the American capital and a perfect stomping ground for urban treks. Over 90 miles' worth are described and mapped in this guide, including a 12-mile grand circuit centered on downtown D.C. and the National Mall that I've audaciously dubbed as a **"a national jaunt."** Seriously, if we can have a National Zoo, National Cathedral, National Arboretum, National Symphony, National Airport, National Christmas Tree and a Nationals baseball team, why not, in this fantabulous footloose-friendly city, a **National Jaunt**?

While the JAUNT itself is an ambitious 12-mile loop around the National Mall and National Nearby, it's also organized around four shorter loops, or seven bite-sized sections, for those less inclined to knock out a half-marathon of walking in a day. The point is to keep it fun and rewarding, with a mild to energetic workout tossed in for good measure. If a one-day half-marathon (13.1 miles) sounds tantalizing, a couple of extra mini-loops are suggested for those who'd like to give that extra milestone a try. The various options are described and mapped beginning on page 34.

In addition to the JAUNT, this guide

9

Constitution Gardens.

weaves a web of interconnecting walks and hikes from the Mall to the Nearby, including excellent urban treks along the banks of the Potomac and Anacostia Rivers; historic loops through Georgetown, Capitol Hill and Old Town Alexandria just across the water; scenic saunters around Chinatown, Dupont Circle, Embassy Row, Adams Morgan and across Key Bridge into Arlington, Virginia; a few treks on some wilder trails in Rock Creek Park and elsewhere; and several short scurries between Metro stations (the subway). The Metro system, by the way, is almost always the quickest and easiest way to get around the city (*see* **Getting Around D.C.,** *p. 24*).

Given so many choices, the hard part may be deciding where to begin. Well, that's really what this book is about. Browse the tables on p. 5 and 103 to narrow the choices, or begin with the JAUNT on p. 39 and see where it takes you. As explained later, the Navy Memorial on Pennsylvania Avenue—"America's

Main Street"—offers an optimal starting point for the grand circuit.

Residents and new arrivals to the Mid-Atlantic region might want to hike each route over a season or two, just to become better acquainted with the geography of this extraordinary, though in some ways, underappreciated city. Washington, D.C., after all, is about much more than politics and monuments.

First-time visitors, on the other hand, could spend Day 1 aimlessly running around the Mall, arms waving, screaming for joy. Once you catch your breath and ease off on the throttle a little, you can begin to get a better sense of it all, and maybe, by jaunting the JAUNT, see some of what you missed the first time. (*See tips for visitors on p. 22-24.*)

If you love the outdoors and go giddy like I do discovering new places, then I hope this guide helps you engineer a footloose frenzy of your own in D.C.'s eminently jauntable outdoors.

—*Ken Wilcox*

A National Jaunt

Every year, millions of visitors from every state and countless nations across the globe come to experience America's national capital. With so much to see in Washington, D.C., the choices can be both thrilling and daunting, especially to first-time visitors.

Some may be satisfied to catch a glimpse of the five "majors," the points of the compass, so to speak, centered on the Washington Monument: Lincoln Memorial (west), the U.S. Capitol (east), the White House (north) and Jefferson Memorial (south), along with a quick tour of a few museums. Others might spend weeks (or years) intent on seeing it all, including the parks, trails, plazas, waterfront areas and gardens, thereby adding some grassy green to all the red, white and blue.

Whatever your intentions, it helps to have a game plan. The JAUNT is one such plan. This isn't to say that aimless wandering doesn't have its rewards, but so does a little trip planning over a map and a cup of joe. To get you started, overview maps of the JAUNT are provided inside the front and back covers. The more detailed maps and directions begin on p. 38.

The JAUNT weaves a highly walkable course through the best of D.C. You set the pace. Avid hikers who enjoy a challenge may want to dive in and knock it out as one continuous circuit in a day or two. Or you can tackle the seven bite-sized sections or four smaller loops one at a time to better fit your interests or time available. Shorter and longer alternatives are described, as well as shortcuts back to the Mall or to the nearest Metro Station, in the event you need to bail out midway.

The JAUNT passes near ten Metro stations and countless bus stops, including those of the new D.C. Circulator route serving Union Station and the National Mall. So it's easy to begin or resume your adventure at almost any point along the way.

As noted, the JAUNT as one big loop is a dozen miles long. That's about five to six hours of walking at a moderate pace, stopping only for traffic, or eight to ten-plus hours at a more leisurely pace. The four smaller loops cover essentially the same ground and vary in length from about two to four miles each, or one to three hours of walking to complete each loop. (The extra bit of walking needed to close each loop adds 2.7 miles, which bumps the total, if you do them all, to 14.7 miles.)

To combine the walking with more extended sightseeing and carousing about the museums, monuments and the multitude of attractions (and distractions) surrounding the Mall, a good strategy may be to go at it loop-by-loop or section-by-section, stopping to

Jefferson Memorial.

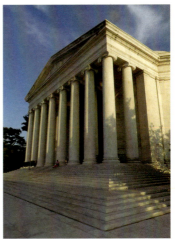

browse, laze or explore when something piques your interest. Again, the options are summarized on p. 34 and 103, and directions are provided for each potential starting point.

If you're not the consummate "outdoorsy" type, not to worry. The terrain is gentle around much of D.C., including the Mall, and the walking is always relaxed, as well as kid and adult-friendly. Nearly all of the routes described are ADA-accessible, with alternates noted so that wheelchair hikers and others can avoid the occasional steps and stairs. Some restrooms and water fountains are noted, except for the obvious ones inside museums and the like. Rest benches and shady spots are widely available for pausing to watch the world go by.

As you explore beautiful Washington, D.C., do carry along a pocketful of common sense. Employ due caution around thunderstorms, busy traffic and those proverbial dark alleys, of course, and safeguard your valuables, as you would in any city. While there is relatively little to worry about crime-wise in the areas described, it never hurts to keep an eye out for the unexpected. A few basic safety tips are provided on p.29.

As noted on the Contents page, use this guide at your own risk! The author accepts no responsibility for wrong turns, stubbed toes, sunburned faces, lost parents, temporary security or construction closures, delayed Metro trains, parking tickets, jaywalkers, goose droppings, ice cream dribbles, acts of Congress or sudden dizziness caused by acute wonderment.

As a nifty new guide, it's possible something important or useful could be missing, so feel free to share any burning thoughts with the author. Corrections and suggestions are always welcome (*see p. 2*).

Walkable D.C.

With the population of D.C. now above 650,000 and surrounding parts of Maryland and Virginia boosting the metro area to more than six million, it's a good thing we all aren't driving cars everywhere. Especially during the commute, when several hundred thousand Virginians and Marylanders head into D.C. for work each day. Amazingly, another 20 million visitors from afar also find their way into D.C. annually.

Counting visitors and residents, the National Mall sees 25 million visits a year. And an astounding 28 million (including repeat customers), walk through the doors of the Smithsonian museums—fortunately, not all at the same time. Thanks to the early work and big ideas of Pierre Charles L'Enfant, the master designer of our spacious U.S. capital, there's plenty of room to roam, both within and around the Mall.

And lucky for us, Washington, D.C.,

Pennsylvania Avenue.

Canine pals out for a morning stroll.

is a highly walkable city. In fact, it's consistently rated as one of the most pedestrian-friendly cities in America. More than a third of D.C. households don't even own a car. It helps that the setting is rather magnificent and the Metro stations are nicely spaced, but wander a bit and you'll soon notice how easy and enjoyable it is to move around the city on two feet. It doesn't matter much whether you amble, ramble, strut, stroll or gavot, D.C. is one of those places where it just feels good to be upright and mobile.

In D.C. proper, you'll generally find comfortably wide sidewalks, pleasant surroundings and a cool city vibe from downtown to uptown to Georgetown, with sufficient wads of greenspace, plazas, sculptures, statues, fountains, historical sites, murals, contemporary urban art (we could use more of that) and stunning architecture scattered throughout. Barrier-free facilities are commonplace and obstructions can be easily avoided in most areas. Or check out the wilder parts of the city

via the extensive trail systems at Rock Creek Park, along the Potomac and Anacostia Rivers, and beyond. Add to that the seasonal foot ferries, or water taxis, leading from D.C. to abundantly walkable Old Town Alexandria just across the Potomac River, or National Harbor located downriver on the Maryland side.

This is not to say that the city planners and sidewalk engineers have achieved mobility perfection and can all retire now, but we can certainly celebrate our metropolitan walkability. We still have our fair share of up-turned bricks on quaint, old sidewalks, trails that need work, and a few too many Walk/Don't Walk signs on timers that defy all logic, but I'm confident the experts will sort it all out in due time.

In a city where the great indoors—the art galleries, Smithsonian museums, the U.S. Capitol, the monuments and the rest—can be downright humbling, there's also a big outside here well worth the rambling. For most of us, the place to begin is on the National Mall.

Potomac Heritage Trail.

Pond at Constitution Gardens.

• •

The National Mall

The National Mall is one of those iconic landscapes that helps define America. It's been called "America's front yard," where we come to honor, celebrate or raise hell about the things we care about. We listen to music and fly our kites here, and pay tribute to our heroes and others who've passed. We mark time and history with our monuments, and enrich ourselves and coming generations with trees, gardens and world-class galleries and museums. But like the city that surrounds it, it's been a work in progress for over two hundred years, and it remains so today.

Once the domain of several Algonquian tribes, native villages were known to exist nearby on the Anacostia River and along both shores of the Potomac River, including a place that would later be known as George Town. Colonists from Europe began moving into the region in the mid-1600s, as the first tobacco plantations were established in the Maryland and Virginia Colonies. With them came a great deal of conflict, not just between natives and settlers, but among the settlers themselves, who also unwittingly delivered the misery of alien diseases to the native population. The tribal clans who survived these calamities were largely forced to seek out safer harbors elsewhere.

When Americans declared their independence from Britain in 1776, Georgetown and Alexandria were already bustling tobacco ports reliant on slave labor. But there was no Washington, D.C. then. In fact, much of the land that would later become the National Mall was river bottom and swamp land leading eastward to a rise of dry ground that one day would be called Capitol Hill.

In 1790, Congress granted President George Washington the task of locating a capital city within a new federal district, up to ten miles square, somewhere on the Potomac River. He naturally chose his familiar stomping grounds around Alexandria, a little north of his family estate at Mount Vernon, Virginia. Yet the site had much going for it. It spanned both sides of the river and included the two port towns and several other waterways near the Potomac River's limit of navigation (and tidal influence). It was also located well inland from Chesapeake Bay and the Atlantic Ocean, which offered relative protection from sea marauders and British invaders.

The district's first cornerstone was

Inscription at Freedom Plaza.

laid in 1791 at the site of the future Jones Point Lighthouse just south of Old Town Alexandria. The boundary was surveyed in the shape of a diamond and marked with a heavy stone at every mile. The district was called Columbia, an early colloquial name for America. The commission assigned to create the new capital decided to name the city itself after the first president.

Washington hired the French-born, New York architect Pierre Charles L'Enfant to lead the design of the city. Thomas Jefferson helped supervise the work, while also seeking to rein in L'Enfant's exuberance for a grand and sprawling capital. According to L'Enfant's plan, "Congress House" would connect to the "President's House" by way of a broad avenue named for Pennsylvania. A standard street grid would be enhanced with diagonal avenues named for other states, crossing at circles and squares that could host parks, plazas and monu-ments to remember our heroes.

L'Enfant also envisioned a 400-foot wide, mile-long boulevard lined with trim gardens extending west from Con-gress House. Someone would later refer to that space as the "Mall."

Only a year into his work, L'Enfant was fired. He'd been too pushy with his big ideas, and though many of them stuck, he'd managed to alienate both the commission and the president. It was a messy breakup and Pierre (or Peter, as he might have called himself) struggled for years just to get paid for his work. Congress eventually relented and gave him a meager stipend to get him out of their hair.

George Washington, meanwhile, re-tired to Mount Vernon, passed the pres-idential baton to John Adams in 1797, then passed away suddenly in December 1799 after a short illness and dubious medical care. The White House was nearly complete and the Adams family

15

moved in the following autumn. The north wing of the Capitol was finished the same year. The south wing, joined to the other by a wood structure, would take another decade to complete.

With the White House and Capitol now occupied and standing like lonely outliers on an oil canvas, the British set them afire in 1814. They were soon rebuilt, however, and in the 1820s, a center section and small dome were added to the Capitol.

In 1835, President Andrew Jackson received word that an English fellow named Smithson, an unmarried scientist, had left his fortune—about $12 million in today's dollars—to the people of the United States. According to the will, the money was to be used for "the increase and diffusion of knowledge." An institution was formed and its members haggled over how to spend the cash.

Other than some limited parks and gardens, little more was done to implement L'Enfant's vision for the Mall until 1848, when the cornerstone was laid for a ginormous monument to George Washington. Ironically, L'Enfant had suggested only a modest pedestal with a sculpture of George on a horse. The obelisk was barely a third finished when funding ran out in 1854.

The Smithson money, however, had found a lasting purpose. By 1855, the Smithsonian Castle was completed, thanks to the magnanimous generosity of the bachelor scientist. The Castle rekindled some of the L'Enfant enthusiasm for grandeur and set the stage for the veritable parade of palatial buildings lining the Mall today, including 11 of the Smithsonian's 19 museums and galleries.

The Capitol was also expanded north and south, and the original dome, which now looked rather puny on such a big building, was replaced by a much larger dome. In December 1863, with much fanfare and in the midst of a Civil War, the 7.5-ton statue of Lady Freedom was hoisted by former slaves to the top of the dome. Just months earlier, President Lincoln had signed the law ending slavery in the capital. Thousands of Union soldiers camped on the Mall before the war ended in 1865.

In 1876, an old cobblestone street named for Pennsylvania was paved in asphalt. The Smithsonian's National Museum (now the Arts and Industries Building) was completed in 1881. Seven years later, the Washington Monument was finally finished.

Also in the 1880s, the Potomac River was dredged for improved navigation and to fill a vast area of mosquito-laden wetlands adjacent to the city, creating more than a square mile of dry land between Washington Monument and the river bank we see today. The Tidal Basin came 20 years later. Up on Capitol Hill, the spectacular Jefferson Building of the Library of Congress opened in 1897.

By 1900, the U.S. had emerged as a major world power, with Washington,

Smithsonian's first Secretary, Joseph Henry.

Inside the Library of Congress.

proposed new Union Station. The Plan also envisioned new parks elsewhere around the city, plus major parkways along Rock Creek and the Virginia side of the Potomac River, reached by a new Memorial Bridge across the river.

Pierre L'Enfant must have sat up in his grave in awe. His grandiose vision for the city had at last garnered some posthumous respect. The details would be substantially modified and the scope broadened, now that the dry land around the Mall had grown considerably, but the late architect's central concepts remained. In 1908, L'Enfant's body was exhumed from a grave in Chillum, Maryland, so he could be reinterred as a national hero at Arlington National Cemetery.

Despite deep disagreements over the enormous cost to implement the Mc-Millan Plan, the construction of Union Station was the first major project to be authorized. It was completed in 1907. The U.S. Department of Agriculture's regal building on Jefferson Dr. followed in 1908, then the Smithsonian Museum of Natural History in 1911. In 1912, 3,000 cherry trees, a gift from Japan, were planted around the Tidal Basin. The Lincoln Memorial, begun in 1914, was finished in 1922.

The new U.S. Supreme Court building, crafted with marble from Spain, Italy, Georgia, Vermont and Alabama, opened in 1935. In 1938, FDR attended the groundbreaking for the Jefferson Memorial. In subsequent years, other monuments, sculptures, museums, galleries and government buildings joined the parade, along with the parkways, Memorial Bridge and the greater city that surrounds them.

Over the past century, much of what we see today has blossomed from the vision of those who kept the L'Enfant and McMillan fires burning. Though we

D.C. at the center of it all. A great city should also look like one, some insisted, rather than the partly glorious, partly ramshackled place that it was. Many residents and members of Congress were eager to see more rapid progress and renewal, especially around the Mall. Modern times and a multitude of ideas warranted a fresh assessment of the possibilities. A Senate Park Commission, sponsored by Michigan Senator James McMillan, was assigned the task in 1901. Commission members spent six weeks in European cities gathering ideas before coalescing around a new vision.

Completed in 1902, the McMillan Plan recommended an expanded Mall with more natural landscaping, sprawling lawns, hundreds of trees, major monuments, reflecting pools, prominent museums and stylish government buildings. It called for the removal of rail lines and tackier commercial structures that had cropped up over the years, and relocation of the train station to a may have differed at times on the finer details and squabbled over what to leave natural and what to put where—the statues, fountains, gardens, the newer museums, monuments and memorials—most of the parts do seem to complement the whole quite swimmingly.

That's not to say there aren't challenges. The landscape and many of the monuments and public facilities within the National Mall were not designed to handle such heavy use by millions of visitors, including very large (and wonderful) outdoor events that have been occurring regularly now for years. To consider ways to preserve what we love about the Mall while accommodating such high use, the National Park Service embarked on a major planning effort in 2006. This work resulted in the *2010 National Mall Plan* (www.nps.gov/nationalmallplan). The plan's purpose is to allow the Mall to:

> ". . . *evolve as the nation's premier civic, symbolic, historic, and commemorative space.... respectfully rehabilitated and refurbished, with improvements to the pedestrian environment.... so that the needs of all visitors can be met in an attractive, high-quality, energy-efficient, and sustainable manner.... while respecting the planned historic character and visions of the L'Enfant and McMillan plans."*

Improvements will be ongoing for many years. Many of the changes will be minor, such as better (and more) restrooms, improved sitting, viewing and exhibit areas, refurbished lawns and gardens, better lighting, separated bike paths and improved surfacing along walkways. But more conspicuous and ambitious changes are also envisioned, including a much smaller reflecting pool below the Capitol Building, with more hard surfacing and restrooms to accommodate larger gatherings without damaging so much turf.

A new indoor/outdoor performance venue is planned near the Washington Monument (where the Sylvan Theater is now), along with a major visitor facility at the east end of Constitution Gardens. A new welcome plaza is planned near the Smithsonian Metro Station, as well as an underground visitor center at the

Potomac River and Jefferson Memorial from Washington Monument.

Vietnam Memorial, new horse stables for the Park Police, and continuing upgrades to the seawall around the Tidal Basin and along the shore of the Potomac River.

Some of these projects are being carried out in partnership with the **Trust for the National Mall**, a nonprofit entity established in 2007 to help raise $350 million needed to implement the plan (www.nationalmall.org). The Trust has been a pivotal force in restoring the Reflecting Pool at Lincoln Memorial and the seawall at Jefferson Memorial, as well as repairing earthquake damage to Washington Monument and installing acres of new and improved turf west of the Capitol.

While much has been accomplished already by the Park Service and the Trust, visitors will soon notice other changes as well, not all of them without controversy. Most of the projects seem reasonable and sensitively designed, although opinions on that may vary.

For example, some observers (including the author) are not particularly enamored with a proposed design for rehabilitating Constitution Gardens. While it's all well intended, plans have included an oversized, odd-looking rectangular structure that would seem to crowd the east end of the pond, altering a part of the area's unique, natural ambience and what is now a sublime view of Washington Monument. The hefty structure would seem to contribute little to surrounding architecture or the American story. On the bright side, today's designers are getting very good at innovative solutions for sensitive sites (we hope).

Apart from the 2010 National Mall Plan, a striking, new African American Museum of History and Culture, adjacent to the American History Museum, opened in the

fall of 2016. A controversial design for a new Dwight D. Eisenhower memorial has stalled that initiative, but it may yet come to be behind the Air and Space Museum. Other memorials are also being contemplated, but they are typically spearheaded by separate entities and not the Park Service. They also tend not to be part of a current, overarching vision for the Mall, which, oddly enough, doesn't actually exist.

Taking another view on the challenges facing the Mall is the **National Mall Coalition** (www.nationalmallcoalition.org), which has pointed out not only the absence of a common vision among multiple interests and jurisdictions, but also the lack of a clear definition of where the Mall's boundaries are. They argue that too much of the planning and site improvements around the Mall and nearby areas along the Potomac River are being done piecemeal by the various agencies and institutions, without a holistic vision of the Mall's future.

To develop that more unified vision, the Coalition believes it's time to establish, in the third century of the National Mall, a new independent commission, akin to that of McMillan in 1902. The idea has gained some traction, but requires an act of Congress to get rolling. In the meantime, the Coalition seeks to

National Museum of African American History and Culture, completed in 2016.

East Potomac Park—an addition to the Mall?

Regardless of our own personal sentiments about what the Mall should or shouldn't be, it's a good thing that so many are even concerned about it. It's an awesome place. Now, more than two centuries since Pierre L'Enfant thunk up the original idea, the National Mall has not only become integral to our mind's image of the nation's capital, it embodies much of the collective spirit of who we are as Americans, and we wouldn't be the same without it.

• •

The National Nearby

With all the jaw-dropping sights and picturesque greenspace that define the National Mall, it might seem a little odd to ask what else there is to see in D.C. But zoom out from the Mall and the walking spaces expand exponentially—from bustling Chinatown, Dupont Circle and Georgetown, to the architectural gems of Embassy Row and Old Downtown, and from the artful quarters of

provide a voice for citizens and advocates for preserving what we love about the Mall and adhering to the L'Enfant and McMillan visions, while also thinking out of the box a little to address evolving needs and concerns.

The Coalition strongly supports, for example, putting a substantial share of parking underground and expanding the Mall outwardly, particularly to the south, to encompass other surrounding greenspaces. A thoughtful expansion of the Mall could, in fact, provide a comparable sense of natural open space, while also including suitable sites for future museums, monuments and public events that don't overly stress the limited space we currently regard as the Mall. For example, the broad L'Enfant Promenade, from the Smithsonian Castle to the Benjamin Baneker Overlook, would seem to offer a perfect extension of the Mall to the developing Southwest Waterfront.

A new commission could nurture consensus for these and other initiatives, large and small. It certainly makes sense to this writer that we at least try to understand in a holistic way what we really have here and how we can sustain it through the generations.

On Embassy Row.

Adams Morgan, U Street, Barracks Row and Eastern Market, to the spacious, green corridors at Rock Creek Park and along the Potomac and Anacostia Rivers.

The National Nearby really knows no bounds, and much good sauntering awaits, none of which requires a car to access. On the Virginia side of the Potomac River, the Metro will take you from downtown D.C. to Arlington in ten minutes and historic Old Town Alexandria in 20, or a scenic water-taxi ride a bit longer. Or you can bike or strut across the river to reach the Mount Vernon Trail for more good walking (and biking), or to explore the native forest and wetlands of Theodore Roosevelt Island. Dozens of outstanding monuments and memorials from Arlington to Alexandria can also be easily reached on foot.

Upriver, the Chesapeake and Ohio (C&O) Canal Towpath leads from Georgetown across Maryland almost to Pennsylvania. Extensive trails follow tributaries of the Anacostia River and other waterways around the city, while the Capital Crescent Trail connects Georgetown to Bethesda and Chevy Chase. Although this guide is mostly focused

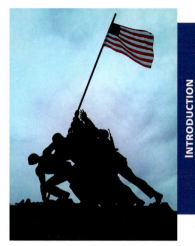
U.S. Marine Corps/Iwo Jima Memorial.

on the urban core and more immediate surroundings, there's a wealth of good hiking trails within an hour or two's drive of D.C. Several great guidebooks by others provide the details.

Newcomers to D.C. looking to see the sights will enjoy the biggest bang for the buck by hiking all or part of the NATIONAL JAUNT. But once you've experienced this introduction to the capital city, other jaunts in the National Nearby will, in many ways, leave you with a more genuine sense of what the city is about. Recent arrivals wanting to get better acquainted with this big, scary metropolis can begin by exploring some of the 18 additional routes described on p. 103 through 174. You'll not only begin to make sense of the geography, you might even have a nice time doing it.

Miller Cabin, Rock Creek Park.

"It is sometimes called the City of Magnificent Distance, but it might with greater propriety be termed the City of Magnificent Intentions."
—Charles Dickens, 1842

How to Use This Guide

The main focus of this guide, of course, is the NATIONAL JAUNT. Detailed directions and maps are provided for each section so you can easily navigate any or all of it. The same goes for all the other jaunts described, which together represent some of the best walking in and around D.C. If you haven't walked a lot of miles lately, be sure of your abilities before you tackle too much at once. Maybe try one of the shorter walks first as a test run.

For each walk, a summary of sights along the way, the distance covered and estimated time required are provided up front. The tables on p. 5 and 103 should help get you started. If desired, you can keep track of your progress by turning to the log on the last few pages of the book and checking off the walks and points of interest as you see them.

If this is your first visit to Washington, D.C., the information here on **Where to Begin**, **Getting Around D.C.**, **Safe Travels**, **Weather and Seasons**, and **Photography Tips** may help you ease into things with minimal fuss. The short section on **Getting Around D.C.** includes tips on biking and using the Metro to get around.

TIPS for first-time visitors—

◆ Pick up a map of D.C., including the National Mall, downtown, Potomac River and some portion of Rock Creek Park. Freebies are easy to come by at information booths, hotels, etc.

◆ Grab a Metro map and SmarTrip card at any Metro station (see p. 26).

◆ Wear comfortable walking shoes. Your feet will thank you later. (Depending on weather and terrain, try sandals, boots or light hikers. If you're prone to blisters, add thin liner socks.)

◆ Bring along sunblock, a sunhat, possibly an umbrella or light poncho if there's a serious threat of rain.

◆ Go light, carry only what you need. If you lug a bag or daypack, you'll need to stop at the security bag check as you enter museums. It's nice to stroll right in. Expect tighter security in government buildings (no food, liquids, large bags, sharp objects, etc.).

◆ Busier times at museums seem to be mid-morning through mid-afternoon (spring and summer), though crowds are highly variable, depending on school and tour groups. Note some museums and galleries are open later than others.

◆ Most major monuments can be visited after dark and many are great at sunset, especially from Lincoln Memorial to Washington Monument.

◆ Major monuments have restrooms, but museums and galleries may have nicer facilities. Metro stations do not have restrooms, except Union Station.

◆ Keep a refillable water bottle at your side on hot summer days. Drinking-water fountains are also widely available around the Mall and elsewhere.

◆ Carry a smartphone, if possible, and perhaps a separate camera, if desired. You can often find an outlet for charging at local eateries and coffee shops while enjoying a break or a meal.

Where to Begin?

The quick answer is turn to p. 39 and start walking! Or you can browse the possibilities and find recommended starting points in the route descriptions for each walk. Jumping-off points are mostly based on easy access to a Metro station or a D.C. Circulator stop. This is true for each loop or section of the JAUNT, as well as all of the other 18 walks in the National Nearby.

The JAUNT is described counterclockwise, starting at the Navy Memorial on Pennsylvania Ave near 7th St NW and next to the Archives Metro Station (*map, p. 36-37*). The Navy Memorial is an ideal central location just off the Mall. From there, you can head up Pennsylvania past the towering Old Post Office and Freedom Plaza on the way to the White House. The Archives Metro Station is also handy for a group or family meet-up. There are good coffee shops and light breakfast spots close by for an a.m. perk-me-up, as needed. To begin the walk elsewhere, browse the descriptions and maps for another convenient starting point and follow the directions from there.

Starting the JAUNT earlier in the morning helps avoid the mid-day heat and crowds in the busy summer season, and promises the best overall lighting conditions for photography. And it offers the chance to do something fun before the museums open. But that's not meant to discourage

• Tag along on a free ranger-led tour for good stories and insight.

• Frequent tours are offered at many public buildings, such as the U.S. Capitol, Library of Congress, U.S. Supreme Court, Washington Monument, Bureau of Engraving and Printing, and at museums and galleries. Free tickets may be required so check the websites or information desks for details.

• Commercial tours are another great option, on foot or by bike, Segway, hop-on/hop-off bus, amphibious "duck" or foot ferry. Promotional brochures are easy to find. Watch for coupons and online deals.

• Pets must be leashed at the Mall and are often more restricted near monuments. Watch for signs or ask a ranger.

• Keep a few dollar bills handy for tipping street musicians. Stop and listen, enjoy the moment.

• Take a lot of breaks.

The National Park Service would like us all to cut back on the use of disposable water bottles in our parks. The volume of discarded plastic bottles, even when dropped in recycle bins, can be overwhelming in popular areas like the National Mall. So think "refillable" and use the water fountains.

later starts either. In fact, in most areas late afternoons and warm nights can be a blast as well. (See also the **Photography Tips** on p. 31.)

To help you keep track of the many sights along each leg of the JAUNT, the last couple of pages of this guide contain a checklist of all points of interest highlighted in the text. Make it your **D.C. Bucket List** if you like—a tally of the places you've visited. There's more to be seen in the capital city than what could possibly be included here, but it's a darn good start nonetheless.

• •

Getting Around D.C.

Once you've landed in D.C., there are any number of ways to get your itchy feet around the metropolis or over to the Mall. If you arrived by air, then busses, shuttles, taxi or rail will take you into the city, depending on the airport. Affordable, express Metrobus service is available to and from the Dulles and Baltimore-Washington airports (routes 5A and B30, respectively; carry a SmarTrip card or $7 exact change). Reagan National Airport is closer in and served by the D.C. Metro (subway). Taxis, ride-hailing and airport shuttles are pricier, but easy to arrange on arrival.

If you came by car, you'll do well to leave it at the hotel or at a regional park-and-ride lot. Unless you know your way around the city, driving in D.C.'s big-city traffic can be a pain in the neck. To avoid the snarls and parking nightmares, think public transit, which in D.C. is quite excellent overall, though we love to complain when things don't go smoothly.

Despite a few quirks, it's hard to beat

• •

TOO MUCH information!

This guide is meant to help you map out the more interesting and scenic routes leading through this world-class landscape. While the routes described connect all the best sites (and sights), I've tried not to regurgitate the boatloads of information widely available in other books, brochures, interpretive displays, websites and the like. That said, a few tidbits are provided to give you a better idea of what you're looking at. The year of completion of a structure or monument is shown in parentheses for most points of interest identified in the text.

Still, it's nice to have the deeper scuttlebutt at your fingertips, so carry along a D.C. travel guide (many excellent choices) or a smartphone or tablet for quick internet access. Several online resources deserve mention here. The Smithsonian maintains an excellent, mobile-friendly website at www.si.edu, and Wi-Fi hotspots are available in many of their facilities, including most of the Smithsonian museums and galleries. The National Art Gallery (www.nga.gov) also has Wi-Fi and an informative app with audio tours.

Another great source of instant info is the National Park Service's app for the National Mall, which includes a rich supply of background information on a great number of monuments, memorials and historic sites around the Mall, as well as maps, directions and schedules for ranger talks and tours. An online search for "NPS mall app" should get you to the download page. See also www.nps.gov/nama.

For more general travel information about Washington, D.C., www.washington.org is a good place to start. You'll find more online sources for walks, hikes, sights to see and just enjoying D.C.'s outdoors on p. 198-199.

the relative convenience of Washington's Metrorail subway system. Fast and frequent trains serve 90+ stations. It's all underground in the downtown area, with subway tracks rising to the surface in the outlying areas. Trains run early and late, and into the wee hours on Friday and Saturday nights. There's no schedule to worry about, since they run so often, especially during rush hours. Just enter a station, swipe your SmarTrip card and hop on the next train going your way. For more about using the system, see **D.C. by Metro** on p. 26.

All the walks in town can be reached by Metrorail, Metrobus or the D.C. Circulator bus, some more readily than others. See specific route descriptions and maps to find the nearest Metro stations. For points between Washington Monument and the U.S. Capitol, stations are conveniently located at National Archives/Navy Memorial, Federal Triangle, Smithsonian and L'Enfant Plaza. West of the Monument (toward Lincoln Memorial) and around the Tidal Basin, stations are not so handy. However, in 2015, the DC Circulator began offering bus service from Union Station to 14 stops around the Mall (www.dccircula-tor.com). You can ride for a buck, with free and discounted transfers if you use your SmarTrip card. Five additional Circulator routes serve other parts of the city. Route maps and schedules are

D.C. Circulator.

available on the bus.

To catch the National Mall Circulator at Union Station, walk out the main entrance past the Freedom Bell and Columbus Fountain to Columbus Circle. Cross here, turn right and follow the circle two short blocks to E St., just beyond Louisiana Ave. A Circulator sign marks the spot. Busses arrive and depart about every ten minutes from 7:00 am (9:00 am weekends) to 8:00 pm (7:00 pm, October-March).

Other options: The Metrobus system is great for downtown, Georgetown and the outlying areas, though they only stop at a few spots near the Mall. Modern busses run frequent schedules citywide and accept either a SmarTrip card or exact change. You can look up wait times for the next bus on your smartphone from any bus stop. Friendly drivers will generally help you find your way. For current status, routes, schedules, fares and how-to information for both Metrobus and Metrorail, visit www.wmata.com.

Hop-on/hop-off tour busses and amphibious "Ducks" offer an excellent means of getting introduced to the city and the sights. Look for their kiosks inside Union Station. Bike rentals are widely available throughout the city (*see* **D.C. by Bike** *on p. 28*). Taxis and ride-hail service are prolific downtown, around the Mall and elsewhere. Rates are controlled by the city and many accept bankcards. Tip-based pedicabs are a fun option for short jaunts around the Mall. Water taxis will shuttle you across the river to/from Georgetown, Old Town Alexandria and National Harbor (*see p. 199*). Segway tours are common and easy to learn for most newbies. Guides are knowledgeable and many also lead bike tours. And, of course, you can always walk, depending on where you've landed.

Where Am I?

Regardless of how you choose to get around, it helps to know a bit about the general layout of the city. As originally conceived by George Washington's hired architect, Pierre L'Enfant, numbered streets run north and south, beginning at the Capitol. Lettered streets run east and west. All are modified by NE, NW, SE or SW, depending on what quadrant of the city you are in. The Capitol Dome is at the center of the grid. Avenues generally run at a diagonal and are named after the states, the most prominent being Pennsylvania Ave linking the Capitol to the White House, more or less. (Free maps of the city are widely available.)

The geography of downtown Washington, D.C. can seem a little mysterious and complicated for first-time visitors and newly arrived transplants, maybe because of all the diagonal avenues, discontinuous streets and traffic circles that seem designed to get you lost. But there's a method to the madness and like any other unfamiliar city, navigation gets easier once you've gotten acquainted with a few main thoroughfares and landmarks. If you stood by the Washington Monument and could remember this much, you'll be doing well: U.S. Capitol: east; Lincoln Memorial: west; downtown: north; Potomac River: south.

D.C. by Metro

Generally speaking, the D.C. Metrorail system is an ideal way to get around the city, as evidenced by the many hundreds of thousands of riders—commuters and tourists alike—using the system every day. In ridership, D.C.'s Metro is second only to New York City's subway. If you're new to the game, it helps to browse the website beforehand to see how things work. There's always an attendant at the station or a friendly bystander who can also help you sort things out, if needed.

Metro routes are identified by color. Direction is defined by the name of the final stop at either end of the route. For example, if you are leaving Union Station headed for Dupont Circle, you'll be on the Red Line and the train will probably say Shady Grove, but might also say Grosvenor-Strathmore, which means it's not going all the way to Shady Grove, but will still make all the other stops, including Dupont Circle. Next-train info is displayed on the platform at each station.

Metro fares depend on where and when you travel. Pick up a SmarTrip card at any Metro station for $2 (cash or credit) and load enough value on the card to get you by for a few days or at least the minimum number of trips you expect to be taking. It's quick and convenient and may save you a few bucks through discounts and transfers. You can also purchase unlimited one-day and seven-day passes. Each person needs a

Chinatown-Gallery Place Metro Station.

card, however (no sharing allowed). Kids aged 4 and under travel free. Note that the old paper farecards were phased out in early 2016.

A few rules to keep in mind: When using the Metro escalators, always stand right/walk left. If you prefer to stand on escalators, stand to the right so others can pass. You'll soon notice across much of D.C. that a great number of people prefer to walk the escalators (up and down), whether for exercise or just hurrying to catch the next train. You'll also find that some are less diplomatic than others in bringing this unwritten rule to your attention. Smithsonian Station, which is mostly used by tourists, is perhaps the most notable exception.

On the platform, stay back from the edge (duh). A fall could be deadly. The "third rail" is high voltage and trains often enter the stations at high speed. Be sure to stand aside so people can exit the train before trying to board. Then board quickly and hang onto your kids and bags. Often the doors will close after just thirty seconds or so. They aren't like elevator doors, so don't try to hold them open (see *If you get separated* below). In case of emergency, look for the intercom button often near the middle doors.

IF YOU GET separated

When a party of grownups gets separated, common sense usually kicks in and everyone finds a way to happily reunite, like old hounds at dinnertime. If kids are involved (or anyone else who might depend on your assistance), then it's worth having a plan in place before a crisis hits. Pick a spot, perhaps a prominent nearby landmark or your next destination, and agree to meet there if anyone gets separated. Sure, everyone might be carrying a cell phone, but what if it breaks, dies, grows legs or loses a signal on the Metro?

It's especially important that kids know how to find lost parents in a big, scary city. In case there's any doubt, it's always okay to call 911 to report a lost parent or child or other emergency. If the circumstances are Metro-related, call the Metro Transit Police at (202) 962-2121. Cell phones often work in Metro stations, but generally lose service in the tunnels. However, Metro began expanding cell service to the tunnels in 2016, an ambitious effort that will take a few years to complete.

On the Metro, there's a pretty simple solution to getting separated. If you got on the train and the door closed before the rest of your party could board (it does happen), just get off the train at the next stop and stay put. Those who were left behind can board the next train from the same position on the platform. When they arrive at the next station a few minutes after you, voila! You'll be right there waiting for them. Beware, though, that if you stepped off toward the back end of an eight-car train and your friends boarded a six-car train, you may need to hustle up the platform to find them.

If a kid gets left behind, the same strategy may work for the older ones, but for younger kids, here's where I would immediately shriek and ask someone in the car to push the emergency intercom button so you can explain the situation to the train conductor. If the train hasn't left, he or she will simply reopen the door. If that's not an option, they'll work with you and other Metro staff to help get you reunited. In any event, be sure the kids (and adults) know what to do in the event of an unplanned separation.

If you find yourself on a crowded platform downtown during rush hours, there's no need to fret about squeezing onto a full train. Chances are a half-empty one will arrive within a couple of minutes. On the other hand, if it's after 7:00 pm or a sports event has just ended, you might want to join the crowd, due to longer wait times at night. If you happen to get on the wrong train or miss your stop, just get off at the next stop, reverse your direction and discombobulate accordingly. Note also that track and equipment upgrades or repairs often occur on weekends, which can cause brief (or longer) delays.

D.C. by Bike

Exploring D.C. by bicycle is an awesome way to see the sights and expand your horizons inside or outside the Beltway. A growing web of dedicated bike paths and bikelanes offer hundreds of miles of good riding, including many paths around the Mall and along the major waterways. For in-city routes, look for the free *D.C. Bicycle Map* at bike shops and visitor info kiosks, or find it online at www.ddot.dc.gov. If you want to cruise for more than a couple of hours, you can rent a quality bike from local bike shops or other rental outfits like www.bikeandrolldc.com and www.

Lovely day for a ride.

bikestoborrow.com, to name a couple.

D.C. seems to become even more bike-friendly every year. You certainly can't miss all the Capital Bikeshare stations around D.C. (www.capital-bikeshare.com). Called bike "docks," there are now more than 350 of them scattered around the metro area where you can easily grab a quick ride when you need it (with a credit card). The clunky-looking, seat-adjustable, red and black bikes have become seriously popular for short-hops around the city. But take note that they are really meant for very short-term use, say, an hour or two at a time, or less (the first 30 minutes of each trip are free with a membership). If you keep a bike much longer than that, be prepared to pay up the nose. But for quick-zipping between museums, landmarks, Metro stations, night spots and the like, Capital Bikeshare is a clear favorite. Helmets, of course, are highly recommended, though you'll need to provide your own.

For longer rides, excellent off-street touring on paved paths can be found on the Mount Vernon Trail (18 miles), Capital Crescent (13 miles), Rock Creek trails (varied lengths), Custis Trail (4 miles and hilly), Washington and Old Dominion (W&OD) Trail (45 miles), Four Mile Run Trail (7 miles), Sligo Creek Trail (10 miles), Anacostia River Trails (15 miles), C&O Canal Tow Path (184 miles, mostly unpaved) and others.

If you can only choose one ride, the family-friendly MOUNT VERNON TRAIL, maintained by the National Park Service, is among the best, with easy access from Georgetown via Key Bridge, Lincoln Memorial via Memorial Bridge, Jefferson Memorial via the I-395 bridge, or from the riverfront in Old Town Alexandria (*see p. 159*). Or you can reach the trail from the Rosslyn, Arlington Cemetery or Crystal City Metro Stations. However, no bikes are allowed on trains during the commuter rush (*Mon-Fri 7:00-10:00 am, 4:00-7:00 pm*). There are some busy, but generally easy, road crossings along most routes, so keep the kids close.

You'll also find good biking at Rock Creek Park. Major sections of Beach Dr. and other connecting roads are closed to cars every weekend, making the park toadly bike and ped-friendly (for details, visit www.nps.gov/rocr). The C&O Canal, Capital Crescent and W&OD trails are other local favorites. This is not meant to be a cycling guide, however, so try a little online sleuthing or a local bike shop to locate area guides, maps and details.

● ●

Safe Travels

While due caution would be advised in any big city, areas described in this guide tend to be among the safest in the District. From spring through fall, you'll find early-morning joggers, commuting footsters and families at sunset cruising around most areas of the Mall. Although the winter chill might keep a lot of folks indoors, it's not unusual to find thousands of people milling about on warm summer nights.

Security might seem higher in areas around the Mall and near the many government buildings downtown and around the Capitol (for obvious reasons), which, along with friendly patrols by officers on horses, bikes and Segways, probably helps keep the petty and not-so-petty offenders at bay. It also helps just having lots of people around. If the Mall is the first stop on your D.C. visit (as it should be if this is your first time here), you aren't likely to get too lonesome out there.

Indeed, a quarter-century ago, Washington, D.C. had an unenviable reputation as a crime-ridden city. But

that's pretty old news now. It's not quite Shangri-la yet, but violent crime rates have fallen considerably since the 1980s and 1990s—well over 400 homicides occurred annually in the early-1990s, falling to around 100 yearly since 2011—even as more than 1,000 new residents flocked to D.C. each month, though this high rate of growth may be slowing. That's much better than some big American cities, and the overall trends still seem to be improving, notwithstanding an upward spike in 2015-2016. Sadly, the most economically depressed parts of the city seem to suffer the most violent crime.

While there is little to fear in the areas covered by this guide, be mindful, of course, that D.C. is a large metro area and crazy things can happen. So trust your instincts, go where the happy people are and avoid wandering into isolated or unpeopled areas, especially at night. Be discreet with your money and your valuables (or leave them in a safe place) and grip (or pocket) your cell phone or tablet on crowded streets and around Metro stations. If anyone does try to mess with you while you're using Metro, the Metro Police welcome your call at (202) 962-2121. Call **911** for emergencies.

For what it's worth, I've yet to be hassled on a train or bus, or for that matter on a sidewalk, trail or in a park, anywhere in D.C. But keeping an eye on your surroundings is good practice just the same. For other tips on enjoying the D.C. area hassle-free, check out the D.C. Metropolitan Police Department's website at www.mpdc.dc.gov.

Perhaps a bigger threat is getting whacked by a vehicle when crossing the street, as in jaywalking against a walk signal. D.C. footsters are notorious for ignoring those pesky, flashing Don't-Walk signs. Way too many of us dash through traffic with a smartphone stuck to one ear, oblivious to the guy in the sports car who just stomped on it from the alley so he could squeeze in ahead of that bus over there. Doggonit, he just didn't see you in time....

The traffic police seem to rarely enforce the rules around jaywalking (though they can ticket you in a nano-second if you mis-park your car). I'm not so straight and narrow to suggest that everyone must abide by the almighty traffic light at all hours, but it's a very poor habit to routinely ignore the signals, especially with traffic present, not to mention setting a bad example for the wee ones. It only takes one tee-ny-tiny misstep to ruin a lovely day, or worse, and I don't like those odds. Serial jaywalkers don't stop to realize we're each allowed only one serious mistake. So keep your precious body off the one-in-a-thousand probability curve and wait for the light.

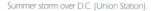

Weather & Seasons

So what about the weather? When can I jaunt the JAUNT?

Barring blizzards and hurricanes, enjoyable jaunting around D.C. can be had pretty much anytime of the year. Spring and fall are awesome under blue skies and colorful foliage. There might be a nip in the air early or late, so dress accordingly. The heights of summer and winter can be poaching hot or crispy cold, but there's nearly always some-where cool or cozy to duck into.

In spring, D.C.'s famed cherry blos-soms normally peak for about a week in late March or early April, depending a lot on how long and cold the winter was. The blossoms mark the end of the cold season about as reliably as any self-ef-facing groundhog. The National Park

Service maintains a website (www.nps.gov/cherry) in early spring that predicts when peak flowering will likely occur. When it does, sizable crowds begin to fill up the cherry tree-lined walkways around the Tidal Basin each morning before sunrise, ballooning to tens of thousands by lunchtime if the weather's good. So grab your camera and be there at first light—you won't regret it. Or stick around for the late-afternoon and pre-sunset show when the crowds are a little less daunting and lighting can still be perfect for photos.

Late for the cherry blossoms? Not to worry. By the time the delicate petals have blown away in a breeze, everything else is on the verge of blooming, as an explosion of green begins to envelop the city.

In summer, most mornings are reasonably comfy, but start early to avoid the mid-day heat. Sudden thunderstorms are both common and exciting—and potentially dangerous if you get caught in the middle of one. Duck indoors to be safe. Carry an um-brella (often sold on the street) if storms are in the near-term forecast. Warm nights around sunset and later are a joy for Mall wandering, as our national landscape is artistically transformed by

Summer storm over D.C. (Union Station).

Sunset over the Tidal Basin.

the soft illumination of trees, walkways, pools, old buildings and monuments. At night, the views of Washington Monument and the Capitol from Lincoln Memorial and the WWII Memorial are stunning.

Fall can be especially gorgeous, with generally milder temperatures, bluer skies due to less humidity, fall foliage and waning crowds. But keep an eye on frequently changing weather forecasts and wide temperature swings from one day to the next.

As for winter, the crowds are gone, but snow and ice and occasional frigid temperatures can present some obvious challenges to footsters. Pick a dry, ice-free day, wear suitable shoes and your favorite warm and fuzzy accoutrements and enjoy. Then seek out a lonely museum, gallery or coffee shop for a warm-up.

Photography Tips

Washington, D.C. is quite a photogenic place. Photographers will find a tremendous amount of subject material all along the JAUNT and most other routes described in this guide. Some of the more unusual or interesting photo ops are highlighted in the text. You don't need to be an expert to go home with a proud portfolio of images. For outdoor photography, the job gets a little easier when you're surrounded by such a diversity of urban art, architecture and expansive land and waterscapes, which are almost everywhere you look across much of D.C.

Unless you're an expert already, notice when (or before) the lighting looks good and head out with a camera that can focus and think for itself, which means about all that's left for you is the composition.

Photo Tips:

- Early morning, late afternoon or around sunset generally offer the best lighting.

- Cloudy days help diffuse the light and tame the contrasts.

- Don't forget to look over your shoulder. Sometimes the best perspectives and lighting are behind you.

- Take lots of shots. Delete the duds later.

- Look for odd angles, perspective, juxtapositions, unusual encounters.

- Experiment with the automatic and manual settings.

- Carry a charger or extra battery.

- Power down and enjoy the view.

Experiment with perspective (Supreme Court).

When to shoot

To jumpstart your quest for great images, below are some of the more iconic buildings and monuments and desirable times to be there:

- Lincoln Memorial (east-facing), morning or after dark

- Martin Luther King, Jr. Memorial (southeast-facing), morning, midday or after dark

- FDR Memorial (north, west and east-facing), midday or later

- Jefferson Memorial (north-facing), early morning or mid-afternoon to sunset

- Washington Monument (everywhere-facing), anytime

- U.S. Capitol (east and west-facing), morning or mid-afternoon to sunset

- Supreme Court (west-facing), mid-afternoon to sunset

- Library of Congress (west facing), late morning to sunset

- White House (north and south-facing), mid-morning to sunset

- Smithsonian Castle (north and south-facing), mid-morning to sunset

- Smithsonian Arts and Industries (north, south and west-facing), mid-morning to sunset

- National Archives (north and south-facing), morning or mid-afternoon to sunset

- Old Post Office (north and west-facing), morning or mid-afternoon to sunset

- Union Station (south-facing), mid-morning to sunset

- National Cathedral (west and north-facing), mid-morning to sunset

- Basilica of the National Shrine of the Immaculate Conception (south, east and west-facing), morning to sunset

Okay, enough with the introduction to D.C. On with the JAUNT:

How Long Will It Take?

It depends. Strong, fast hikers can knock out the JAUNT in a few hours. Others may spend several days taking it all in. If the full, 12-mile circuit sounds too arduous, consider doing it in four servings, as in four shorter loops, or mini-jaunts, that cover all the same ground in more manageable chunks (*see map, p. 94*). Or, walk the full circuit section-by-section, spending an hour or two exploring each. Call it a jauntlet.

The route descriptions and maps also include a number of shortcuts and alternate routes that are still scenic and interesting, but which allow you to reduce or extend the walking. Obviously, you can vary your route considerably, so the purpose here is to suggest more interesting connections in case you need to bail out of your walk in a sudden thunderstorm or dash over to the Capitol building because the lighting for photos just got really good.

Distances and estimated walking times are provided for the entire JAUNT, each section, and the four suggested loops. Faster times assume a brisk 2.5 to 3 MPH pace with minimal stops or traffic delays. Slower times are for more leisurely walking (1.5 MPH), with occasional stops to read the plaques, soak up the views and snap a few photos. The more serious photographer or history buff should allow more time than indicated to absorb it all.

By the way, 0.1 mile is 528 feet, or about 200-250 paces for most adults. At 1.5 MPH, each 0.1 mile traveled requires about four minutes to walk (or a mile in 40 minutes). At 3 MPH, assume two minutes to walk 0.1 mile (or a mile in 20 minutes). Then add some for stops.

Deciphering Directions

The directions for each walk are written as sequentially as possible with references to street names and landmarks at every turn. If you drift off-route, the maps should help you get back on track. Running distances are in bold type, followed in italics by the distance traveled within a specific section. The U.S. Navy Memorial, our official starting point, is MILE **0.0**. If you're new to the D.C. area, you might find that it helps to check the maps and reread short sections as you walk them. Look back over your shoulder now and then, not only to confirm your route, but to catch a view you might have otherwise missed.

Is the JAUNT ADA-accessible?

Yes! Stairs may be encountered, but alternative routes without obstacles are described so anyone in a wheelchair or electric scooter (and strollers too) can enjoy the entire JAUNT. There are a few minor hills, especially near the U.S. Capitol (on Capitol Hill), but grades are gentle and rest benches are abundant throughout. Construction, special events, presidential motorcades, UFO landings or other temporary closures can blow these route suggestions out of the water. However, there's always a way around and most D.C.-ers are happy to help with directions.

Sights to See

In addition to the dozens of monuments, memorials and museums located on or near the National Mall, you can expect to encounter countless other sites of historic or cultural importance while you're jaunting the JAUNT. Below is a summary of sites and sights you'll see along the seven sections. (Each of the four loops includes a similar list, beginning on p. 95.)

SECTION 1:
U.S. Navy Memorial to the White House

Points of interest:

U.S. Navy Memorial, Naval Heritage Center, National Archives, FBI, Old Post Office, Federal Triangle, Environmental Protection Agency, Woodrow Wilson Plaza, Freedom Plaza, General Pulaski Monument, Pershing Park and General Pershing statue, Bald Eagle Memorial, White House Visitor Center, William Tecumseh Sherman Monument, U.S. Treasury, Alexander Hamilton statue, The Extra Mile, Marquis de Lafayette statue, Lafayette Square, White House–North Portico

SECTION 2: The White House to Lincoln Memorial

Points of interest:

White House–North Portico, Lafayette Square, President Andrew Jackson Memorial, St. John's Episcopal Church, General Von Steuben statue, Decatur House, General Jean de Rochambeau statue, Blair House, Renwick Gallery, Eisenhower Executive Office Building, Corcoran School of the Arts, First Division Monument, President's Park, White House–South Lawn, National Christmas Tree, Zero Milestone, The Ellipse, Ellipse Visitor Pavilion, Boy Scout Memorial, Enid Haupt Fountains, German-American Friendship Garden, Second Division Memorial, Lockkeeper's House, Organization of American States, Daughters of the American Revolution, American Red Cross, Amerigo Vespucci sculpture, Art Museum of the Americas, Simón Bolívar Monument, José Artigas statue, Constitution Gardens, Memorial to the Signers of the Declaration of Independence, Vietnam Veterans Memorial, Lincoln Memorial and Reflecting Pool

SECTION 3: Lincoln Memorial to Jefferson Memorial

Points of interest:

Lincoln Memorial and Reflecting Pool, Vietnam and Korean War Veterans Memorials, John Ericsson Memorial, West Potomac Park, U.S. Park Police Horse Stables, Ash Woods, District of Columbia War Memorial, Martin Luther King, Jr. Memorial, Tidal Basin, Franklin Delano Roosevelt Memorial, George Mason Memorial, Jefferson Memorial

SECTION 4: Jefferson Memorial to the Smithsonian Castle

Points of interest:
Jefferson Memorial, Tidal Basin, Bureau of Engraving and

Printing, U.S. Holocaust Museum, Floral Library, Survey Lodge, John Paul Jones Memorial, WWII Memorial, Sylvan Theater, Washington Monument, Museum of African American History and Culture, U.S. Department of Agriculture, Freer Gallery of Art, S. Dillon Ripley Center, Arthur M. Sackler Gallery, Enid A. Haupt Garden, Smithsonian Castle

SECTION 5: The Smithsonian Castle to the U.S. Capitol

Points of interest:
Smithsonian Castle, Enid A. Haupt Garden, Smith-

sonian Arts and Industries Building, Voyage Model Solar System, Smithsonian Carousel, Mary Livingston Ripley Garden, Hirshhorn Museum and Sculpture Garden, National Air and Space Museum, Phoebe Waterman Haas Public Observatory, National Museum of the American Indian, Capitol Reflecting Pool, Mid-Atlantic Regional Garden, U.S. Botanic Garden and Conservatory, Bartholdi Park and Fountain, James Garfield Memorial, Ulysses S. Grant Memorial, Peace Monument, Summerhouse, U.S. Capitol—West Lawn/West Steps

SECTION 6: The U.S. Capitol to Union Station

Points of interest:
U.S. Capitol (West Lawn/West Steps, East Plaza and Capitol

Visitor Center), U.S. Supreme Court, Court of Neptune Fountain, Library of Congress, Folger Shakespeare Theatre and Library, Sewall-Belmont House and Museum, VFW, Capitol Hill Neighborhood, Stanton Park, General Nathanael Greene statue, Federal Judicial Center, Christopher Columbus Fountain, Union Station

SECTION 7: Union Station to the U.S. Navy Memorial

Points of interest:
Union Station, Postal Museum, National Guard Memo-

rial Museum, Holodomor Memorial, Freedom Bell, Christopher Columbus Fountain, Senate Park and Fountain, Japanese-American Memorial, Robert A. Taft Memorial and Carillon, U.S. Department of Labor, John Marshall Park, Canadian Embassy, Newseum, Andrew Mellon Memorial Fountain, Federal Trade Commission, National Gallery of Art, National Sculpture Garden and Ice Rink, Smithsonian Museum of Natural History, National Archives, Grand Army of the Republic Memorial, Temperance Fountain, General Winfield Scott Hancock statue

A NATIONAL JAUNT & FOUR LOOPS

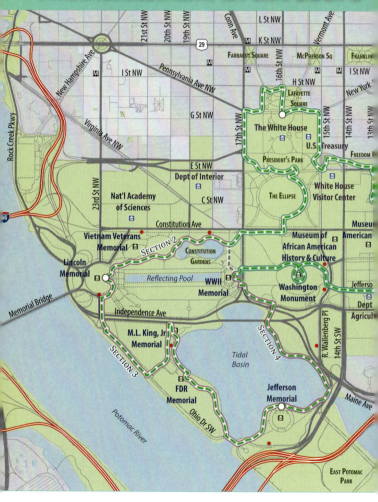

- – – – – – **NATIONAL JAUNT CIRCUIT**
- - - - - - **LOOP CONNECTOR**
- Ⓜ Metro Station
- ● DC Circulator Stop

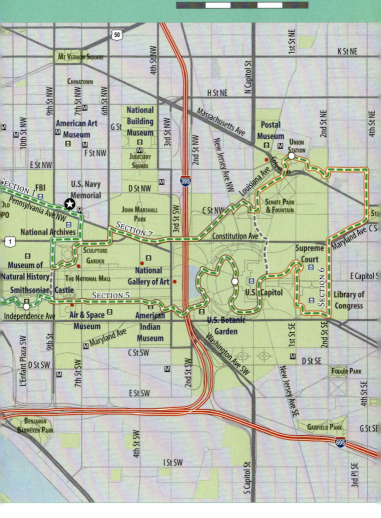

0   0.1   0.2   0.3   0.4   0.5 mile

50

Mt Vernon Square

Chinatown

National Building Museum

Massachusetts Ave

Postal Museum

Union Station

American Art Museum

G St

Judiciary Square

F St NW

9th St NW
7th St NW
6th St NW
10th St NW

4th St NW

3rd St NW

2nd St NW

N Capitol St

1st St NE

K St NE

2nd St NE

4th St NE

H St NE

New Jersey Ave NW

E St NW

SECTION 1

FBI

U.S. Navy Memorial

D St NW

C St NW

Louisiana Ave

Senate Park & Fountain

Pennsylvania Ave NW

OLD PO

John Marshall Park

SECTION 7

National Archives

Constitution Ave

Maryland Ave, C S

Supreme Court

SECTION 6

Library of Congress

1

Sculpture Garden

National Gallery of Art

The National Mall

Museum of Natural History

Smithsonian Castle

SECTION 5

U.S. Capitol

E Capitol S

Independence Ave

Air & Space Museum

American Indian Museum

Maryland Ave

U.S. Botanic Garden

3rd St SW

2nd St SW

1st St SE

2nd St SE

D St SE

Folger Park

Washington Ave SW

9th St SW
7th St SW

L'Enfant Plaza SW

D St SW

C St SW

E St SW

New Jersey Ave SE

4th St SE

Benjamin Banneker Park

4th St SW

I St SW

S Capitol St

Garfield Park

G St SE

695

3rd Pl SE

WEST LOOP
WEST-CENTRAL LOOP
EAST LOOP
EAST-CENTRAL LOOP

1 | THE COMPLETE CIRCUIT: SECTION 1
U.S. Navy Memorial (MILE 0.0) to the White House (MILE 1.3)

▶ *Distance:* 1.3 miles (allow 1 to 1.5 hours)

▶ *Start:* U.S. Navy Memorial, near Pennsylvania Ave and 7th St NW

▶ *Nearest Metro:* Archives–Navy Memorial–Penn Quarter (*next door*)

Points of Interest: **U.S. Navy Memorial • Naval Heritage Center • National Archives • FBI • Old Post Office • Federal Triangle • Environmental Protection Agency • Woodrow Wilson Plaza • Freedom Plaza • General Pulaski Monument • Pershing Park & General Pershing statue • Bald Eagle Memorial • White House Visitor Center • William Tecumseh Sherman Monument • U.S. Treasury • Alexander Hamilton statue • The Extra Mile • Marquis de Lafayette statue • Lafayette Square • White House–North Portico**

START/FINISH AT
U.S. NAVY MEMORIAL

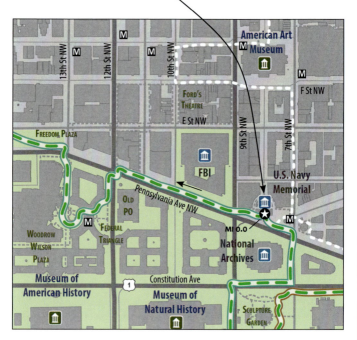

The Lone Sailor, U.S. Navy Memorial.

Navy Memorial

Spend a few minutes taking stock of the fountains, the intricate bronze bas-reliefs (like miniature sculptures, over two dozen of them), the **Lone Sailor** and other maritime features. Every spring during the **Blessing of the Fleet,** a bit of water from the world's seven seas and the Great Lakes is dribbled into the pools of the Navy Memorial. Military bands often perform here in the evening during the warmer months (free).

If you have a Navy vet in the family, maybe peek inside the **Naval Heritage Center** in the big curvy building to the right (9:30-5:00 daily). Browse exhibits and search for, or leave, information about veterans you may know.

Let the JAUNT begin!

. . . .

The **U.S. Navy Memorial**, dedicated in 1987, is a perfect place to kick off a Washington, D.C. walkabout. The memorial is next to the **Archives–Navy Memorial–Penn Quarter Metro Station**, centrally located at 7th St NW and Pennsylvania Ave, and between the museums on the National Mall and downtown Washington. If you're walking over from the Mall, 7th St is about midway between the U.S. Capitol and the Washington Monument.

The easy ramble from here to the White House is 1.3 miles, which for most mortals requires about an hour of leisurely walking. Among the highlights are great plazas, squares, lesser known monuments and outstanding architecture.

Look for the giant map of the globe sprawled across the circular plaza of the Navy Memorial near the top of the Metro escalators. Technically, it's a map of the world's oceans called **The Granite Sea**. Interestingly, the memorial is exactly where Pierre L'Enfant, the 1790s architect of the city, thought it should be—a tangible example of his extraordinary legacy.

Before departing the plaza [MILE 0.0/0.0], look south across Pennsylvania Ave to the **National Archives** (1935). Inside this striking edifice you can view the original *Declaration of Independence* and *U.S. Constitution*, among countless other historic documents (*open 10:00-5:30*). It's well worth a visit before or after your jaunt. Enter from Constitution Ave on the opposite side of the building.

Put a big toe on the map of the globe somewhere near your home, snap a selfie and start walking. Head west toward 9th St NW (away from the escalators) along the wide, treed sidewalk of Pennsylvania Ave.

Cross 9th St NW to a veritable forest of street trees and pass the **FBI's J. Edgar Hoover Building** (1974) on your right. The building, one of the largest in D.C., has been controversial since it was built, mainly for its mundane architecture. Plans are in the works to redevelop the site with something more lavish and move the FBI closer to the Capital Beltway. For now, try to look innocent and keep marching.

Across Pennsylvania Ave is the more stylish **U.S. Department of Justice** building (1935), named for Robert F. Kennedy in 2001. On the next block (left) is the headquarters of the **Internal Revenue Service** (1936), also controversial, but not for its architecture. You might keep a hand on your wallet as you walk by.

After crossing 10th St NW [MILE 0.3/0.3], crane your neck up and left to admire the century-old clock tower of the **Old Post Office** building (1899), a historic marvel of Romanesque architecture that in 2016 was converted to a luxury, albeit controversial, hotel. By

An unusual collection of historic American flags flutter above the sidewalk at the FBI building.

America's Main Street

Also known as **America's Main Street, Pennsylvania Avenue** is a designated National Historic Site. It's been at the center of countless national events for over 200 years, from major parades and festivals to large demonstration marches and the grand presidential procession on Inauguration Day, when hundreds of thousands of onlookers line the street. Even since the good old days when Pennsylvania Ave was lined with sketchy bars, brothels and makeshift housing, it's remained a major artery in the heart of downtown Washington.

You can ignore the hotel and still admire the Old Post Office building. In fact, an elevator ride to the observation deck above the giant clock ought to be on your D.C. bucket list.

Ben Franklin statue near 12th St.

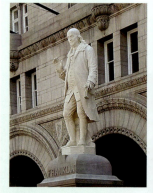

Old Post Office, west side.

Federal Triangle

The **Federal Triangle** is a cluster of federal office buildings built in the 1930s and contained within the triangle of 15th St NW and Pennsylvania and Constitution Avenues. The Old Post Office was included within the redevelopment footprint and was supposed to be demolished way back when to accommodate the architectural symmetry of a Great Circle between the buildings. But citizens loved the Old Post Office and demanded that it be saved. Thankfully, it was.

The upshot? There's only three-quarters of a circle of building facades here, which makes the Old Post Office something like a square peg in a round hole inside a triangle, and all within the big diamond known as D.C.

Curving walkway, Federal Triangle.

agreement with the developer, the historic character will be preserved, as will future public access to one of D.C.'s more prominent national landmarks (*see* www.nps.gov/opot).

At 315 feet high, the Old Post Office is the third tallest building in D.C., after the Washington Monument (555 feet) and the Basilica of the National Shrine of Immaculate Conception (328 feet). The National Cathedral is just a shade lower at 301 feet. All are spectacular and worth visiting (*see p. 192 for more about the basilica and cathedral*).

Cross Pennsylvania Ave at 11th St NW and look straight ahead for a small sign describing some of the history of the area. Continue along Pennsylvania Ave to a marble statue of **Benjamin Franklin** (1889; relocated here in 1982). Cross 12th St NW, then turn immediately left and briefly head south along 12th St to the arched corridor just ahead. Enter and follow the tunnel-like curving walkway to the right for some interesting photo ops. This building was originally designed to replace the Old Post Office, but is now the headquarters of the **Environmental Protection Agency**. Note the view back at the Old Post Office and surrounding **Federal Triangle**. Another sign nearby offers nuggets of history that complement the earlier sign.

Amid this near circle of buildings, continue along the curved wall to the **Federal Triangle Metro** escalators. The JAUNT heads right past the escalators. (Incidentally, if you continued down 12th St to the next traffic light, you would find the Museums of Natural History on the left and American History on the right.)

At the Metro escalators, the one-quarter circle mark of the curved facade, turn right through more archways and into the great circular space of **Woodrow Wilson Plaza**, a fine place to lunch or linger. Free noontime concerts are common here on weekdays in summer (nice acoustics). Straight across the plaza from the escalators is an entrance to the **Ronald Reagan Building and International Trade Center** (1998), the largest building in D.C. You'll find 3.1 million square feet of floor

A NATIONAL JAUNT

space here in which to swivel your chair and ponder your export strategy.

The building also houses a humble, but interesting, **Woodrow Wilson Memorial** to our 28th President. Some of his personal effects are on display, along with video and stories of Wilson's progressive efforts to protect workers, reel in financial abuse, help bring an end to WWI, and establish the League of Nations, for which he received a Nobel Prize. Yet his stature was ignobly diminished by his support for racial segregation. To enter you'll need to pass through a quick security check. Once inside the main entrance, a food court and large atrium will be dead ahead. The memorial is to the left.

Woodrow Wilson Plaza.

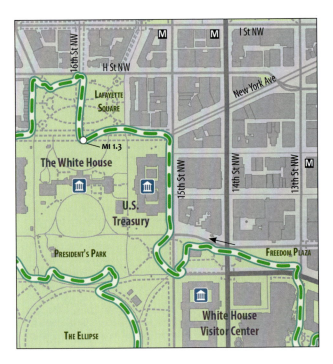

General Pulaski was an effective strategist and horseman during the Revolutionary War and is considered to be the "Father of the American cavalry." He was bestowed honorary U.S. citizenship in 2009.

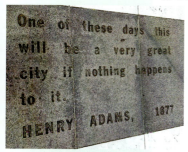

Inscription at Freedom Plaza.

General Pershing—Pershing Park will get an upgrade soon, and official status as a WWI Memorial.

To exit Woodrow Wilson Plaza, follow the pedestrian corridor north to Pennsylvania Ave. If you're unsure which way is north, stand in the middle of the plaza facing the Metro escalators and turn 90 degrees left.

Cross Pennsylvania Ave to the north and saunter left across the unexpected expanse of **Freedom Plaza** [MILE 0.6/0.6]. Near the east end, **General Casimir Pulaski** sits on his mighty horse watching over the place. Pulaski was a Revolutionary War hero credited with saving George Washington's life during the Battle of Brandywine near Philadelphia. Pulaski died in another battle at Savannah in 1779.

Looking at your feet as you meander across the plaza, you'll notice that a large map of D.C., **Pierre L'Enfant's 1791 plan** for the capital, is inlaid into the granite and marble surface (*see the front cover photo*). The map is surrounded by notable quotes about the high stature of this fair and worldly city. To the right is the **National Theatre** (1923), which operates as a nonprofit. Left across Pennsylvania Ave is the **Wilson Building** (1904), hosting D.C. government offices, including the mayor and city council. Be sure to look back down America's Main Street for a good telephoto shot of the Old Post Office and U.S. Capitol (better with afternoon light).

Continuing across Freedom Plaza, angle slightly right to its northwest corner at 14th St NW. Cross 14th St to **Pershing Park** (1981). Beyond the little grassy slope is a treed and sunken public square lying a few feet below the street level. Occasionally, you'll find outdoor music here as well. A statue of **General John Pershing**, venerated leader of American forces during WWI, stands to the left.

Close by on the north side of Pennsylvania Ave is one of the classier hotels in D.C., the historic **Willard** (1901). It's hard to believe that, as recently as the 1970s, it was so forlorn and neglected it was threatened with demolition. Its lobby is where the term 'lobbyist' was coined. A display in the back of the hotel (near F St) shares some of its stories.

Continue to the northwest corner of Pershing Park at 15th St NW and look for the small, yet striking **Bald Eagle** sculpture donated by the National Wildlife Federation in 1982.

If you're on a tight schedule, you could cross 15th St here to the General Sherman Monument. However, the JAUNT jogs south briefly to catch the nearby **White House Visitor Center**. Walk downhill on 15th St (or through Pershing Park) to the next light; cross Pennsylvania Ave and walk left a few yards to the entrance for the Visitor Center, just inside the **Department of Commerce** building (1932). A recent $12.5 million renovation included new exhibits, video, an interactive model of the White House and immaculate restrooms. The White House Visitor Center opens early (*7:30-4:00*), offering a nice morning activity before the museums open. However, tours of the White House must generally be arranged far in advance (*see* www.nps.gov/whho).

Return to 15th St NW, cross and wander right for a quick spin around the **William Tecumseh Sherman Monument** [MILE 0.9/0.9], a solemn reminder of the brutal end days of the Civil War. Then ramble north (uphill) on 15th St past the **U.S. Treasury** (1869). Out front is the prominent statue of the first Treasury Secretary and close advisor to George Washington (and recent Broadway star), **Alexander Hamilton**, mortally shot in the famous 1804 duel with his nemesis, Vice-President Aaron Burr.

Across the street, should you wish to scoot back across 15th St, a series of large bronze medallions are embedded in the sidewalk in what's known as **The Extra Mile**. The markers commemorate many individuals whose work has contributed great things to America and the world—Clara Barton, Rachel Carson, Cesar Chavez, Frederick Douglas, Samuel Gompers, Helen Keller and John Muir, to name a few. (The Extra Mile leads up 15th St, then turns right at G St.)

Once past the Treasury, just beyond G

Bronze Bald Eagle.

General Sherman Monument.

Alexander Hamilton and the U.S. Treasury, familiar icons on a $10 bill.

Along The Extra Mile.

Marquis de Lafayette.

White House North Portico.

St, turn left and stroll west on the broad pedestrian avenue (a closed street) a block to **Lafayette Square** (1824) on the right. A statue of the **Marquis de Lafayette**, a French officer and dear friend of George Washington and the American Revolution, greets you at the corner. The two cherubs at Lafayette's back hint at the struggle for America in its infancy in the 1770s.

Keep walking to enjoy your best view of the **White House** (1800), front and center, including the **North Lawn and Portico** [MILE 1.3/*1.3*]. When heads of state come knocking, they typically enter from this side. The presidential motorcade also zips through here on occasion, although the police will have chased you off well beforehand. You can credit Frederick Law Olmsted, Jr. for the landscaping around the White House.

If you're not continuing on to SECTION 2 and the Lincoln Memorial right away, you can find a number of eateries and hangouts beginning a block or two north of Lafayette Square via Connecticut or Vermont Avenues (leading from the Square's far corners away from the White House). Connecticut Ave also takes you to Dupont Circle, a 15-minute walk. The nearest Metro stations, Farragut West and McPherson Square, are close by on I St, at 17th St NW or Vermont Ave. (*For a stroll to Foggy Bottom, see p. 187.*)

A NATIONAL JAUNT

2 THE COMPLETE CIRCUIT: SECTION 2
White House (MILE 1.3) to the Lincoln Memorial (MILE 3.3)

▶ *Distance:* 2.0 miles (allow 1 to 1.5 hours)

▶ *Start:* Continue from SECTION 1, or start in front of the White House–North Portico, near Lafayette Square

▶ *Nearest Metro:* Farragut West (three blocks); from 17th St NW & I St, walk a block east on I St and one block south on Connecticut; walk through the center of Lafayette Square toward the White House. From McPherson Square, exit at Vermont Ave and walk southwest a block to Lafayette Square and the White House.

Points of Interest: **White House–North Portico • Lafayette Square • President Andrew Jackson Memorial • St. John's Episcopal Church • General Von Steuben statue • Decatur House • General Jean de Rochambeau statue • Blair House • Renwick Gallery • Eisenhower Executive Office Building • Corcoran School of the Arts • First Division Monument • President's Park • White House–South Lawn • National Christmas Tree • Zero Milestone • The Ellipse • Ellipse Visitor Pavilion • Boy Scout Memorial • German-American Friendship Garden • Second Division Memorial • Lockkeeper's House • Organization of American States • Daughters of the American Revolution • American Red Cross • Amerigo Vespucci • Art Museum of the Americas • Simón Bolívar Monument • José Artigas statue • Constitution Gardens • Memorial to the Signers of the Declaration of Independence • Vietnam Veterans Memorial • Lincoln Memorial**

White House from Lafayette Square.

This anti-nuke peace vigil near the White House has been sustained since 1981. Conchita, who was there almost from the beginning, passed away in early 2016 at the age of 80. Others now maintain the vigil.

Andrew Jackson Memorial.

A NATIONAL JAUNT

SECTION 2 of the JAUNT dabbles at the edge of downtown Washington, before cruising over to the west end of the National Mall. There is much to see and plenty of distractions, including an extra mini-loop with a Latin American flair.

Begin this White House–Lincoln Memorial two-mile saunter at the iron fence in front of the **North Portico** of the **White House** (1800), opposite **Lafayette Square**. To score a tour inside, you'll have to contact your member of Congress (or visit their website) for tickets one to six months in advance.

Fast walkers will require less than an hour to reach Lincoln Memorial. But if you like to savor and dally, you might want to allow at least a couple. It generally makes sense to combine this section with the next for a no-hurry, three-hour-plus adventure. Or consider the 4.6-mile WEST LOOP on p. 97.

First up is the White House. Imagine the good old days of 1829 when President Andrew Jackson, in his brash yet neighborly Tennessee way (he was also a prolific slave owner), simply invited everybody, you and I included, to park the horses, kick the mud off our boots and c'mon into the White House, even to the Inaugural Ball. Fences were for keeping the cows out—or in, as the case may be. How times have changed. These days, you'll have to settle for a selfie outside the gate. So, put your gown and tuxedo away and wish the current president happy thoughts before heading north, away from the White House fence [MILE 1.3/0.0] and into the middle of **Lafayette Square**.

Aim for the prominent statue of our controversial 7th president, **Andrew Jackson** (1853), a man of the people, or some people anyway, on his rearing horse above the cannons. Keep walking north through the Square, not quite to H St, the street bordering the park, and prepare to hang a left on the curving red-brick path. The small grey and white building to the right contains restrooms—not the finest loo

47

in Washington, but it may have to do in an emergency. (Maybe we could designate it the National Loo to coax Congress into freeing up funds for an upgrade?) The big yellow church across H St is **St. John's Episcopal** (1816).

Now follow the red-brick path leftward to the northwest corner of Lafayette Square and a statue of **General Von Steuben** (1910), another devoted friend of General Washington and Revolutionary America. Across Jackson Place is the **Decatur House** (1818), sometimes open for free tours and exhibits (*see* www.whitehousehistory.org/plan-your-visit). The Latrobe-designed house was built for Stephen Decatur, Jr., a Naval war hero of high status. He died here after being shot in the gut in a duel with a fellow officer. Perhaps they should have settled for a card game.

Head left along Jackson Place back toward the White House to a statue of another Revolutionary War hero and French army commander, **General Jean de Rochambeau** (1902). Turn right at the corner to pass **Blair House** (1826) and the French-inspired **Renwick Gallery** (1863) at the corner of 17th St NW and Pennsylvania Ave (*10:00-5:30 daily*) [MILE 1.6/0.3]. The gallery is named for the building's architect, James Renwick, Jr., the same gent who designed the Smithsonian Castle. The World Bank, Edward R. Murrow Park and the Mexican Embassy are close by just off Pennsylvania Ave, if you choose to wander a bit (*see p. 187*)

Next, head left down 17th St to the far end of the imposingly elegant **Eisenhower Executive Office Building** (1888) on your left. Pass a security post just beyond to find a path on the left. Before taking this path, look across the street to the former Corcoran Gallery (1897).

Thousands of contemporary works of art from the Corcoran were absorbed into the National Gallery of Art in 2015, while the historic building is remade into George Washington University's **Corcoran School of the Arts and Design**. A new **Corcoran Gallery** is planned as part of the building renovations (lasting into 2017) and will remain accessible to the public.

St. John's Episcopal Church, attended by all presidents since James Madison, Lincoln in particular.

Decatur House.

Recently emerged from a two-year renovation, the Renwick Gallery hosts classical and contemporary works of fine American artists. Once known as the Corcoran Gallery, it was originally regarded as the "American Louvre," despite its modest size.

Eisenhower (a/k/a Old) Executive Office Building. President Nixon would hide out in an office here, to escape the business and busyness of the Oval Office.

First Division Monument.

White House, South Lawn.

National Christmas Tree.

In the meantime, student works may be on display just inside (up the steps on 17th St).

If you need to make a beeline for the Mall, continue down 17th St. Otherwise, take the curved walkway on the left (noted above). It leads past a tall monolith topped by a golden figure. This is the **First Division Monument** (1924) originally commemorating Army veterans of WWI.

At a sidewalk intersection head left, cross a driveway and continue toward the black iron fence. As you might notice by the gathering of onlookers, there's another good view of the **White House** here, this time looking across the **South Lawn** [MILE 2.0/0.7]. The Kitchen Garden (they really do grow vegetables here) is tucked against the trees to the left. In Andrew Jackson's day, you could clippety-clop your buggy right up to the door and say howdy. Today, not so much.

Keep walking along the fence a short distance, then cross the drive rightward at a designated spot between the security fences. As soon as you get to the other side, look to the right for the **National Christmas Tree** (1973), also encircled by a fence. During the winter holidays, choo-choo trains chug charmingly around the cheerful tree—fun for the kids, especially after dark. Mosey over for a closer look and to find a small pedestal nearby that marks the **Zero Milestone** (1923), the point from which highways and places throughout America could theoretically be measured,

49

except that they're not—a good idea that got a little complicated.

Now, facing Washington Monument, note the giant circular lawn here called **The Ellipse**. Walk left (clockwise) on the obvious perimeter path, passing the **Ellipse Visitor Pavilion** (1994), a low building with pudgy white columns (also restrooms, refreshments). About 80 yards past the Pavilion, look to the left for a thrifty-brave-and-reverent-looking monument hidden in the trees—an idealized tribute to the **Boy Scouts of America** (1964).

Ellipse Visitor Pavilion.

That big government building over there opposite 15th St is the **Department of Commerce** (1932), later named for Herbert Hoover. There's not too much to see there besides the White House Visitor Center, so keep on ellipsing till you're halfway around.

If you love lawn, the big one here ought to really spin your mower. The Washington Senators played baseball here in 1860. Union troops camped in the area during the Civil War, before it became a dump. Conversion to a park began in 1879. The vast Ellipse is sometimes abuzz as a gathering place, but can also be a bit of a yawner. To jazz it up for everyday use, perhaps we could add a lawn-bowling green or (because jazz is uniquely American) a giant labyrinth in the shape of a saxophone?

Keep circling till you reach an intersection near the main avenue between The Ellipse and the Washington Monument. The White House should be due north. Turn left and look for two square, low-profile, granite fountains—the **Haupt Fountains** (1969)—adjacent to Constitution Ave. These were donated by Enid Haupt, an avid urban gardener, philanthropist and friend of Lady Bird Johnson. Cross Constitution Ave to the tidy **German-American Friendship Garden**, dedicated by President Reagan and German Chancellor Helmut Kohl in 1988. Turn right.

From this vantage point, the **Washington Monument** (1888) towers majestically above the sweeping lawn. You can head that way if you need to cut your walk short. Otherwise, follow Constitution Ave west to the next

Boy Scouts Memorial. If you're not a boy, take heart that the Extra Mile markers mentioned in SECTION 1 of the JAUNT include Girl Scouts' founder Juliette Gordon Low (on G St near 15th St; photo, p. 45).

German-American Friendship Garden.

The stone Lockkeepers House primarily served Pierre L'Enfant's C&O and Washington Canals, crucial to commerce in the 1830s. The old canals, now buried under Constitution Ave, were a primary means of moving goods around in the good old days, before better roads and steam trains assured their demise.

John Hancock's famous signature appeared with that of our second president, John Adams, both willing to dedicate, as the Declaration states, "our Lives, our Fortunes and our Sacred Honor" to the idea of America.

Constitution Gardens.

intersection at 17th St NW. On the way, you'll pass the gilded flaming sword of the **Second Division Memorial** (1936) across the street. Cross 17th St to the old stone **Lockkeeper's House** [MILE 2.7/1.4].

Across Constitution Ave is the **Organization of American States** (1910) representing all 35 nations of North, South and Central America. For a short, photo-friendly sidetrip that takes in several more sights between 17th and 18th Sts NW, see the AMERICAS MINI-LOOP on the next page. (If doing the entire 12-mile JAUNT and you want to bump up your mileage to a 13.1-mile half-marathon, the added 0.6 mile for this loop will get you that much closer.) Or skip it to continue the JAUNT.

The old stone **Lockkeeper's House** (1835) once fronted the C&O Canal and the Potomac River, the latter lapping at the shore right outside the building—until a massive dredging and landfill project in the 1880s created a full square mile of new upland, including much of what's now the west end of the National Mall. A sign near the building illustrates where the river's edge used to be (*see p. 110 for more on the C&O Canal*).

Next, take the curved path heading up a gentle slope away from the Lockkeeper's House to a four-way junction. (You could cut left here to the WWII Memorial visible through the trees. Or wait till SECTION 4 of the JAUNT, when you'll reach it from the other side.)

From the four-way junction, the JAUNT makes a soft right leading down the hill to the large duck pond and **Constitution Gardens**. Follow its northern (right) perimeter to a small island visible up ahead. The island hosts a **Memorial to the 56 Signers of the Declaration of Independence** (1984) [MILE 2.9/1.6]. Their signatures, including John Hancock's very own "John Hancock," are etched in the rocks.

Along the water's edge, take a moment to look back and reflect on the beauty of the **National Mall**. From Washington Monument to Lincoln Memorial, the landscape's softer edges, gentle slopes, open water and scattered trees give the west end of the Mall the sense

A NATIONAL JAUNT

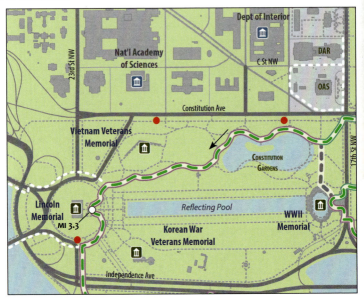

The AMERICAS MINI-LOOP

From the **Lockkeeper's House**, cross Constitution Ave for what amounts to a 0.6-mile walk around the block. Shuffle north on 17th St NW, passing the ornate headquarters of the **Organization of American States** (OAS) to your left. The OAS comprises all 35 nations of North, Central and South America and the Caribbean and seeks to promote peace, justice and collaboration.

At C St, you'll find the columned edifice of the **Daughters of the American Revolution** or DAR, a/k/a Memorial Continental Hall (1905), and the adjacent **Constitution Hall** (1929). The DAR, run entirely by women, has a museum, extensive library and exceptional period rooms depicting early American life

DAR Continental Hall

(*open Mon-Sat, hours vary—see www. dar.org*). Constitution Hall hosts conferences, galas and performances throughout the year.

Continue on 17th St to the next corner for a glance at the striking bright edifice of the **American Red Cross** (1917), then retrace your steps to C St. Turn right to pass by the Continental Hall's semicircle of columns. Across the street on the OAS lawn is an interesting bust of **Amerigo Vespucci,** (2012) the Italian merchant, navigator, mapmaker and man of big hair (or hat) for whom the Americas were named. Now imagine what we'd be called if they'd used his last name instead.

Continue on C St to 18th St. The blocky fortress ahead and right is the **U.S. Department of Interior** (1936). Turn left here, or continue straight a

A Vietnam veteran (the author's big brother, in fact) remembers a Marine Corps chopper pilot and crew who were lost in the war. The "Wall" is an elegantly simple memorial inscribed and imbued with a moving dose of wartime reality.

that it might actually be "America's Front Yard." That said, the placid scene is at risk due to ambitious plans to upgrade the paths and pond. Let's hope the designers are thoughtful enough to preserve these unique qualities.

March on to the far end of the pond, staying right at a concession booth. In 60 yards more, pass a round restroom building on the left (water fountain close by). Fifty yards farther, you could stay left at a fork to avoid possible congestion near the black granite wall of the **Vietnam Veterans Memorial**, or go right to pass a memorial to the women who served and to visit the hallowed wall. You'll find an index of inscribed names near each end. Either path will get you to the **Lincoln Memorial** and plaza, now just moments away.

As you arrive at Lincoln Memorial, pause for a moment on the plaza above the Reflecting Pool. This is perhaps the best known, best loved place on the Mall, with a view that ought to get every American's patriotic juices flowing. On your way up the grand

A NATIONAL JAUNT

half block to visit the once respectable, but in 2016 skimpy **Interior Museum** on the right (*Mon-Fri 8:30-4:30; photo ID required*). A major collection of American art and thousands of artifacts lie in storage limbo. At least the gift shop is nice. Check the website for a murals tour (www.doi.gov/interiormuseum).

Back on 18th St, walk south to the end of the long hedge on your left to the **Art Museum of the Americas** (1976), a part of the OAS (*Tue-Sun 10:00-5:00*). You'll find a gorgeous Mayan loggia (like an atrium) inside, plus a small, but outstanding collection of works by Latin American artists. New works cycle through every three months.

Across 18th St from the art museum stands heroic **Simón Bolívar** (1959), the Liberator, on his fearless horse. Wander

Amerigo Vespucci

over for a look, then follow Virginia Ave back to 17th St (*see also p. 188*). Pass a monument to **José Artigas** (1950), Uruguay's revered liberator, and an array of sculptures outside the OAS. Cross Constitution Ave at the light to return to the Lockkeeper's House. (*Add 0.6 mile to your log if you're keeping track.*)

American Red Cross

staircase [MILE 3.3/2.0] to visit our monumental 16th president, look for the engraved words where Martin Luther King, Jr. stood in the summer of 1963 to deliver his "I have a dream" speech. Above sits the president's realistic portrayal, carved from marble and immersed in stunning Roman architecture.

A tiny bookstore is off in one corner. Exhibits, restrooms and an elevator can be found below the memorial, reached from the left side of the steps (when looking upward). The exhibit area is open early and late. If the weather's nice, you'll likely have plenty of company, even ranger talks, till 11:00 pm or later.

End this leg of the JAUNT with a walk around the outside terrace among the columns for a good look at the Potomac River and the glassy skyline of downtown Rosslyn, Virginia—a part of Arlington. Not a bad spot for a shady respite from the crowds. Walk a bit more and Memorial Bridge is also conspicuous, with the Arlington National Cemetery at its far end. (See the five-mile RIVER LOOP on p. 105 for a refreshing two or three hour trek over the bridge, along the MOUNT VERNON TRAIL, and back across Key Bridge to Georgetown.)

Return to the plaza to continue with SECTION 3 of the JAUNT, including a pleasant walk along the Tidal Basin to Jefferson Memorial. If you need to skedaddle, the D.C. Circulator stops left of the memorial.

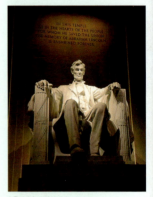

Washington Mall from Washington Monument: WWII Memorial, Lincoln Memorial and Reflecting Pool, Memorial Bridge (upper left), Constitution Gardens (center right). →
JOSH FITZGERALD PHOTO

President Lincoln.

Lincoln Memorial, stunning by day and by night.

3 THE COMPLETE CIRCUIT: SECTION 3
Lincoln Memorial (MILE 3.3) to Jefferson Memorial (MILE 5.1)

▶ *Distance*: 1.8 miles, allow 1.5 to 2 hours

▶ *Start*: Continue from SECTION 2, at the Lincoln Memorial plaza

▶ *Nearest Metro*: The D.C. Circulator offers easy access to Lincoln Memorial. By Metro, it's a 15 to 20-minute walk. From Arlington Cemetery Metro Station (0.9 mile), walk northeast across Memorial Bridge (south side), aim rightward to the memorial. From Foggy Bottom (0.8 mile), just keep walking south on 23rd St NW

Points of Interest: **Lincoln Memorial & Reflecting Pool • Vietnam & Korean War Veterans Memorials • John Ericsson Memorial • West Potomac Park • U.S. Park Police Horse Stables • Ash Woods • District of Columbia War Memorial • Martin Luther King, Jr. Memorial • Tidal Basin • Franklin Delano Roosevelt Memorial • George Mason Memorial • Jefferson Memorial**

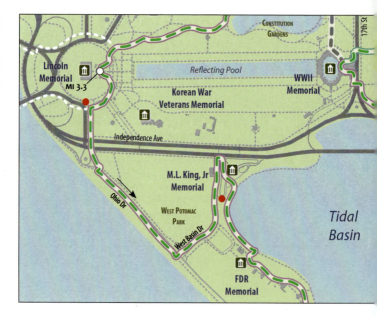

Lincoln Memorial.

From the Gettysburg Address.

Vietnam Memorial, near the wall.

T he 1.8-mile walk from Lincoln Memorial to Jefferson Memorial is among the best on the Mall, passing through a sea of urban greenspace and five iconic memorials, including these two heavyweights (Lincoln and Jefferson), as well as stirring memorials to Korean War veterans, Martin Luther King, Jr. and President Franklin D. Roosevelt. You'll also pass several lesser known, but nationally important sites, amble along the shore of the Tidal Basin, and catch a wide view of Northern Virginia from the shore of the Potomac River.

This segment of the JAUNT can also be done as part of the 4.1-mile WEST LOOP, as described on page 97. The National Mall Circulator bus conveniently stops at both ends of the walk and at the M.L. King Jr. Memorial.

Start where SECTION 2 left off, at the center of the plaza below the steps leading up to Mr. Lincoln's cozy columnar quarters. The numbers are hard to fathom, but millions of visitors climb the steps of the **Lincoln Memorial** (1922) each year—a mandatory ascent when you're this close. A ramp and elevator, if needed, can be found left of the steps (restrooms also).

On the terrace, many of our 16th president's most ponderable words, including the Gettysburg Address, are etched in stone, not to mention the ponderous president himself. Interpretive rangers and information kiosks are available to further enrich your visit.

Once you've admired the big man inside and hoisted your jaw back into place—this truly is an awesome memorial—take in the setting above the 2,000-foot-long reflecting pool and the broad greenspace at the far west end of the Mall above the Potomac River. Be sure to visit the **Vietnam** and **Korean War Veterans Memorials** on either side of the **Reflecting Pool** (a typical stroll through both memorials adds less than a half-mile to your walk).

Two options for the initial part of SECTION 3 of the JAUNT are described below. The first

A NATIONAL JAUNT

57

includes a short stretch along the Potomac River. The second skips the river portion and is more direct (0.3 mile shorter.)

Option 1 (Recommended): From the center of the plaza below the steps of the Lincoln Memorial [MILE **3.3**/*0.0*], look toward the memorial then head left to the far end of the plaza. Cross the drive to the bike rental station and a slightly curved walkway leading toward the golden horses marking the east end of **Memorial Bridge**. But only follow this path to the next corner (23rd St) and turn left. Take this to Independence Ave; cross and continue straight, passing the **John Ericsson Memorial** (1926) amid a traffic island to your right. Ericsson was the Swedish engineer who designed the Navy's first ironclad warship, the mighty *USS Monitor*, launched in January 1862 and lost at sea in a storm eleven months later.

Continue a short distance to where the path curves left to a crosswalk; cross Ohio Dr and head left along the river (right leads to Kennedy Center, Georgetown and Rock Creek Park; figure about three miles to Connecticut Ave from here; *see also p. 128*). Across the river, you'll notice joggers and cyclists on the MOUNT VERNON TRAIL (*see p. 105 and 168*). Those thin, sweeping blades rising above the trees are at the Air Force Memorial near the Pentagon (*see p. 191*).

A quarter-mile after Mr. Ericsson's statue, reach a crosswalk intersection [MILE **3.8**/*0.5*]. Notice an inconspicuous stop on the right for the **seasonal water taxi** to Old Town Alexandria and National Harbor (a schedule may be posted here for an impromptu adventure; you can buy a ticket when you board). Head left to recross Ohio Dr and continue briefly along West Basin Dr to the **Martin Luther King, Jr. Memorial** (2011) on your right. A bookstore and gift shop are to the left [MILE **4.1**/*0.8*].

If you chose Option 1 above, skip ahead to the M.L. King Memorial on the next page.)

Option 2: Again, from the plaza below Lincoln Memorial look east toward Washington Monument, then drift rightward to the wide paths just beyond the last little staircase

Korean War Memorial, with an almost eery assemblage of soldiers silently making their way across uncertain terrain.

John Ericsson Memorial.

Martin Luther King, Jr. Memorial.

Say howdy to the U.S. Park Police.

Ash Woods in winter.

WWI Memorial, dedicated to D.C. residents lost in the war.

Design of the Martin Luther King, Jr. Memorial is based on a line from King's 'I Have a Dream' speech: "Out of a mountain of despair, a stone of hope."

above the **Reflecting Pool**. Stay right of the circular path that leads down to the pool and keep walking through a grove of small trees. The next left is the route for Option 2. But first check out the **Korean War Memorial** just ahead. Then return to the walkway just noted and continue east and parallel to, but well above, the Reflecting Pool.

After a couple of minutes' walking, you'll pass the **U.S. Park Police Horse Stables**, slated for an upgrade that should eventually allow more enjoyable interactions between man and beast. Until that happens, there's not a whole lot to see here. All's not lost, however. In fair weather, there's a pretty good chance you'll encounter at least a pair of amicable park officers and their mounts on patrol somewhere along your journey.

Just after the stables, notice **Ash Woods** on the right, the closest thing to a forest anywhere on the Mall. Continue another hundred yards and turn right at the **District of Columbia War Memorial** (1931), the small domed structure surrounded by Ash Woods. When you reach Independence Ave, amble a short distance to the right (west) to a crosswalk at the traffic light. Cross and enter the **Martin Luther King, Jr. Memorial**. Options 1 and 2 converge here. The bookstore and restrooms are to the right.

A NATIONAL JAUNT

Though it was a long time coming, the Martin Luther King, Jr. Memorial finally opened in August 2011. Walk through the mountain to admire this fitting tribute to a great American leader, one whose own monumental work changed a nation. A selection of his best tenets on justice and civil rights are preserved in the surrounding stoneworks.

After due contemplation, walk to the edge of the **Tidal Basin** and head right for the Jaunt. Japanese cherry trees crowd much of the shoreline, a-bloom in late March or early April. Peak flowering lasts only a few days to a week at most (*see* www.nps.gov/cherry).

Notice there are no railings and no swim ladders for escape if you happen to tumble in. So keep the kids on a close leash and puzzle like I do why there isn't some kind of subtle railing or posts and black chains in place (like in other areas of the Mall) to help keep our collective keisters out of the drink.

Fun fact about the Tidal Basin: Reconstructed in 1949, much as it appears today, the Basin was designed to use a pair of automatic tide gates and two or three feet of local tidal influence on the Potomac River to help flush the

Cherry Blossoms

During the spring bloom, expect the Tidal Basin to be swarmed, with many experiencing the spring spectacle for the first time. For best lighting and more manageable crowds, be there with your camera before sunrise. Anywhere around the basin will do (areas near the M.L. King and FDR Memorials are local favorites).

You can thank Eliza Scidmore for needling officials for two decades (a century ago) to plant these trees. Having traveled to Japan, she thought cherry trees offered a perfect spiffer-upper for what was a recently reconstructed waterfront. Finally in 1912, over 3,000 cherry trees and a stout Japanese lantern were shipped to the U.S., a gift from Japan. The first two trees were planted by First Lady Helen Taft and Viscountess Chinda, wife of Japan's Ambassador. To see the lantern and first trees, detour left along the basin from the M.L. King Memorial, then retrace your steps to continue the JAUNT.

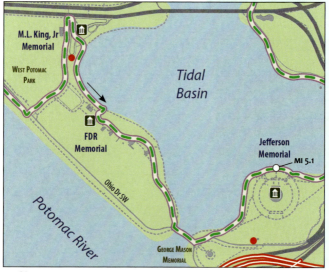

Peak cherry blossoms and Tidal Basin near the Martin Luther King, Jr. Memorial. KRIS WILCOX PHOTO (ABOVE)

FDR Memorial.

extra sediment and goose poop out of the Washington Channel boat harbor southeast of the Basin. (*For a walk to the harbor and Southwest Waterfront, see p. 66.*)

From the Martin Luther King, Jr. Memorial, look across the Tidal Basin to your destination, the domed Jefferson Memorial, and head right. One could enjoy a perfectly nice walk along the water's edge all the way to Jefferson's haunt, but then you would miss the expansive and artful FDR Memorial, certainly among the best places to visit on the Mall. So, when you've walked around the Basin about 300 yards from the M.L. King Memorial, turn right up a stairway (or wheelchair ramp) leading into the **FDR Memorial** (1997). The building off to the right contains restrooms and a bookstore with an entrance on the opposite side [MILE 4.3/1.0].

Atop the steps, saunter left for the JAUNT and to explore the memorial's elaborate walls, alcoves, pools, waterfalls and sculptures. The 32nd president's immortal words are carved into heavy granite blocks. Keep an eye out for **Eleanor**, another American icon, and **Fala**, the First Family's Scottish terrier. You'll find oodles of places to laze around before continuing your trek to Jefferson. Additional restrooms are at

61

Recalling the Great Depression, at the FDR Memorial.

the south end as you leave the memorial.

From FDR, the path traverses lawn and trees above the Tidal Basin before merging with the shore path just short of the bridge and tidal gates. Continue over the bridge to find an obvious left fork in the trail leading to Jefferson Memorial. But before you gallop over there, another point of interest can be quickly reached (0.1 mile round trip) by turning right at the crosswalk immediately before the fork. Cross Basin Dr and jog slightly left into the **George Mason Memorial**, tucked in the trees [MILE 4.9/*1.6*].

You can thank this Virginia statesman for authoring the *Bill of Rights*, including a few things we often take for granted, like freedom of speech, press and religion. Mason insisted these ideas be made part of the *Constitution*— or dadgummit, he wasn't signing. Though he was a slaveholder (as were Washington and Jefferson), he tended toward abolition and is highly regarded as a Founding Father.

Head back to that fork in the trail noted earlier and saunter on over to Jefferson Memorial. Occasional flooding of the old shore path nearby begs one to wonder about an ever-rising sea and the local effects of climate change.

At the **Jefferson Memorial** (1943), swing around to the water side, climb the steps and savor the view [MILE 5.1/*1.8*]. Ascend the steps

The Roosevelts' Fala.

George Mason Memorial.

The high steps at Jefferson Memorial make good bleachers for occasional summer music events.

to the 19-foot tall statue of the third U.S. president and principal author of the *Declaration of Independence*. Again, you'll find a number of his more profound exaltations etched in marble. An elevator is available for those who might like an upward assist to the main terrace to visit with Mr. Jefferson. The elevator, along with a gift shop, exhibit area and restrooms are hidden in a tunnel below the memorial.

The next section continues around the south end of the Tidal Basin and takes you to the WWII Memorial, Washington Monument, Smithsonian Castle and the nearest Metro, Smithsonian Station. Or walk back out to the road for the Circulator stop near a concession stand. A bike rental station is also close by.

A NATIONAL JAUNT

At sunset, the columns at Jefferson Memorial come alive in cream, yellow and orange light.

4 THE COMPLETE CIRCUIT: SECTION 4
Jefferson Memorial (MILE 5.1) to Smithsonian Castle (MILE 7.1)

▶ *Distance*: 2.0 miles, allow 1.5 to 2 hours

▶ *Start*: Continue from SECTION 3, Jefferson Memorial, bottom of the steps

▶ *Nearest Metro*: The D.C. Circulator, a hop-on/hop-off tour bus or a bicycle offer easiest access to the Jefferson Memorial. By Metro, from Smithsonian Station (25 minutes away), walk or bike west 0.3 mile to 15th St NW; cross and turn left on the walkway. Cross Independence Ave at the next light and continue along 15th St (also called Raoul Wallenberg Pl) 0.2 mile south to Maine Ave SW; cross and continue left around the Tidal Basin another 0.3 mile to the Jefferson Memorial. You'll duplicate part of this route when you leave the memorial.

Points of Interest: **Jefferson Memorial • Tidal Basin • Bureau of Engraving & Printing • U.S. Holocaust Museum • Floral Library • Survey Lodge • John Paul Jones Memorial • WWII Memorial • Sylvan Theater • Washington Monument • Museum of African American History & Culture • U.S. Department of Agriculture • Freer Gallery of Art • S. Dillon Ripley Center • Arthur M. Sackler Gallery • Enid A. Haupt Garden • Smithsonian Castle**

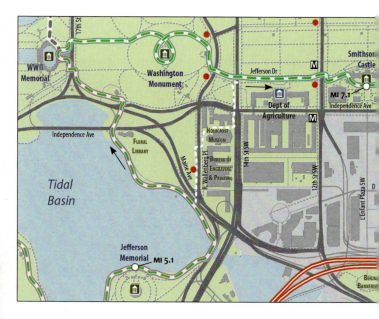

Inside the Jefferson Memorial.

Need tickets?

If you plan to snag an elevator ride up the **Washington Monument** on this leg of the JAUNT, or catch a tour of the **Bureau of Engraving and Printing** (weekdays only), it's best to grab your free, same-day tickets in the morning—earlier the better in the busy season (March-October). At the monument, lines can form before 7:00 am, or reserve in advance for a nominal fee at www.nps.gov/wamo. Tickets are for specific times, so allow some extra if you plan to get a walk in beforehand (don't be late). See the map for ticket booth locations.

H ighlights of this two-mile stretch of the JAUNT are, of course, the Jefferson Memorial, the east end of the Tidal Basin, and your choice of the WWII Memorial and Washington Monument, or the Bureau of Engraving and Printing (closed weekends) and Holocaust Museum—or all of the above.

Begin this section of the JAUNT in the plaza at the base of the steps leading up the Jefferson Memorial. If you are there already, you can skip to the next paragraph. If you are not there, easiest access is by way of the D.C. Circulator bus. As noted above, the nearest Metro station, Smithsonian, is near Smithsonian Castle, which is not terribly convenient, although you could grab a bike at the Bikeshare station near the escalator (or elsewhere), ride over to Jefferson and leave the bike there (see **D.C. by Bike**, p. 28).

The **Jefferson Memorial** was completed in 1943 and dedicated by FDR, although the bronze statue wasn't finished and installed until after WWII. The design of the building was borrowed in part from the ancient Pantheon in Rome, which was also the model for the University of Virginia's Rotunda, designed by none other than Thomas Jefferson, the founder of the university (after his presidency). You might say our third prez was a versatile fellow.

Once you've fist-bumped Mr. Jefferson [MILE 5.1/0.0] and thanked him for all his help cre-

A NATIONAL JAUNT

Jefferson Memorial and cherry blossoms on the Tidal Basin.

ating an actual country, look to the **Tidal Basin** and saunter right. For future reference, the large columned building across the water is the **Bureau of Engraving and Printing**. Continue along the water for a bit, then follow the main path slightly upward through the trees to a bridge over the outlet channel of the basin.

Optional: For a ten-minute sidetrip to the oldest **fish market** in the country, turn right at the sidewalk just before the bridge and backtrack slightly to a crosswalk. Cross and follow the path leftward to the overpass and turn right to follow Maine Ave to the boat harbor and market. Return to the Tidal Basin via Maine Ave. (*See also p. 188*.)

Back at the bridge over the outlet channel, cross and take the left fork that descends to the shore again. Follow this to a junction and decision point just before the paddle boat dock [MILE 5.4/0.3].

Option 1 (Recommended): For Washington Monument and the WWII Memorial, keep going along the water past the **paddle boat rental dock** (restrooms and refreshments close by; boats for two to four people are rentable by the hour, but are best reserved online). Continue to the far end of the long, skinny parking area on the right. Then scroll down four paragraphs to continue with *Option 1*.

Option 2: For a shorter route to Smithsonian Castle (almost a mile shorter), or to visit the **Bureau of Engraving and Printing** (BEP) or **Holocaust Museum**, turn right at the junction near the paddle boat dock. Cross Maine Ave (three crosswalks' worth) and head up the hill a long block to a crosswalk at the far end of the 24-columned BEP building (1914). Cross Raoul Wallenberg Pl SW here. The BEP ticket booth is there on the corner, open weekdays only.

Walk briefly left for the Holocaust Museum (1993) and wheelchair entrance. The main entrance to the museum (where you can learn how Raoul Wallenberg saved the lives of tens of thousands of Jews), as well as the usual entrance to the BEP, are on the 14th St side.

A narrow pedestrian corridor leads between the Holocaust museum and an older red brick

Bridge over the outlet channel.

The money factory, Bureau of Engraving and Printing.

Holocaust Museum.

Pedestrian corridor to 14th St.

Smokey Bear.

Floral library

Gnarly tree and Survey Lodge.

building next door known as the Yates Federal Building (1880). It once housed the BEP and has served as headquarters for the U.S. Forest Service since 1990. Follow this skinny corridor to 14th St. Turn right to enter the Holocaust Museum, and a half block more for the money factory (BEP).

If you're aiming for the Smithsonian Castle or Metro station, head left on 14th St from the end of the narrow corridor and walk a block and a half north to Jefferson Dr. The **Forest Service Visitor Center** on the left is small, but cute, for a quick diversion. Otherwise, turn right. (*Options 1 and 2 converge here.*)

Jefferson Dr will take you past the marbled headquarters of the **U.S. Department of Agriculture** (1908) containing another small **visitor center** just inside (*weekdays, 9:00-3:00*) and a vegetable garden outside. The **Freer Gallery** and **Smithsonian Castle** are just beyond. The Smithsonian Metro escalator is across the street from the Freer Gallery.

Resuming Option 1 to Washington Monument: At the end of the long, skinny parking area and just short of Independence Ave, cross the driveway and look for the **Floral Library** to the right. In dozens of plots maintained by National Park Service staff, the "library" is a splashy garden of tulips in spring, transitioning to other showy flowers in summer.

Cross Independence and Maine Aves in the general direction of Washington Monument. After the third crosswalk, turn left at the gnarly tree to check out the **Survey Lodge Ranger Station** (1886) [MILE *5.8/0.7*]. Built from leftover stone and misfit rocks from the Washington Monument, the building houses a Park Service information desk and some nice rangers. It once contained a steam plant to power the old elevator inside the Monument.

Walk down the sidewalk left of the Lodge, curving past a memorial to **John Paul Jones** (1912), an American naval war hero during the Revolution and a patriarch of the U.S. Navy.

At the traffic light, cross to the **WWII**

A NATIONAL JAUNT

WWII Memorial.

Memorial [MILE **6.0**/*0.9*], dedicated in 2004 after a decade of controversy about where to put it and what it should look like. The states and territories of 1948 are all represented, and the fountains and other features provide good subject matter for photos. You might stumble on a bit of authorized graffiti ("Kilroy was here") engraved in the rock. From here, it's an easy shot back up the center of the National Mall to the base of George's famed obelisk, the **Washington Monument**. The outdoor stage off to the right below the monument is the **Sylvan Theater**, slated for an upgrade soon. Free concerts are common here in summer.

The monument at night.

At 555 feet in height, **Washington Monument** (1885) [MILE **6.4**/*1.3*] is the world's tallest obelisk. The 12-ton cornerstone was set in 1848 and contained a time capsule, though it's now thought to be buried 20 feet underground and encased in concrete. The monument was only 150 feet tall after six years of construction when funding ran out. The Civil War delayed further progress until 1877. Marble was brought in from a different quarry, thus the slight difference in coloration above the 150-foot level. Another factoid: the monument weighs over 40,000 tons.

While the monument lines up perfectly with the U.S. Capitol and Lincoln Memorial, it stands about 100 yards east of the White House-Jefferson Memorial axis, due to once swampy ground at that location. (Look downhill about 100 yards to the northwest for a small marker

In August 2011, a rare 5.8 magnitude earthquake, centered 80 miles from D.C., caused considerable damage to the monument. Although it was mostly cosmetic, the damage was serious enough to close the monument for nearly three years while repairs were made. It reopened to the public in May 2014.

A cloud-splitting monument.

Department of Agriculture

Smithsonian Castle.

known as the **Jefferson Pier**, at a point due south of the White House and due west of the Capitol.)

For a free ticket to the top and the eagle-eye view, you'll need to visit the **Washington Monument Lodge**, the little stone building located downslope and 500 feet to the east. The entire day's tickets can disappear in a hurry in the busy season, so plan to arrive early at the ticket window (or order online well in advance at www.nps.gov/wamo).

From Washington Monument, circle left and down to reach the ticket lodge, which also contains a bookstore and restrooms. On the way there, you could also cross 15th St NW to access the new **National Museum of African American History and Culture** (brand new in 2016), or the **Museum of American History** (1964) next door to the east. Both are on the north side of the Mall, and like all the museums, are highly recommended. Otherwise, continue south past the ticket lodge and up to the next traffic light at Jefferson Dr.

Cross 15th St and follow Jefferson Dr to 14th St [MILE **6.8**/*1.7*]. Cross both streets to the **Department of Agriculture** on the corner, then continue along Jefferson Dr (watch for a cherry tree planted by Hillary Clinton in 1999). After two blocks, reach the **Freer** (1923) and **Arthur M. Sackler** (1982) **Galleries** of Asian Art and the **Smithsonian Castle** (1855) just beyond [MILE **7.1**/*2.0*]. The Smithsonian Metro Station is across the street from the Freer Gallery. The Smithsonian's **Museum of Natural History** (1910)—the most heavily visited museum in North America—is directly across the Mall from the Castle.

To continue with SECTION 5 to the U.S. Capitol Building, aim for the Enid Haupt Garden behind the Castle. Or, if you're in no hurry, you could consume a couple of hours exploring the three intermingled art galleries close by: the Freer and Sackler Galleries or the adjacent S. Dillon Ripley Center with varying exhibits and a kid-friendly Discovery Theater. The nearest D.C. Circulator stop is on Jefferson Dr at the Hirshhorn Museum, a long block east of the Castle.

5 THE COMPLETE CIRCUIT: SECTION 5
Smithsonian Castle (MILE 7.1) to U.S. Capitol (MILE 8.4)

▶ *Distance*: 1.3 miles, allow 1 to 1.5 hours

▶ *Start*: Continue from SECTION 4, or begin at the Enid A. Haupt Garden behind the Smithsonian Castle (near the southside entrance to the Castle). To reach the garden, either strut on through the front entrance of the Castle and out the back, or take the wide walkway through a gate between the Castle and the smallish green dome of the S. Dillon Ripley Center.

▶ *Nearest Metro*: Smithsonian Station is less than five minutes away, opposite the Freer Gallery. The Castle is visible from the Metro entrance, just east on Jefferson Dr.

Points of Interest: **Smithsonian Castle • Enid A. Haupt Garden • Smithsonian Arts & Industries Building • Voyage Model Solar System • Smithsonian Carousel • Mary Livingston Ripley Garden • Hirshhorn Museum & Sculpture Garden • National Air & Space Museum • Phoebe Waterman Haas Public Observatory • National Museum of the American Indian • Capitol Reflecting Pool • Mid-Atlantic Regional Garden • U.S. Botanic Garden & Conservatory • Bartholdi Park & Fountain • James Garfield Memorial • Ulysses S. Grant Memorial • Peace Monument • Summerhouse • U.S. Capitol–West Lawn & West Steps**

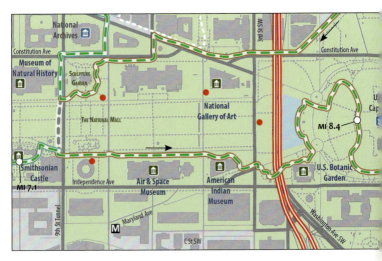

The Smithsonian Castle

The first of the great museums built on the National Mall, the **Castle** was designed by the young, prolific architect, James Renwick, Jr., who also designed St. Patrick's Cathedral in New York and the building that houses the Renwick Gallery near the White House. The castle was made of red sandstone from a quarry near the C&O Canal, 30 miles outside Washington, D.C. The tallest tower is 145 feet high.

The institution is named for **James Smithson,** a well-to-do English scientist who died in 1829 and willed his fortune to the people of the United States for the "increase and diffusion of knowledge." The impetus for his generosity remains a mystery—Smithson had not even visited America.

his leg of the JAUNT is straight-forward and hardly requires a description, since you are merely walking from the Smithsonian Castle to the U.S. Capitol Building—perhaps the two most conspicuous buildings in the neighborhood. However, with a few extra twists, turns and minor detours, you'll see some worthwhile tidbits that others may pass by unaware. Plan on a 1.3-mile stroll, which most folks will knock out in an hour or so, not counting, of course, museum stops, etc.

Before you begin, do walk through the **Smithsonian Castle** (1855) for some interesting history of the Smithsonian Institution, its improbable beginning and prime benefactor, **James Smithson**. A tall statue of **Joseph Henry**, the first Secretary of the Smithsonian, is across the street from the entrance (*photo, p. 16*). Just inside, you'll find the crypt containing Smithson's remains, shipped here from Genoa, Italy, in 1905.

The Castle was designed and built to house the offices of the Smithsonian Institution (Smithson himself chose the name), along with the growing collections of specimens from around the world. As the collections expanded, so did the associated work of preserving and displaying them in order to meet Smithson's vision of diffusing all this scientific knowledge to the public. Thanks to his enormous gift, and that of many others over the years, the Smithsonian Institution's facilities, most of which line the National Mall, have grown to represent the largest museum complex in the world.

As inviting as it looks, the Castle is the Smithsonian Institution's main office, so the upper floors are generally off limits, unless you're able to score a member tour of the building. Be sure to wander down the long hall to the exhibit area in the **West Wing**. Exhibits include a sampling of what you'll find at the other museums, plus 3D models and historic photos of the Castle and National Mall in 1863.

Also inside are an information desk, gift

A NATIONAL JAUNT

73

shop, deli, restrooms and Wi-Fi. For more history, museum details, research and education materials, Imax movie showtimes and upcoming events, you'll find a wealth of information online at www.si.edu (mobile friendly).

The Smithsonian Castle is perhaps more fun to gander at on the outside. So head out the back door to the big garden where this leg of the walk begins. The back forty, or should we say the back four acres, is known as the **Enid A. Haupt Garden** (1987), trimmed out in Victorian style with tidy flower beds, walkways, sculptures, fountains and sitting areas. Ms. Haupt, a New York publishing mogul, donated the $3 million to establish the gardens, which incidentally double as the roof of the art galleries below. You can explore the underground galleries by entering through the **S. Dillon Ripley Center**, the small, green-patina domed structure just outside the garden's west gate.

After poking around the gardens, start this section of the JAUNT near the big double doors behind the Castle [MILE 7.1/0.0]. Mosey eastward (left while facing the main garden) on the brick path leading between the Castle and the rather spectacular **Arts and Industries Building** (1881). Though currently vacant, this was the Smithsonian's first official museum.

Known in its day as the U.S. National Museum, the design of the Arts and Industries Building is a delightful exercise in 19th century architecture, making it one of the more striking

In the Castle's West Wing

With a couple of large, romantic buildings rising above the Haupt Garden, photographers will find plenty to point their lenses at here.

If the Smithsonian has a plan for the Arts and Industries Building (currently an events venue), they aren't talking, not yet anyway. Well, how about a National Museum of Merriment, with interactive (non-digital) fun, humor, games, toys of the world, magic and attitude—to match the architecture, of course.

S. Dilllon Ripley Center provides access to extensive galleries underground.

Smithsonian Castle.

Enjoy a short walk at the Ripley Garden amid much floral diversity. Most of the plants are nicely labeled.

Hirshhorn Museum fountain.

historic buildings in Washington. The building has been extensively restored, and though glorious on the outside, it still needs additional work inside and apparently a purpose and a suitor before it can reopen—a crisp $30 million might just do it.

Follow the red brick walkway around the east end of the Castle to the **Folger Rose Garden** and Jefferson Dr. Watch for a small interpretive sign for **Pluto** near the streetside corner of the building. This is the far end of an outdoor exhibit called **Voyage: A Journey through Our Solar System**. The location of each planet is spaced along Jefferson Dr at a one-to-ten-billion scale, beginning here with poor Pluto, relegated to a dwarf planet, a lowly plutoid, in 2006. You'll pass by the rest of the Voyage exhibit as you make your way to the Sun near the Air and Space Museum. (Do that walk ten billion times and you'd have walked the distance to real Pluto.)

Cross the street here to the Smithsonian's **National Carousel** and read the plaque for a surprising tidbit of American history. Adults can ride too, by the way. Amble east to another crosswalk just past the Arts and Industries Building and cross back to the south side of Jefferson Dr. The **Mary Livingston Ripley Garden** is straight ahead. You can follow this cozy, meandering garden walk to its end, in about 100 yards, and back for a camera-friendly array of flowering plants—like the voodoo lily and Dutchman's pipe. Even the rest benches are eye-catching.

As you exit the Ripley Garden at Jefferson Dr, turn right (and add 0.1 mile to your log if you walked to the end and back). Close by, look for **Neptune**, the first bonafide planet in the scale model of the solar system and a mere 2.7 billion miles from the sun.

Continue along the south side of Jefferson Dr to the steps leading up to the plump, hovering cylinder known as the **Hirshhorn Museum** (1974), a gallery of modern and contemporary art—think Mastisse, Picasso, et al [MILE 7.3/0.2]. A wide load of curious objects and art forms are displayed on several levels,

75

so enjoy a look-see now or later. In the plaza beneath the cylinder, you'll discover the round mass is not solid, but more like a giant donut or spacecraft surrounding a pulsating fountain. Back across Jefferson Dr and below the street level is the **Hirschhorn Sculpture Garden**. Cross for a short loop among abstract human forms, or view it from above.

Keep on trucking eastward on Jefferson Dr and cross both Jefferson and 7th St SW to find **Uranus** near the corner. **Saturn** comes next along Jefferson Dr, by the entrance to the **National Air and Space Museum** (1976). Air and Space is one of the iconic museums of the Smithsonian and, like the Museum of Natural History nearby, is among the most heavily visited museums in the world, in some years second only to the Lourve in Paris (or more likely, third behind Natural History).

Just inside Air and Space is *Columbia*, the real-life Apollo 11 command module that carried Armstrong, Aldrin and Collins back from the Moon in July 1969. You'll also find John Glenn's legendary capsule, *Friendship 7*, the Wright Brothers' *Wright Flyer*, Charles Lindbergh's *Spirit of St. Louis* and plenty more.

If a peek inside the museum hasn't rearranged your plans for the day, continue east from the entrance and look for a small plaque on the wall commemorating the first telegraph dispatched from the air—a **message to President Lincoln** via balloon. Nearby is **Jupiter**, the fifth marble from the Sun, soon followed by the **Asteroid Belt**, then **Mars**, **Earth**, **Venus** and **Mercury**, all clustered around a grapefruit-sized **Sun**. You are now 3.7 billion miles from Pluto—not bad for a leisurely stroll.

You can further your celestial pursuits nearby in the **Phoebe Waterman Haas Public Observatory**, although hours are seasonal and limited (*see* www.airandspace.si.edu). To find it, keep walking past the east end of the Air and Space Museum, turning right on 4th St SW and right again on Independence Ave. Inside the smallish, white dome, a telescope is often trained on the moon or solar corona in midday (*12:00-3:00*), with occasional viewing of the

Lindbergh's *Spirit of St. Louis* and Apollo Lunar Module at the Air and Space Museum. You can spend all day browsing exhibits, famous airplanes, rockets, spacecraft and 3D films, and still feel like you barely saw the place.

An author favorite (my dad was an airplane mechanic, also named Don).

The Sun always shines at the Mall.

American Indian Museum.

U.S. Capitol and Reflecting Pool.

Mid-Atlantic Garden paths invite a closer look at native trees, shrubs, and flowers found in this part of the U.S., including greater D.C.

moon and planets at night. Return to Jefferson Dr to continue the JAUNT.

Heading more or less toward the Capitol Building, cross 4th St SW to the **National Museum of the American Indian** (2004). Follow the walkway along the left (north) side of the museum, passing totems, a waterfall, outdoor sculptures and a natural wetland near the main entrance. This is another museum you can lose yourself in, so enjoy it now or later (check out the Mitsitam Native Foods Café inside—we love the fry bread).

Past the museum's main entrance overhang is Maryland Ave. Jog left there to cross 3rd St SW. The **Capitol Reflecting Pool** is just ahead to the left—a good photo op. But come back to this corner to cross Maryland Ave.

After crossing, walk left a few steps and turn right at the gate for a spin around the **Mid-Atlantic Regional Garden** [MILE 7.8/0.7], a mandatory stop if you're of the native plant ilk, or to escape the buzz of traffic on the avenues. Most of the garden is wheelchair-friendly and many plants are labeled. If you arrive late and the gate is closed, just continue up the sidewalk, which is also lined with a rich assortment of Mid-Atlantic flora.

Whether from the garden or the street, aim for the left side of the **Conservatory** of the **U.S. Botanic Garden** (1933), originally established in 1820 at another location on the Mall. The main entrance off Maryland Ave is adjacent to a nice plaza and sitting area. Free concerts sometimes occur at the Conservatory in summer and during the winter holidays, so check the website (www.usbg.gov) or information desk for a schedule.

The Conservatory offers a good reprieve whether it's muggy or freezing outside, and contains plants from other parts of the globe,

A NATIONAL JAUNT

77

from desert to tropical. If you do duck inside, take a stroll through the Jungle, including the canopy catwalk above, accessible by stairs or elevator. From the catwalk windows, you might also notice, across the street to the south, another outdoor garden and a striking fountain within Bartholdi Park.

Bartholdi Park (1932) is an extension of the Conservatory, though few tourists seem to wander over to view the flowers and one of the more exotic fountains in D.C. The sculptor was Frederic Bartholdi who incorporated gas lamps in the original design. Bartholdi is better known as the Frenchman who designed the Statue of Liberty in New York. To visit the park (undergoing restoration in 2016), walk around the Conservatory, either along the street on the east side or a path on the west side (if the gates to the Mid-Atlantic garden are open).

Leaving the Conservatory's main entrance, angle right a little toward the dark statue in the traffic circle. Pause for a moment to acknowledge this sculpture and **Memorial to President James Garfield** (1887). Four months after his inauguration, a crazed and destitute political minion who had supported Garfield in the election and expected to be awarded a diplomatic job in return, was rebuffed, so he bought a gun and shot the president. Garfield later died from an infection that may have resulted from poor medical care. Soon thereafter, the assassin was tried and promptly executed.

Cross Maryland Ave at the crosswalk (left of the Garfield Memorial) and aim for the nearest corner of the Capitol Reflecting Pool, descending three steps to the waterside walkway. (For wheelchair access, keep right on the sidewalk and take the next left.)

Follow the water's edge to explore the **Ulysses S. Grant Memorial** (1922), one of the more distinguished monuments on the Mall. Grant, of course, was commander of the Union Army during the Civil War before becoming the 18th U.S. president in 1869. Step up onto the terrace for a closer look at the Cavalry (north) and Artillery (south) and a commanding view of the **U.S. Capitol** (1800).

U.S. Botanic Garden.

President James Garfield Memorial. Garfield's inaugural ball was held inside the Arts and Industries Building (near the Castle), just as it was being completed in 1881.

Ulysses S. Grant Memorial.

Peace Monument.

At Summerhouse, enjoy a cool, stone seat and a refreshing swig of the Potomac River (D.C.'s water source).

U.S. Capitol, West Steps.

Exit via three steps at the northeast corner of the pool (wheelchairs can exit near Ulysses). Walk right a few yards to a crosswalk and, facing the Capitol, cross 1st St NW. The **Peace Monument** (1877) will be in the traffic circle on your left. Carved in marble in Italy, it commemorates the lives lost at sea during the Civil War. The draped figure facing the Capitol is Peace. The two above are Grief and History.

Rather than bounding up to the Capitol Building from the Peace Monument, continue north a few steps around the circle to the next wide walkway. Take the right fork up the hill past an enormous **willow oak** tree. The rotund stone pillar in the bushes nearby is part of the Capitol's old ventilation system. Although the JAUNT stays right toward the Capitol steps, first make a quick detour left about 50 yards to the low-profile, six-sided, red brick structure known as **Summerhouse** (1880), designed by Frederick Law Olmsted. Olmsted also laid out the grounds of the Capitol. Summerhouse is a perfect water stop on a hot day, and little birds seem to agree. Wander over to see why.

Return to the stone pillar and follow the curving path toward the **West Steps** of the Capitol [MILE **8.4**/*1.3*]. This iconic building and dome (the latter fully restored in 2016) are a stunning monument to American democracy. Insight into the building's history and what it represents comes with a free and highly recommended docent tour that begins at the underground visitor center on the opposite (east) side of the building (*see p. 82*).

SECTION 5 of the JAUNT ends here, at the terrace overlooking the West Lawn and National Mall. Washington Monument is 1.3 miles away, Lincoln Memorial is just over two. Free concerts by military bands, the National Symphony Orchestra and others are often held here in the warmer months, with the biggest events during the Memorial Day, 4th of July and Labor Day holidays.

SECTION 6 will take you around the south side of the building to the East Plaza, Supreme Court, Library of Congress and beyond.

A NATIONAL JAUNT

6 THE COMPLETE CIRCUIT: SECTION 6
U.S. Capitol (MILE 8.4) to Union Station (MILE 10.3)

▶ *Distance*: 1.9 miles, allow 1.5 to 2 hours

▶ *Start*: Continue from SECTION 5, or begin at the Capitol's West Steps above the West Lawn. The D.C. Circulator's Mall route stops on 3rd St NW behind the Capitol Reflecting Pool. Head up toward the Dome from there.

▶ *Nearest Metro*: Capitol South Station (15 minutes away); walk north on 1st St NE a block and a half to Independence Ave. Cross and follow the walkway left then right into the Capitol's East Plaza, or continue downhill left of the Capitol to reach the West Steps overlooking the Mall (the JAUNT comes back up this hill).

Points of Interest: **U.S. Capitol (West Lawn/West Steps, East Plaza) • Capitol Visitor Center • U.S. Supreme Court • Court of Neptune Fountain • Library of Congress • Folger Shakespeare Theatre & Library • Belmont-Paul Women's Equality Monument • VFW • Capitol Hill Neighborhood • Stanton Park • General Nathanael Greene Statue • Federal Judicial Center • Christopher Columbus Fountain • Union Station**

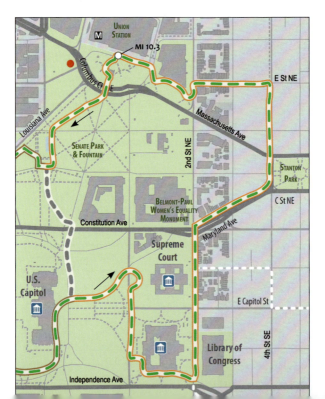

The female figure atop the Capitol dome is Freedom, looking toward the sunrise, welcoming visitors

U.S. Capitol and east steps; below, lampposts lining the East Plaza.

The JAUNT from the U.S. Capitol to Union Station takes you by some of the more stunning civic architecture in the city, if not the nation, including the U.S. Supreme Court, the Library of Congress, Union Station and, of course, the magnificent U. S. Capitol Building. The 1.9-mile walk also offers a glimpse of everyday life on Capitol Hill, as it's the only section of the JAUNT to dip into one of the city's older, established neighborhoods. Much worthwhile exploring is possible nearby, such as an easy ramble to Barracks Row and Eastern Market (*see p. 147*). The free tour of the Capitol Building is highly recommended (reserve online or take your chances—sometimes the lines do move quickly).

Begin the walk above the **West Lawn** of the **U.S. Capitol**, near the tiered fountain in the central alcove at the base of the steps [MILE 8.4/0.0]. This is more or less where presidents stand on a really big soapbox to deliver their inaugural speeches. Looking up at the building, the **Capitol Dome** and Rotunda are at the center (duh), with the **Senate** to the left and the **House** to the right. Head right (south) to enter a lawn area and pass a water fountain. Notice the **horse-chestnut tree** sapling on the left, planted in 2014 to honor Anne Frank and the chestnut tree she wrote about in her famous diary.

Choose the left fork at a stone pillar, then stay left again to continue up the broad walkway that climbs a long, gentle slope around the south end of the Capitol. At the top of the hill, mosey left into the sprawling **East Plaza**, or what's essentially the Capitol's front yard [MILE 8.7/0.3]. Elaborate friezes adorn the gables and two intriguing figures guard the central door, as do the Capitol Police. Parts of the **Capitol** were still in the throes of a multi-year restoration effort in 2016.

Toward the back of the plaza is a line of six large, ornate **lampposts**. Look for signs nearby for the **Capitol Visitor Center**, which is located beneath the plaza (*8:30-4:30, closed Sundays and some holidays*). Browse **Exhibition Hall** and statues of high achievers from the states, plus the original plaster model of **Freedom**.

The 45-minute tour of the Capitol, always led by a knowledgeable guide, should be on everyone's must-do list. Timed tickets can be reserved in advance online, but you'll still want to arrive early to get through security (*see* www.visitthecapitol.gov). Visit the website for more details and to learn how you can get a ticket to the galleries while **Congress** is in session.

Note that if you do head down to the Capitol Visitor Center and go through the security check, you can take an underground pedestrian tunnel to the Library of Congress, perhaps without having to go through security again. The tunnel works vice versa too, in case you decide to come back to the Capitol when leaving the library. But for the Supreme Court, you'll need to stay above ground.

So if you're still in the East Plaza, look eastward (away from the Capitol toward 1st St NE). The Library of Congress is the double-domed building to the right, and the U.S. Supreme Court is to the left. Head there next by walking past the leftmost ornate lamppost noted above and following a left-curving walkway to a crosswalk. Cross 1st St NE here to the plaza fronting the **Supreme Court** (1935). The seated figures out front are the **Contemplation of Justice** (female) and the **Authority of Law** (male). The gender association could make for some lively conversation.

Although you cannot enter through the giant doors above the plaza—each door weighs over six tons—you can still climb the steps and enjoy mingling among the marble columns. The building really gleams in late afternoon sunlight. The public entrance to the court's **Great Hall** and exhibits, and if your timing is good, a potential tour of the courtroom, is below and right of the great stairs and columns (wheelchair access is to the left). When the court is in session, long lines form early to observe the justices in action, amid the legal

Statuary Hall, U.S. Capitol.

Full-size model of Freedom.

Above the columns in the West Pediment are Lady Liberty in the center, Chief Justices Taft (left) and Marshall (right). The sculptor, Robert Aitken, surprised folks by including himself in the work (second from the right).

U.S. Supreme Court. The building was sited here within view of the Capitol as a not-too-subtle reminder of the checks and balances in democratic government guaranteed by the Constitution.

Court of Neptune Fountain.

wranglings of the parties involved. Visit www.supremecourt.gov for details.

Leaving the steps of the Supreme Court, head south down 1st St to the **Library of Congress** (1897). Keep to the sidewalk long enough to check out the **Court of Neptune Fountain** (1898), a dramatic sculpture of mythical figures in a pool, inspired by the 18th century Trevi Foundatin in Rome. Hike up the steps, about three flights' worth, to the Library's entrance above an archway (wheelchairs enter below).

There's much to explore inside the Library, also known as the Jefferson Building—old books like *Gideon's Bible*, old maps like the first to say "America," George Gershwin's piano, many exhibits, murals, columns, stairways and a spectacular ceiling. The **Reading Room** is also quite the thing. More than 35 million books

Library of Congress,
Thomas Jefferson Bu[...]
The retired presiden[...]
nated his massive pe[...]
collection of books t[...]
new national library [...]
1814. It's since beco[...]
the largest library in [...]
world, with more th[...]
160 million items ar[...]

are shelved and catalogued here, though you can't exactly check them out. Browse the website (www.loc.gov/visit) for details. Do wander inside for a look or a docent tour, or save it for later as the case may be. (Note the long tunnel on the lower level that can take you back to the Capitol Visitor Center, if desired.)

For the JAUNT, continue walking past the Neptune Fountain and the Library's entrance and turn left either at Independence Ave, or on a walkway that parallels Independence Ave closer to the Library. Follow this to 2nd St NE where the JAUNT turns left [MILE 9.2/0.8]. To your right begins Pennsylvania Ave SE, with a number of local hotspots over the next several blocks if you have an urge to chill or chow down.

To add an hour or two of additional exploring, see p. 147 for the 2.8-mile CAPITOL HILL LOOP from here to Barracks Row and Eastern Market. Otherwise, cross 2nd St and head left (north) to continue the JAUNT.

After passing the back side of the Library of Congress (backside sounds impolite), the next building on the right at the end of the block is the **Folger Shakespeare Library and Theatre** (1932), highly recommended if you're the literary type (*open 10:00-5:00 most days*). Watch

Ceiling inside the Library of Congress.

Outside Folger Shakespeare Library.

Belmont-Paul National Monument.

At Stanton Park, General Greene's right index finger points down Maryland Ave to the Capitol.

for the statue with a catchy quote. Inside the Folger's East Capitol St entrance is a small, but interesting exhibit hall and a perfect Elizabethan theater for taking in a play. If you poke around there, walk back to 2nd St to continue the JAUNT.

Next up, on the left after crossing East Capitol St, is the highly decorated rear end the Supreme Court building. Notice the immortal words near the gable or East Pediment. Among the figures are Moses, a tortoise and a hare.

In another block, cross 2nd St and turn right, or jog left first to visit the **Belmont-Paul Women's Equality National Monument**, designated in 2016 to honor women's suffrage and the home of the National Women's Party since 1922 (the building dates to 1800). Open for tours only (*Thur-Fri-Sat, 11:00, 1:00, 3:00*). If you stopped in for a look, re-cross 2nd St NE to the **Veterans of Foreign Wars** (VFW), founded in 1899 after the Spanish-American War.

From the VFW [MILE **9.6**/*1.2*], follow Maryland Ave for two blocks, admiring an array of 19th century architectural styles. At 4th St NE. the JAUNT turns left. Or take the crosswalk over to **Stanton Park** and the statue of Revolutionary War hero, **General Nathanael Greene** (1877). Greene was recognized as a brilliant military strategist, second only to George Washington.

Back at 4th St, cross Massachusetts Ave and continue north two blocks before turning left at E St. In two blocks more, cross 2nd St NE. Then take the short sidewalk angling up the grass and turn right on another path at the end of the hedge. Follow this past the **Federal Judicial Center** to a cluster of flagpoles and a walkway on the right leading to **Union Station** dead ahead [MILE **10.3**/*1.9*]. If you haven't already wandered inside, be sure to explore the lavish interior of Union Station before moving on to the next and last leg of the JAUNT to Penn Quarter and the Navy Memorial.

Approaching Union Station.

7 THE COMPLETE CIRCUIT: SECTION 7
Union Station (MILE 10.3) to U.S. Navy Memorial (MILE 12.0)

▶ *Distance*: 1.7 miles, allow 1.0 to 1.5 hours

▶ *Start*: Continue from SECTION 6, beginning near the big Freedom Bell in front of Union Station

▶ *Nearest Metro*: Union Station (and Archives–Navy Memorial Station at the end)

Points of Interest: **Union Station • Postal Museum • National Guard Memorial Museum • Holodomor Memorial • Freedom Bell • Christopher Columbus Fountain • Senate Park & Fountain • Japanese-American Memorial • Robert A. Taft Memorial & Carillon • U.S Department of Labor • William Blackstone Statue • General George Meade Monument • John Marshall Park • Canadian Embassy • Newseum • Andrew W. Mellon Memorial Fountain • Federal Trade Commission • National Gallery of Art • Sculpture Garden & Ice Rink • Smithsonian Museum of Natural History • National Archives • Grand Army of the Republic Memorial • Temperance Fountain • General Winfield Scott Hancock Memorial**

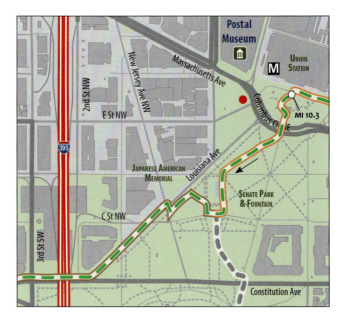

At Union Station.

Union Station is as awesome as it is large—long enough, in fact, that if you stood it on end it would be taller than the Washington Monument.

Inside Union Station.

A NATIONAL JAUNT

After much good walking on the National Mall, around the Tidal Basin, past a plethora of iconic buildings and through the Capitol Hill neighborhood, SECTION 7 of the JAUNT changes pace. We now ease back into downtown Washington for another perspective on the workaday world and urban treasures of our multi-dimensional city, and dip into the National Mall once more before the finish. It's a fun stretch to walk, meandering slightly to take in the most interesting sights and ending at the cusp of D.C.'s happening nightlife. The route offers another good lesson in geography that might help visitors and newbies mentally connect the National Mall with both downtown D.C. and our starting point here at Union Station.

If you haven't already peered inside **Union Station** (1907) [MILE 10.3/0.0], by all means do. The beaux-arts building was nearly lost to neglect by 1980, but was carefully restored (a couple of times) to preserve what is truly one of America's grand architectural marvels. The **Main Hall** is 96 feet high and leaved with 70 pounds of gold guarded by 36 Roman legionnaire statues.

The respectable nudes and near-nudes, including six more outside the main entry, are the work of American sculptor Louis Saint-Gaudens. A century ago, political correctness collided with anatomical correctness here, resulting in the artist's begrudging addition of a handheld shield to each male form. Archways, ornate trim and lighting, circular stairs, marble floors and an old Roman clock add to the glamour.

It's not uncommon for more than 100,000 people to pass through the station in a day, mostly Amtrak, light rail, regional bus and Metro commuters. Besides people, you'll find upscale shops, travel and visitor services, dozens of eateries, including a large food court on the

87

lower level, and sufficiently decent restrooms. Just inside the main entrance, you'll also find ticket counters for hop-on/hop-off D.C. bus tours, and a big reader board for regional train departures. When you've seen enough inside, move to the plaza outside to ogle the exterior décor.

Begin your walk outside the main entrance to Union Station in the long, arched corridor or loggia. Before ambling over to the big Freedom Bell and Christopher Columbus Fountain dead ahead, first look right, down the photogenic corridor. It leads directly to the Smithsonian's **Postal Museum** just across 1st St NE, a worthy side trip. If you don't mind a little extra pre-JAUNT wandering, two other sites of interest are located a block farther down Massachusetts Ave at the corner of North Capitol St: the **National Guard Memorial Museum** (1991) and the new **Holodomor Memorial** (2015) across the street. If you decide to visit these nearby sites (a 0.4-mile side trip), backtrack to Union Station and the Freedom Bell to continue the JAUNT.

Postal Museum, west entrance.

Holodomor Memorial.

The **Freedom Bell** (1981) is an enlarged replica of the Liberty Bell in Philadelphia. Walk around it and the **Christopher Columbus Fountain** (1912). Wheelchairs can make a wide detour left or right. Notice the figures to either side of Columbus representing the Old and New Worlds. Columbus, of course, is the namesake for the District of Columbia.

Following Columbus' nose, head south across Columbus Circle (toward the U.S. Capitol) via the extra-wide crosswalk. At the median, drift over to the right-hand crosswalk leading to the line of flagpoles. Then take a soft right on the diagonal walkway that cuts through a long, shady corridor of spring-flowering trees and shrubs. Many of the larger and older trees in the surrounding **Senate Park** were dedicated to former presidents. Some are tagged with little placards noting the common and Latin names for each species.

At the far end of this restive corridor, take the obvious crosswalk left, then aim for the nearby reflecting pool for a nice mirror-im-

More than a century ago, tens of thousands attended the Columbus Fountain's dedication and Knights of Columbus parade that followed. Despite that momentous beginning, the actual fountain has been out of commission for years, apparently in need of a serious plumbing job, and probably a benefactor.

At the Senate Fountain, the upthrusting water columns mimic the Capitol Dome.

Japanese American Memorial.

U.S. Department of Labor (right).

age of the Capitol rising above the **Senate Fountain** [MILE **10.6**/0.3]. This is also a great place for cherry blossoms in spring, with some varieties blooming later than the more famous trees around the Tidal Basin. Walk around the pool and head up the steps to the main fountain for a look. (*Note that the EAST LOOP heads over to the Capitol's East Plaza from here; see p. 99.*)

Return to the base of the stairs and with your back to the lower fountains follow a diagonal path angling left to Louisiana Ave. (Wheelchair hikers can explore the picturesque lower fountains, but to access the upper fountain, you'll need to find the ramp over at 1st St NE, a block east of the fountains; return the way you came; *see map on p. 86.*)

The diagonal path descends a few steps to Louisiana Ave; turn left (wheelchairs can stay near the reflecting pool before turning left at the street). Cross Louisiana Ave at New Jersey Ave, the first intersection downhill. Then take a few steps right to visit the **Japanese American Memorial** (2000). While walking through this peaceful memorial, you'll find the story of the internment camps during WWII, the subsequent Presidential apology, and a list of Japanese Americans who died serving in the U.S. military during WWII. A humbling place.

Return to Louisiana Ave and turn right to cross New Jersey Ave, then C St and 1st St NW. If you hear a bell tolling, it's probably the 100-foot belltower visible in the trees to the left, otherwise known as the **Robert A. Taft Memorial and Carillon** (1959). Taft, a stalwart conservative, was a U.S. Senator from Ohio and son of President Taft.

Continue along Louisiana Ave another block, where it merges into Constitution Ave near a gaggle of white-potted trees. Look a little right and cross 2nd St to a red brick walkway. Take this briefly uphill past the **U.S. Department of Labor** (1975) for a slightly better view of the Mall. The building is named for Labor Secretary Frances Perkins, the first woman cabinet member and still longest serving Labor Secretary

A NATIONAL JAUNT

(1933-1945). She was pivotal in implementing FDR's New Deal.

Ahead, the dome and angular buildings to the left across Constitution Ave are the West and East Buildings of the **National Gallery of Art** (1941 and 1978). While admission is free, they are not part of the Smithsonian, but rather a gift to the American people by banker-collector-philanthropist Andrew Mellon. The curvier buildings on the right at the corner belong to the federal court system.

Now cross 3rd St NW and follow busy Constitution Ave to a couple of statues just ahead. **Sir William Blackstone** (1943), a highly influential 18th century English legal scholar is hiding out on the right, followed on the left by a robust monument to **Union General George Meade** of Gettysburg fame.

Union General George Meade.

A short distance beyond the General, reach **John Marshall Park [MILE 11.2/0.9]**, dedicated to the supremely influential 4th Chief Justice of the U.S. Supreme Court. (*The OLD DOWNTOWN-CHINATOWN LOOP described on p. 142 heads north through this two-block long park.*)

Just ahead is a big building flying maple leaf flags—the **Canadian Embassy** (1989), the nearest foreign embassy to the U.S. Capitol. Should you feel like snooping, the steps lead up to the main entrance (wheelchairs stay right), where you'll find an intriguing sculpture from British Columbia. The **Spirit of Haida Gwaii** appears to float in a pool. (*For more embassies, see p. 119 for a trek through EMBASSY ROW.*)

Embassy of Canada.

Walk down Pennsylvania Ave another half block to the **Newseum** (2008) and the mesmerizing daily newspaper display of America's front pages (and a few other countries' too). This museum's outstanding exhibit areas inside are not free, but the museum is award-winning and a popular stop for many. A really big reminder of our **First Amendment rights** is printed on the face of the building.

Here's Mom browsing the front pages at the Newseum.

At this point, near 6th St and Pennsylvania Ave, you're just a block away from the end of the JAUNT at the Navy Memorial. But before you make a mad dash to the barn, there are

Mellon Fountain and National Gallery of Art—West Building above, East below.

just a few more sights to see on this last leg of the last leg of the NATIONAL JAUNT.

Cross Pennyslvania Ave at 6th St and pass between the **Andrew Mellon Memorial Fountain** (1951) on the left and the **Federal Trade Commission** (1938) on the right. Continue across Constitution Ave to the **West Building** of the National Gallery of Art (1941) and turn right. (For a quick look inside, at least head up to the second floor rotunda. Also, the West Building is joined to the angular **East Building** (1978) by a rather joyful underground light tunnel. A major renovation and expansion of the East galleries, including a new rooftop terrace, were completed in 2016. Visit them now or later. (*Open most days 10:00-5:00; details at* www.nga.gov.)

As you walk past the West Building toward 7th St, notice the 1942 statue next to the Federal Trade Commission depicting a big man (society) struggling to tame a mighty horse (trade).

Cross 7th St to a corner gate leading into the **National Sculpture Garden** (1999) [MILE

A NATIONAL JAUNT

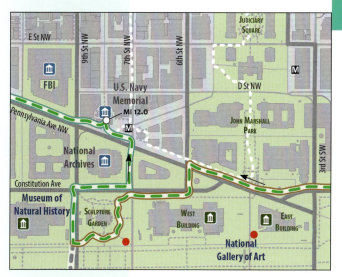

11.5/1.2]. A spin around the garden is time well spent (*open most days 10:00-5:00*). Friday evening outdoor jazz concerts are popular here in summer. The large fountain at the National Sculpture Garden converts to an ice skating rink in late fall and winter (*open mid-morning to 9:00 pm or later; skate rentals available*).

Exit the south side toward the Mall (near the tree sculpture) and walk right to cross over 9th St NW. If you arrived after the gates are closed, you can easily walk left around the perimeter to spot the metallic tree.

Ahead on the right is the renowned **Smithsonian Museum of Natural History**, one of the most popular museums on the planet, and deservedly so. But to complete the JAUNT, hang a right down a curvy path though the **Butterfly Garden** immediately west of 9th St. Where the path rejoins the sidewalk, keep walking north to re-cross Constitution Ave. Turn right to pass in front of the **National Archives** (*open daily 10:00-5:30*). The visitor entrance to access the exhibit areas, including handwritten originals of the *Declaration of Independence* and *U.S. Constitution*, is left of the steps (*details at* www.archives.gov/museum). Lines can form early during the busy season.

At the next corner, across from the gate where you entered the Sculpture Garden, turn left. Walk up 7th St (away from the Mall) and cross Pennsylvania Ave. The obelisk on the right is the **Civil War Memorial** to the Grand Army of the Republic (1909), surrounded by several historic buildings of D.C.'s Old Downtown, now more commonly known as **Penn Quarter**. The **Temperance Fountain** (1884), crowned by a heron, is close by.

The last stop between you and the Navy Memorial finish line is the **General Winfield Scott Hancock Memorial** (1896) across 7th St from Temperance. Hancock was a decorated Union general during the Civil War, and was prominent in the Battle of Gettysburg. He later ran for president against James Garfield, but lost by a whisker.

Finally, mosey over to the **Navy Memorial** and plaza map of the oceans (the **Granite Sea**)

"Graft," the stainless steel tree at the National Sculpture Garden.

Now dry, the Temperance Fountain was an ice-cooled drinking-water fountain meant to discourage excessive alcohol consumption.

Civil War Memorial to the Grand Army of the Republic.

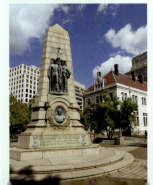

to soak it all in [MILE 12.0/1.7]. You're done!

If you just completed the entire JAUNT, congrats! You've probably seen more of the National Mall and its surroundings than most D.C. visitors (and quite a number of locals) may ever see. If you haven't already, take a look at the D.C. Bucket List at the back of this guide to browse or record your experience.

Then go have an ice cream.

General Winfield Scott Hancock.

Bronze bas reliefs and fountain at the U.S. Navy Memorial.

A NATIONAL JAUNT

THE FOUR LOOPS

A nother great way to complete the JAUNT is to walk the following four loops over several outings. You'll cover the same ground, plus a little more to close each loop—14.7 miles in total, instead of 12—but in more manageable chunks. Allow a couple of hours for each loop, or take all day if you want to spend time at the museums, galleries and gardens along the way. You'll actually see a bit more via the loop approach than if you did the JAUNT as one complete circuit, but either choice lets you experience the best of everything in and around the Mall.

WEST-CENTRAL LOOP: 4.6 miles, 2 to 3 hours (p. 95)
Navy Memorial ➜ Freedom Plaza ➜ White House ➜ Washington Monument ➜ Smithsonian Museums ➜ National Archives

WEST LOOP: 4.1 miles, 2 to 3 hours (p. 97)
Constitution Gardens ➜ Lincoln Memorial ➜ Vietnam & Korean War Memorials ➜ Martin Luther King, Jr. Memorial ➜ FDR Memorial ➜ Jefferson Memorial ➜ WWII Memorial

EAST LOOP: 2.2 miles, 1.5 to 2 hours (p. 99)
U.S. Capitol ➜ Supreme Court ➜ Library of Congress ➜ Capitol Hill ➜ Union Station ➜ Postal Museum ➜ Senate Park

East-Central Loop: 3.8 miles, 2 to 3 hours (p. 101)
National Archives ➜ Sculpture Gardens ➜ Smithsonian Museums ➜ U.S. Botanic Garden ➜ U.S. Capitol ➜ National Art Galleries ➜ Navy Memorial

West-Central Loop

Navy Memorial → Freedom Plaza → White House → Washington Monument → Smithsonian Museums → National Archives

▶ *Distance*: 4.6 miles, allow 2 to 3 hours

▶ *Start/Finish*: U.S. Navy Memorial (*map next page*)

Points of Interest: **U.S. Navy Memorial • Naval Heritage Center • FBI • Old Post Office • Federal Triangle • Environmental Protection Agency • Woodrow Wilson Plaza • Freedom Plaza • General Pulaski Monument • Pershing Park & General Pershing statue • Bald Eagle Memorial • White House Visitor Center • William Tecumseh Sherman Monument • U.S. Treasury • Alexander Hamilton statue • The Extra Mile • Marquis de Lafayette statue • White House–North Portico • Lafayette Square • President Andrew Jackson Memorial • St. John's Episcopal Church • General Von Steuben statue • Decatur House • General Jean de Rochambeau statue • Blair House • Renwick Gallery • Eisenhower Executive Office Building • Corcoran School of the Arts • First Division Monument • President's Park • White House-South Lawn • National Christmas Tree • Zero Milestone • The Ellipse • Ellipse Visitor Pavilion • Boy Scout Memorial • Enid Haupt Fountains • German-American Friendship Garden • Second Division Memorial • Lockkeeper's House • WWII Memorial • Sylvan Theater • Washington Monument • Museum of African American History & Culture • Museum of Natural History • National Sculpture Garden • National Archives • General Winfield Scott Hancock Memorial • Penn Quarter**

A NATIONAL JAUNT

• •

The 4.6-mile WEST-CENTRAL LOOP catches all of SECTION 1 of the JAUNT, part of SECTIONS 2 and 4, and closes the loop with a short stroll across the National Mall from Hirshhorn Museum to the National Sculpture Garden, Museum of Natural History and National Archives.

Begin by completing SECTION 1 of the JAUNT (*p. 39*) from the **Navy Memorial** to the **White House**, then continue along SECTION 2 as far as the old stone **Lockkeepers House**. At the four-way junction just beyond the stone building, head left (south) to the **WWII Memorial**. You will have walked 2.8 miles to here (or 0.6-mile more if you added the mini-loop on p. 52).

Next, turn to p. 68 for the continuation along SECTION 4. As described, the loop heads east from the WWII Memorial, past the **Washington Monument** and over to the **Smithsonian Castle**. From the Castle, walk east to the **Hirshhorn Museum** at 7th St and check out the **Hirshhorn's Sculpture Garden** directly across Jefferson Dr. From here, wander across the Mall (near 7th St) to the **National Sculpture Garden**, just right (east) of the **Museum of Natural History**. Pass through or around the Sculpture Garden to the **National Archives**. Continue north a block on 7th St to your start/finish line at the Navy Memorial.

Inside the Smithsonian
Museum of Natural History

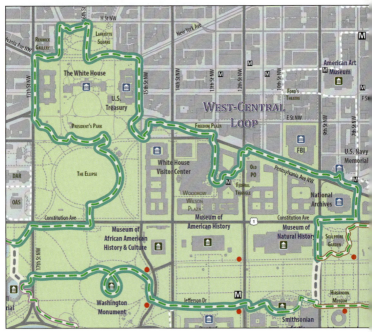

West Loop

Constitution Gardens → Lincoln Memorial → Vietnam & Korean War Memorials → Martin Luther King, Jr. Memorial → FDR Memorial → Jefferson Memorial → WWII Memorial

▶ *Distance*: 4.1 miles, allow 2 to 3 hours

▶ *Start/Finish*: Washington Monument (*map next page*)

Points of Interest: **Washington Monument • WWII Memorial • Constitution Gardens • Signers of the Declaration of Independence Memorial • Vietnam War Veterans Memorial • Lincoln Memorial & Reflecting Pool • Korean War Veterans Memorial • John Ericsson Memorial • West Potomac Park • Martin Luther King, Jr. Memorial • Tidal Basin • FDR Memorial • George Mason Memorial • Jefferson Memorial • Floral Library • Survey Lodge • John Paul Jones Memorial • WWII Memorial • Sylvan Theater • Bureau of Engraving & Printing • Holocaust Memorial Museum**

A NATIONAL JAUNT

The pleasant, 4.1-mile WEST LOOP follows parts of SECTIONS 2 and 4 of the JAUNT and all of SECTION 3. The circuit takes in the west end of the Mall from Washington Monument to Lincoln Memorial, as well as a good chunk of the Tidal Basin and Jefferson Memorial, with a couple of options at the finish.

Begin at the **Washington Monument**. In the warmer months, special events are common here on weekends, from rock concerts and military band performances to festivals, celebrations and protest rallies. (Every 4th of July, this is also ground zero for an amazing fireworks display, but go early to pass through the temporary security gates and stake out a patch of grass. Or avoid all that by watching from somewhere closer to the river.)

From George's giant obelisk, walk west to the **WWII Memorial**. Once there, look for the tall archway at the north end of the memorial labeled "Atlantic." With your back to the fountain, follow the walkway north about 0.1 mile to a four-way junction of wide, paved paths. Turn left and follow this one down to the duck pond (**Constitution Gardens**) and along the right side to the little island up ahead. Then turn to p. 51 for the continuation to **Lincoln Memorial**. Expect a one-mile walk from Washington to Lincoln.

From Lincoln Memorial, follow all of SECTION 3 (around the **Tidal Basin**) past the **Martin Luther King, Jr.**, **FDR** and **Jeffer-**

son Memorials, and SECTION 4 as far as the WWII Memorial. Return to Washington Monument to complete the loop. The WEST LOOP, as you might notice, is the greenest of the bunch—trees, lawns, ponds, the Tidal Basin—almost all of it following off-street trails and walkways.

Martin Luther King, Jr. Memorial.

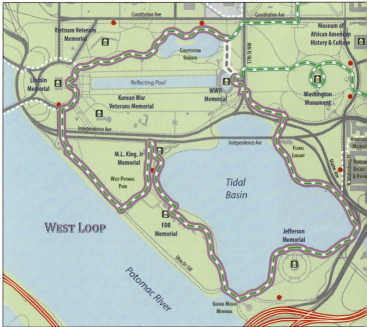

East Loop

U.S. Capitol → Supreme Court → Library of Congress → Capitol Hill → Union Station → Postal Museum → Senate Park

▶ *Distance*: 2.2 miles, allow 1.5 to 2 hours

▶ *Start/Finish*: East Plaza, U.S. Capitol (*map next page*)

Points of Interest: **U.S. Capitol (East Plaza & Capitol Visitor Center) • U.S. Supreme Court • Court of Neptune Fountain • Library of Congress • Folger Shakespeare Theatre & Library • Sewall-Belmont House & Museum • VFW • Capitol Hill Neighborhood • Stanton Park • General Nathanael Greene statue • Federal Judicial Center • Union Station • Postal Museum • National Guard Memorial Museum • Holodomor Memorial • Freedom Bell • Christopher Columbus Fountain • Senate Park & Fountain**

• •

At 2.2 miles, the EAST LOOP is the shortest of the bunch, but with much to see. It largely follows SECTIONS 6 and 7 of the JAUNT, with a short 0.3-mile connector completing the loop.

Start at the **East Plaza** of the **U.S. Capitol** (*see p. 81 for directions, if needed*), then follow the same route description for SECTION 6 from the East Plaza to the **Supreme Court**, **Library of Congress**, **Folger Shakespeare Theatre** and **Union Station** (1.6 miles to there). Next, turn to SECTION 7 and follow that as far as the **Senate Fountain**.

From the upper Senate Fountain (above the steps), face the Capitol and walk a short way toward it, then take the path angling left through large oak trees. That brings you to the corner of Constitution and Delaware Aves. Cross both streets to access the East Plaza beyond the security kiosk. For Metro access, you could also begin and end the loop at **Union Station**.

Historic, walkable Capitol Hill Neighborhood.

A NATIONAL JAUNT

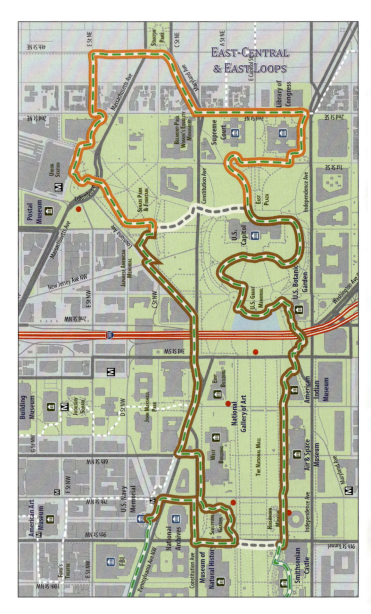

East-Central Loop

National Archives ➜ Sculpture Gardens ➜ Smithsonian Museums ➜ Botanic Garden ➜ U.S. Capitol ➜ National Art Galleries ➜ Navy Memorial

▶ *Distance*: 3.8 miles, allow 2 to 3 hours

▶ *Start/Finish*: Navy Memorial (*map previous page*)

Points of Interest: **Navy Memorial • National Archives • Sculpture Garden • Hirshhorn Museum • National Air & Space Museum • Waterman Haas Observatory • American Indian Museum • Mid-Atlantic Regional Garden • U.S. Botanic Garden • Bartholdi Park • James Garfield Memorial • U.S. Grant Memorial • Peace Monument • Summerhouse • U.S. Capitol • Senate Park & Fountain • Japanese-American Memorial • Taft Memorial & Carillon • U.S Department of Labor • William Blackstone Statue • General Meade Monument • John Marshall Park • Canadian Embassy • Newseum • Andrew W. Mellon Fountain • Federal Trade Commission • National Gallery of Art • Museum of Natural History • National Archives • Grand Army Memorial • Temperance Fountain • General Hancock Memorial**

• •

The EAST CENTRAL LOOP heads south from **Penn Quarter**, swings around the eastern part of the **National Mall** and back **downtown**, beginning and ending, once again, at the **Navy Memorial**. The 3.8-mile route picks up most of SECTION 5 of the JAUNT, and parts of SECTIONS 6 and 7. If you've already completed the first three loops, this one will wrap up the remainder of the NATIONAL JAUNT.

From the Navy Memorial, walk south on 7th St toward the Mall, with the **National Archives** on your right. Take a spin around the **National Sculpture Garden** and continue across the Mall to the cylindrical **Hirshhorn Museum**, where you'll pick up SECTION 5. Turn to p. 75 and follow that route to its end at the **West Steps** of the **Capitol**. Then continue on with SECTION 6, but only as far as the **East Plaza** (2.1 miles to here).

From the East Plaza, head north (right of the Capitol) and pass a security kiosk to the traffic light at Constitution and Delaware Aves. Cross both streets and take the path angling through large oak trees. Then aim for the **Senate Fountain** just ahead. Descend steps on the opposite side and pass the reflecting pool to Louisiana Ave; turn left. Here, pick up SECTION 7 of the JAUNT (*see p. 89*) and follow it to its end at the Navy Memorial—then consider the advice there on p. 93.

More Jaunts in the National Nearby

To experience more of D.C. and the surrounding metro area, here are 18 more walkabouts. Suggested routes range from easy sauntering to light hiking in varied settings. See the map on p. 176-177 for approximate locations.

Senate Park in spring.

▶ **RIVER LOOP & T. ROOSEVELT ISLAND** - *Riverfront hike to Georgetown (p. 105)*
5.0 to 6.5-mile loop / allow 2.5 to 4 hours

▶ **GEORGETOWN LOOP** - *Quaint, fun and historic (p. 113)*
1.6 to 3.8-mile loop / allow 1 to 2.5 hours

▶ **EMBASSY ROW** - *Elegant architecture, international ambience (p. 118)*
1.3 to 2.7-mile loop / allow 1 to 2 hours

▶ **DUPONT CIRCLE TO ADAMS MORGAN** - *Downtown to uptown, and curious (p. 123)*
2.2 miles / allow 1.5 to 2 hours

▶ **ROCK CREEK HIKER-BIKER TRAIL** - *Lazy ramble with a fun zoo finish (p. 126)*
2.7-mile loop / allow 1.5 to 2 hours

▶ **PEIRCE MILL–BOULDER BRIDGE LOOP** - *Easy intro to Rock Creek Park (p. 127)*
4.0 to 6.0-mile loop, allow 2 to 4 hours

▶ **RAPIDS BRIDGE–ROLLING MEADOW BRIDGE LOOP** - *A real hike in the park (p. 130)*
2.2 to 4.2-mile loop, allow 1.5 to 2.5 hours

▶ **NATIONAL ZOO TO DUPONT CIRCLE** - *Via Mount Pleasant and U St (p. 133)*
3.3 to 4.8 miles, allow 1.5 to 3.0 hours

▶ **CHINATOWN TO DUPONT CIRCLE** - *Downtown plazas, circles and squares (p. 137)*
1.7 miles, allow 1 to 1.5 hours

▶ **OLD DOWNTOWN–CHINATOWN LOOP** - *Discover historic, walkable D.C. (p. 140)*
2.0-mile loop, allow 1 to 2 hours

▶ **CAPITOL HILL–EASTERN MARKET LOOP** - *Quaint, funky and beauteous (p. 145)*
2.8-mile loop, allow 1.5 to 2 hours

▶ **ANACOSTIA RIVERWALK** - *Major, recent enhancements and much to see (p. 148)*
2.7 to 3.5-mile loop, allow 1.5 to 2.5 hours

▶ **POTOMAC HERITAGE TRAIL** - *A good, close-in hike with cozy waterfalls (p. 152)*
3.6 to 9.0 miles, allow 2 to 6 hours

▶ **FOUR MILE–BLUEMONT–LUBBER RUN** (ARLINGTON) - *Good rambling paths (p. 156)*
3.7 to 5.5-miles, allow 1.5 to 3 hours

▶ **NEW TOWN/OLD TOWN ALEXANDRIA** - *Urban sauntering into history (p. 160)*
2.5-mile loop, allow 1.5 to 2 hours

▶ **OLD TOWN ALEXANDRIA–LOWER LOOP** - *Footsteps of the founding fathers (p. 164)*
1.4-mile loop, allow 1 to 1.5 hours

▶ **MVT/MEMORIAL BRIDGE–CRYSTAL CITY–OLD TOWN** - *Got your 10,000 steps? (p. 169)*
3.3 to 6.7 miles one way, allow 1.5 to 3.5 hours

▶ **MVT/OLD TOWN–JONES POINT–DYKE MARSH** - *Scenic riverfront stroll (p. 172)*
2.8 to 7.8 miles round trip, allow 1.5 to 4 hours

MORE JAUNTS

103

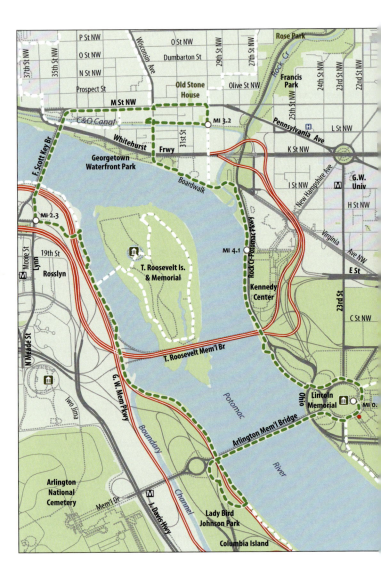

River Loop & Theodore Roosevelt Island

▶ *Distance*: 2.0 to 6.5-miles or 5-mile loop, allow 1 to 4 hours

▶ *Start*: Lincoln Memorial and across Memorial Bridge; or Arlington Cemetery Metro Station; or see below to begin at Rosslyn or Kennedy Center

▶ *Nearest Metro*: Arlington Cemetery or Foggy Bottom (15 minutes away), or Rosslyn to start mid-route

Points of Interest: **Lincoln Memorial • Memorial Bridge • Potomac River • Arlington National Cemetery • George Washington Memorial Parkway • Mount Vernon Trail • Columbia Island • Theodore Roosevelt Island & Memorial • Potomac Heritage Trail • Rosslyn • Key Bridge • Georgetown • Francis Scott Key Park • M Street • Wisconsin Avenue • Old Stone House • C&O Canal & Towpath • Justice William O. Douglas bust • Georgetown Waterfront Park • foreign embassies • Rock Creek Trail • Kennedy Center • Peter's Point**

Mount Vernon Trail in Lady Bird Johnson Park.

*If biking the loop, road crossings require extra caution with kids. On M St, families may want to walk their bikes on the sidewalk for a few blocks. Caution is also advised at the C&O Canal (there's no railing). Browse local cycling guides and websites for more family rides.

This scenic five-mile loop sidles up close to the Potomac River, including two historic bridge crossings, the ever-popular MOUNT VERNON TRAIL, an island preserve, the C&O Canal National Historical Park, Georgetown, and if your timing is right, an optional free performance at the Kennedy Center (6:00 pm nightly). In fact, the RIVER LOOP really could be part of the NATIONAL JAUNT, but is listed separately to keep the JAUNT to a more manageable 12 miles.

The loop starts and ends at **Lincoln Memorial** and mostly follows paved paths through nicely maintained landscapes and boardwalks among wetlands. The return includes a quaintly, if not lively, stroll along historic Georgetown's main drag, M St, with links to other nearby walks. One could also do this as two shorter walks between the Rosslyn Metro Station and the Kennedy Center, where a free shuttle goes to the Foggy Bottom Metro (*see map*). The entire loop is wheelchair-accessible despite a couple of steep spots. It also makes a great bike tour,* except for the Roosevelt Island side trip (closed to bikes).

For the RIVER LOOP, begin at the center of the plaza below the steps of the **Lincoln Memorial** [MILE 0.0]. (*To reach the Memorial, see*

105

p. 56. As an alternative, you could start the loop at the Arlington National Cemetery Metro Station or Rosslyn and adjust the directions below accordingly*.)

From the center of the **plaza**, looking at Lincoln Memorial, walk left to the far end of the plaza. Cross the one-way drive to the bike rental station and walkway leading rightward to 23rd St and the stately **Memorial Bridge** (1932) beyond the trees. The abutments are adorned with golden horsemen from Italy. A wide sidewalk leads across the bridge. Don't forget to look back at the Lincoln Memorial.

The obvious island upriver is Theodore Roosevelt Island. We'll dally there soon enough. Straight ahead on the Virginia side of the river is **Arlington**

Traffic noise detracts, but it's a scenic stroll across Memorial Bridge above the mighty Potomac, second largest river feeding Chesapeake Bay.

National Cemetery (1864), established during the Civil War. The cemetery's 400,000+ burials include countless American heroes, explorers, astronauts and national leaders, notably the Kennedys (John, Jackie, Robert and Ted). The Changing of the Guard at the **Tomb of the Unknown Soldier** often draws a crowd (*on the half-hour April-September, hourly October-March; see also p. 190 and* www.arlingtoncemetery.mil).

The columned edifice on the hill above Arlington Cemetery is **Arlington**

House (1817), a former Lee mansion and now memorial to Confederate General Robert E. Lee. After the Civil War, he stayed in the area, but it's said he would walk by the old house without looking up. In a roundabout way, Arlington, Virginia, got its name from this house. Memorial Bridge symbolically joins Arlington House to Lincoln Memorial as reaffirmation of a unified North and South after the war. Located above the **Kennedy Gravesite**, the House is open to viewing most days of the year.

A little to the left of Arlington House, look for the tall, sweeping arms of the Air Force Memorial (at a distance), rising like a Thunderbirds jet formation (*see p. 191*). At the far end of Memorial Bridge, the path curves left and passes a junction [MILE 0.7]. For the MOUNT VERNON TRAIL, continue straight. (Or head right if you first want to visit Arlington National Cemetery, or to locate the adjacent Metro station, a five-minute walk from this junction*.)

*If starting your hike at the Arlington Cemetery Metro Station, exit the station via the south side escalator, swing right (toward the river) to pass "The Hiker" (a memorial to Spanish American War veterans) and follow the sidewalk to the far end of a big traffic circle. Cross two lanes of traffic at a crosswalk (generally not difficult) to the signed junction for the MOUNT VERNON TRAIL.

MVT and G.W. Pkwy from Memorial Bridge in winter. The MVT was completed in 1972 and is co-managed with the George Washington Memorial Parkway. In 1983, the trail was also designated as part of the Potomac Heritage National Scenic Trail, which could eventually extend from Chesapeake Bay to southwestern Pennsylvania.

From the junction, the trail curves left to cross a busy, one-lane ramp to **George Washington Memorial Parkway**, a unit of the National Park System more commonly referred to as the "G. Dubya Parkway." Cross when safe.

The artful path now meanders southward through **Lady Bird Johnson Park** to a fork. Stay left and cross the Parkway's two northbound lanes at a crosswalk. It's a short crossing and generally quick and easy. If it's busy, be patient, a gap will soon appear. Courteous drivers often stop to let folks cross—just be sure the guy in the other lane is stopping too. Many drivers don't seem to realize they're motoring through a national park. (Don't fret too much over these various road crossings—they're just a little annoying.)

Once across the Parkway, you'll reach the well used **Mount Vernon Trail** [MILE 0.9]; scurry left for the RIVER LOOP. Right would take you three miles south to Crystal City via Reagan National Airport, or six miles to Old Town Alexandria (*see p. 169*). But head upriver to pass beneath Memorial Bridge.

The MOUNT VERNON TRAIL (or **MVT**) is a paved, 18-mile bicycle-pedestrian trail linking Rosslyn, Virginia to George Washington's historic estate at Mount Vernon, south of Alexandria. The next mile of walking will give you a pretty good sense of what the other 17 miles are like (an excellent bike ride).

Another little known fun fact is that this stretch of the MVT is actually on a mile-long island called **Columbia Island**. About 0.4 mile after passing under Memorial Bridge, you'll leave the island when you cross the trail bridge over **Boundary Channel**. The channel marks the boundary between Washington, D.C. and the Old Dominion of Virginia, placing Columbia Island and nearby Theodore Roosevelt Island squarely within D.C.

The next series of highway bridges are for I-66 and U.S. 50, which cross over the south end of **Theodore Roosevelt Island**. At an underpass, the trail meets an elevated boardwalk for a quarter-mile. Pass a junction on the left (goes to D.C. via the I-66 bridge), before reaching a parking area and footbridge to T.R.'s island [MILE 1.9]. A trail map should be posted at the far end of the bridge to help you locate the actual **Theodore Roosevelt Memorial** (1932) hidden in the woods above the footbridge, though it's easy to find (go right at the end of the footbridge, then make the next two lefts).

Boardwalk section of the MVT near Theodore Roosevelt Island.

MORE JAUNTS

It's under a half-mile round trip from the parking lot to the memorial. Or hike there via the **island loop** (right).

The memorial plaza and captivating sculpture of the 26th American president are nicely secluded and well maintained, comparable to sites on the National Mall. Notable quotes are etched in stone, while the protected forest is also a peaceful and fitting tribute.

In the 1700s, the 88-acre island was occupied by a large farm with extensive produce gardens. It was reforested with native trees in the 1930s as a natural memorial to T.R., the old Bull Moose-hunter-conservationist and fifth cousin to FDR. The statue of T.R. was dedicated in 1967. A small herd of deer and other furry things roam the woods, while copious feathered, scaly and sticky things hang out around the wetlands.

If you hiked the island loop to get to the memorial, exit the plaza by in the same direction T.R. is facing, then follow the curving path down and right to reach the footbridge. You might notice a few kayakers enjoying a popular circumnavigation of the island. Many rent their boats in Georgetown near Key Bridge.

After dawdling (or doddering) around the island, return to the MOUNT VERNON TRAIL and continue past the parking lot and briefly upriver. Just before the trail ramps up, notice the unpaved path on the right—the **Potomac Heritage Trail**.

Theodore Roosevelt.

T.R.'s Island Loop

You can burn an hour or more exploring the web of trails around T. R.'s island. For a 1.5-mile loop, cross the footbridge from the parking area, head right 30 yards to a junction and stay right (left goes up the hill to the T.R. Memorial). Follow this path to where it meets a parallel trail above (MILE 0.3); jog left and right to continue on that (the trail you departed goes to a Roosevelt Bridge overpass). Reach a no-frills but adequate restroom and water fountain just ahead, then choose the wide right fork. The trail then circles around to the left past an overpass to begin a half-mile section of elevated boardwalk through extensive wetlands. Watch for cypress knees (wood stubs) hidden in the brush. At the far end of the boardwalk climb a short hill and stay left at the next three forks immediately ahead (short spurs on the right lead to the river). The third left (MILE 1.1) heads up slightly to an easy stretch to the memorial (MILE 1.3).

Kayakers and Key Bridge from T.R. Island.

It leads about ten miles up the river, and while it isn't heavily used, it's scenic enough and is gradually being improved (*see p. 152*). For now, ascend the long ramp, almost a corkscrew, where the climbing path spans the G.W. Parkway. Just beyond, you'll arrive at **Rosslyn**, Virginia, and the north terminus of the MOUNT VERNON TRAIL at the Lynn St traffic light [MILE 2.3]. (If you need to skedaddle to the nearest Metro Station, walk two blocks left, one block right, then briefly left again to reach the Rosslyn Station*. Incidentally, the express bus to Dulles Airport stops at the corner downhill from the Metro entrance.)

To continue the RIVER LOOP across Key Bridge from the MVT, turn right at the traffic light, follow the sidewalk to a one-lane ramp and cross when safe. Then head across **Key Bridge** (1923) to Georgetown. This is D.C.'s oldest bridge over the Potomac. Named for Georgetown's star-spangled poet-lawyer, Francis Scott Key, it affords broad views up and down the river. The expansive white building way down yonder and hiding behind T.R.'s Island is the Kennedy Center; the closer greenspace on the left bank is Georgetown Waterfront Park.

Dead ahead is **Georgetown**, settled in 1751. It may have been named for a king, but not a president, or possibly for a couple of colonial Georges who were neither kings nor presidents (the record isn't clear). The dark spires left of the bridge are part of Georgetown University (1879) (*see p. 113 for a closer look*). Near the north end of Key Bridge, cross one more off-ramp, (when safe), this one accessing the Whitehurst Freeway. Near the end of the bridge, notice the **C&O Canal and Towpath** below.

* If starting the walk at Rosslyn Metro, exit to Moore St and turn left. At the end of the block go right, then left on Lynn St. Cross to the east side of Lynn St and continue across Key Bridge.

As you reach the traffic light at M St [MILE 2.7], amble right through little **Key Park** to find a bust of Mr. Key (1993) near the white columns. Continue along **M St** for several blocks admiring the well preserved architecture, some of it dating to the late-1700s and now home to modern shops, eateries and imbiberies. There's a whole lot of history here, so watch for a couple of historical signs and plaques and walk in the famed footsteps of nation-founders, civic leaders, assorted dignitaries and celebrities, not to mention mere commonfolk like us out for a stroll.

Bust of Francis Scott Key.

When you reach **Wisconsin Ave**, cross M St near the golden dome of the former Riggs National Bank (1922). If time allows, wander up the hill a couple of blocks to enjoy a bit more of the G-town hubbub (*see also p. 113*). Otherwise, cross Wisconsin Ave and keep heading east on M St another block and a half to the **Old Stone House** (1765), D.C.'s oldest building. Find exhibits, period furnishings and a bookstore/gift shop inside, gardens outside.

Continue to the next corner, go right to recross M St and head south down 30th St one block to the Chesapeake & Ohio, a/k/a C&O Canal and TOWPATH [MILE 3.2]. (Venezuela's embassy is

Old Stone House.

close by.) The suggested route for the RIVER LOOP turns right to follow the canal path three blocks west to Wisconsin Ave (again) before heading down to the riverfront. To shorten your journey by a third of a mile, you can skip the walk on the TOWPATH by continuing down 30th St to a large sundial next to the river, then see the continuation on the next page.

From the 30th St bridge over the C&O Canal and TOWPATH, catch a good view of the locks, then head right (upstream) along the canal. Thirty yards from the bridge, look for a bust of **Supreme Court Justice William O. Douglas** (1977) near the canal. Douglas, an avid hiker and conservationist, is credited with preserving the canal and adjoining greenway from development over sixty years ago. His likeness now gazes up the canal at **Lock Number 3** (of 74).

Cross the next street, Thomas Jefferson St, to **Lock 4**. Look for the tired bones of the canal barge *Georgetown*, although it may have disappeared by the time you read this. The old boat offered

Justice William O. Douglas.

enjoyable canal lock tours, but was deemed unsafe several years ago and too costly to fix. (*For a possible canal barge tour at Great Falls, see p. 182.*)

Cross 31st St. (To avoid some stairs up ahead, wheelchair hikers may want to turn left here and head down to the riverfront via 31st St.) After crossing 31st St, continue along the Canal TOWPATH—mules walked these paths for decades towing boats and barges up and down

C&O Canal

In its heyday in the mid-1800s, the C&O Canal was grand infrastruture, a principal transportation corridor that operated for nearly a century. From trade and travel to coal shipments and mail delivery from mills, mines and farms, the C&O served the growing city inside the Capital Beltway, long before there was any notion of a Beltway. Canals were much more efficient than buggies and horses on lumpy, muddy trails—that is, until canal transport was ultimately snuffed out by the big ol' bootheel of steam trains.

Canal construction, begun in 1828, never did make it to the Ohio River at Pittsburgh as originally envisioned, but few would complain. Trains were way cool, and hugely faster. Today, the C&O Canal and TOWPATH are part of a national historical park that extends 184.5 miles from Washington, D.C. to Cumberland, Maryland, all of it walkable and bikable (*see p. 182*).

C&O Canal in Georgetown.

Head left along the river with views across the Potomac to Rosslyn's well funded skyline and the big white Kennedy Center downriver. Rowing teams often kick up wake offshore. The park ends at the end of 31st St and the boardwalk and boat dock, where you can catch a **foot ferry** over to Old Town Alexandria—highly recommended in good weather (*see p. 159*). Continue walking along the **boardwalk** adjacent to a local hotspot, perhaps with a spring break atmosphere if you happen to catch it at the right (or wrong) time. A large oval **plaza and fountain** to the left converts to a winter ice-skating rink.

the canal. Pass under an attractive, arched **stone bridge**, then a few paces beyond, watch for the stone steps hidden on the right and follow them up to Wisconsin Ave. Turn right and head down to the river.

Strutting down Wisconsin Ave toward the river, you'll pass an old stone church (Grace Episcopal) and the Thailand Embassy before crossing K St beneath the Whitehurst Freeway. Enter **Georgetown Waterfront Park**, a veritable national park, near a large fountain and water play area [MILE 3.6]. Kids young and not so young love running through the spray on a warm day, so expect plenty of company if it's hot out.

Riverfront boardwalk.

At the end of the boardwalk (30th St) you'll find the **sundial** mentioned earlier. The Swedish Embassy (2006) is close by and is sometimes open for exhibits on weekends. It shares a bit of space with Iceland's Embassy. From the sundial, walk between the river and the embassy. (Note the boathouse to the right; rentals available.)

Angle left to cross the bridge over **Rock Creek** and stay right on the paved path as it swings away from the traffic light. (At the light, another paved path heads left along Rock Creek Pkwy.; this is the **Rock Creek Hiker-Biker Trail**, which can be followed 2.5 miles to the National Zoo, or beyond; *see p. 126*.)

TOWPATH and stone arch bridge.

Potomac River and Kennedy Center.

The RIVER LOOP parallels the river toward the sprawling white rectangle, the **Kennedy Center for the Performing Arts** (1971). Just before it on the left is the distinctive curlicue architecture of the Watergate Hotel (also 1971) made famous in the Nixon years. The actual water gate was a flow-control structure at the mouth of Rock Creek. Remnants still exist.

Hall of Nations, Kennedy Center.

For a quick tour of the Kennedy Center, turn left to cross Rock Creek Pkwy at the traffic light [MILE 4.1]. Take the sidewalk up the hill to access the entrance on the upper side of the building. Kennedy is worth a visit, especially if you

catch it by 6:00 pm (any evening, all year long). An endless variety of performers from around the world appear at the **Millennium Stage**, always free and no tickets neeed. Check the website (www.kennedy-center.org) for upcoming shows or to stream the ones you missed. A free and frequent shuttle serves the Foggy Bottom Metro Station, in case you are starting or ending your walk here.

Back at the traffic light, finish your last mile of the RIVER LOOP by continuing along the path next to the river, passing under the steel and stone bridges of I-66. Jog around a curvaceously angular plaza at **Peter's Point**, once a welcoming area for visitors arriving by boat. Across the street are several "beach" volleyball courts, heavily used on nice weekends.

The path becomes a sidewalk here and climbs a long, easy grade to a pair of **golden-winged horses** near Memorial Bridge [MILE 4.8]. Cross left at the horses and follow the walkway through a couple of intersections to the north end of the **Lincoln Memorial plaza** [MILE 5.0]. If you started the loop at the Arlington Cemetery Metro Station, walk across the entire plaza, then refer back to the beginning of the RIVER LOOP for your final easy leg across the bridge to the Metro.

Memorial Bridge from near the golden horses and Lincoln Memorial.

Georgetown Loop

▶ *Distance*: 1.6 to 3.8-mile loop, allow 1 to 2.5 hours
▶ *Start*: Northeast corner at M St and Wisconsin Ave (*map, next page*)
▶ *Nearest Metro*: Rosslyn, Foggy Bottom (20-minute walk)

Points of Interest: **M Street • C&O Canal & Towpath • Key Bridge • Car Barn • Exorcist Stairs • Georgetown University • Volta Laboratory • Volta Park • Wisconsin Avenue • Book Hill • Georgetown Library • Duke Ellington School of the Arts • Dumbarton Oaks • Montrose Park • Dumbarton Gardens & Museum • Oak Hill Cemetery • Evermay • Dumbarton House • Rose Park • Old Stone House**

Georgetown, M St at Wisconsin Ave. Many buildings predate the Civil War.

Golden dome and starting point.

When someone says "Georgetown," one of the first things to come to mind is M St. Of course, if you live there, your view is probably more encompassing and maybe all but excludes M St. To be sure, it can get a little crazy sometimes with restaurant goers, tourists and the college crowd. Nevertheless, it's a wonderful old part of D.C. and warrants much aimless exploring any old time.

You can get to **Georgetown** by Metrobus or the D.C. Circulator, which both run frequent schedules. Or walk there from the Rosslyn Metro Station across scenic Key Bridge, or from Foggy Bottom via 23rd St and Pennsylvania Ave. (Consult a city map or ask a fellow pedestrian.)

To extend your experience beyond a lazy stroll on M St, here's a four-mile loop to get you better acquainted with the neighborhood. Hills and stairs will get your pulse up (not wheelchair friendly), though most of the walk qualifies as easy-breezy. It can also be split into two shorter loops, as noted below. Either choice will give you a good introduction to the **Georgetown National Historic District**.

Begin at the old bank with the golden dome at the corner of M St and Wisconsin Ave, the approximate centroid of the Georgetown universe [MILE 0.0]. **Wisconsin Ave** offers an intermediate connector to split up the walk

MORE JAUNTS

if desired. To bypass the lower section, head up the hill on Wisconsin Ave about five blocks to Volta Pl and skip the next six paragraphs. Otherwise, ignore that last sentence, cross Wisconsin and saunter west on **M St**.

Looking across M St, the first red-brick building up from the corner was known as the **City Tavern** (now private), built in 1796. It was a favored Georgetown hangout for George Washington and Thomas Jefferson, among others.

Continue up the block to Potomac St. Cross M St to a specialty market. Jog slightly to the left side and follow the cobblestone alley to a **C&O Canal** overlook (*see p. 110 for more about the canal*). Either cross the footbridge here and head right on the **Towpath**, or pass behind the same building to a narrow alley that leads to the next footbridge at 33rd St. You could cross the canal there, again heading right or upstream.

Follow the C&O Canal TOWPATH

another couple of hundred yards to **Key Bridge** (1923). Pass under the archway and in 100 yards more turn left up an inconspicuous staircase immediately before the next bridge. The stairs lead to a short walkway next to the Whitehurst Freeway, which takes you back across the C&O Canal.

Cross M St at the light to the old **Car Barn** (1895) on the corner [MILE 0.5]. This was the depot for the streetcar trolley system way back when. Walk along the left side of the building and up the **giant staircase** ahead, famous for the filming of a pivotal scene in the 1970s classic, *The Exorcist*. A marker near the top of the stairs highlights films shot in Georgetown over the years.

Turn left on Prospect St then right onto 37th St. At the next corner, head left up the stone-lined stairs for a good look at **Georgetown University**'s historic **Healy Hall** (1879), named for Patrick Healy, a former slave and early president of the university. Stroll past this old stone edifice (also featured in the same scary movie) to a sculpture of the founder, Bishop Carroll. The striking White-Gravenor Hall is nearby. Amble right to the main entrance gate at 37th St. Turn left, then take P St to 35th St.

Turn left at 35th St and walk a block north to Volta Pl NW; turn right. At

Georgetown's White-Gravenor Hall.

the corner, note the **Volta Laboratory**, established by Alexander Graham Bell in 1893. On the next block, pass **Volta Park**, a good place to catch a kids' baseball game in season.

Thirteen-year-old Helen Keller broke ground for the construction of the Volta Laboratory building, and it still houses a nonprofit serving the needs of the deaf.

Upon reaching Wisconsin Ave [MILE 1.3] you'll find an attractive, old **stone church** (Georgetown Lutheran, 1914). Note that your starting point is five blocks down the hill, in case you only wanted to walk the 1.6-mile lower GEORGETOWN LOOP. For the longer (or upper) loop, head north on Wisconsin Ave a block to Q St, before crossing both Q St and Wisconsin Ave at the light.

Continue uphill on the east side of Wisconsin Ave to Reservoir Rd and a curving stairway just ahead. The stairs, nicely landscaped, lead up **Book Hill**,

Giant staircase off Prospect St.

MORE JAUNTS

which by some accounts actually begins at P St. Atop the hill is the **Georgetown Library** (1935), a true neighborhood gem [MILE 1.6]. Pass around the right side of the library to reach R St and turn left. (To cut the walk short by about 0.7 mile, you could turn right on R St, bypassing the scenic hike through Dumbarton Oaks Park. If you skip Dumbarton, walk only to 32nd St and jump ahead five paragraphs for the continuation.)

For the more interesting route, follow R St west (left) across Wisconsin Ave and keep walking two blocks to 35th St; turn right. Notice the **Duke Ellington School of the Arts** (1897) perched on a rise and undergoing major renovation in 2016. It serves as a high school for high performers and is a joint effort of D.C. Public Schools, Georgetown University and the Kennedy Center. A locally-famous, giant Adirondack chair sits at the far left end.

Follow 35th St north past the old **Fillmore School** (1893). Formerly the Corcoran School of the Arts and Design, the building was recently sold to another nonprofit supporting the arts. At Whitehaven Pkwy two blocks ahead, turn right to return to Wisconsin Ave. Down the hill a smidgeon on the right is the **Georgetown Flea Market**, where artists, collectors and other vendors hawk their goods every Sunday, unless the weather's horrid (since 1972). For the loop, however, cross Wisconsin Ave, jog left, then right on Whitehaven St. In a block, the street curves left. Look

for a trail on the right here, signed for **Dumbarton Oaks** and turn right on the unpaved path [MILE 2.2].

Though the trail is well used, the first short section may pass through an area of dense vegetation. Things quickly open up, however, as you descend into a lush valley of meadows and forest. Stay straight at a junction (some steps go left) and before long you'll cross a small tributary of Rock Creek on a skinny footbridge. Just stay on the main path right of the creek. Restoration work is underway. Today's Dumbarton Gardens are somewhat visible on the hillside above (more on that below).

In Dumbarton Oaks Park, traces of extensive gardens and landscaping done long ago are apparent, especially in the surviving rock work along the path, several small bridge crossings and the banks and pools of the stream.

The trail appears to end at an open gate and what sort of qualifies as a four-way intersection. Of the two trails on the left, the leftmost one climbs to Massachusetts Ave. The other leads down to the ROCK CREEK HIKER-BIKER TRAIL at a bridge in under a half-mile and Connecticut Ave 0.2 mile farther (*see p. 126 for a continuation from there to the National Zoo*). But for the GEORGETOWN LOOP, head right up the hill on the narrow paved road known as **Lovers' Lane**. Trudge up the hill on Lovers' Lane to R St. Alternatively, as you're heading up, notice a gravel path on the left leading

Duke Ellington School of the Arts.

more steeply uphill into **Montrose Park** (1911), which fronts on R St. Any of the routes heading upward will take you to R St and the top of Georgetown [MILE **2.6**]. Park restrooms are near the street in a small brick building to the left.

The GEORGETOWN LOOP turns left (east) at R St, but to first explore the **Dumbarton Oaks Museum and Gardens**, turn right on the R St sidewalk to find the garden entrance opposite 31st St. The museum entrance is around the corner at 32nd St. Note the museum was closed for restoration in 2016, though the nearly 10 acres of gardens remained open (*2:00-6:00, Tue-Sun, modest fee; 2:00-5:00 in winter, free*).

So, regardless of where you find yourself on R St, head east to 28th St to continue the loop. You'll pass the securely fenced **Oak Hill Cemetery** (1848) and **stone chapel** on a picturesque hillside with pretty trees and winding paths among hundreds of tilting micro-monuments to the macro personalities of greater Georgetown—a kind of a quintessential cemetery if there is such a thing (*9:00-4:30 most days*).

As you round the bend to 28th St, you'll pass the well preserved **Evermay** mansion (1801), which now houses a foundation and frequent classical music performances. Turn left at Q St, pass the historic **Dumbarton House** (1800), which hosts tours and special events (not to be confused with Dumbarton Oaks noted earlier). Turn right at 27th

The chapel at Oak Hill Cemetery, designed by James Renwick using stone from the same quarry as the Smithsonian Castle.

St [MILE **3.0**], then make an immediate left and quick right to 26th St, lined with unassuming yet classy old townhomes. Follow this a block to P St and turn right, then head left on 27th St.

Much of the surrounding area was once the heart of **Georgetown's African American community**. In 1800, when George Town was a thriving tobacco port, a quarter of its 5,000 residents were slaves. The black population

A quiet street in Georgetown.

increased rapidly following emancipation, despite persistent racism. Gentrification picked up steam around 1950 and the community remains predominantly white today. Imagine the hustle-bustle on these streets before there were cars.

Follow 27th St south three blocks. Go right on N St (near Rose Park), left on 29th, right on Olive St and left on 30th. Walk a block to M St; turn right. Pass the **Old Stone House** (1765) to end the loop at Wisconsin Ave [MILE **3.8**].

When you reach M St, you could also go left to find the nearest Metro station at Foggy Bottom, a 0.8-mile hike. If you're heading that way, stay right to cross the Pennsylvania Ave bridge and walk several more blocks to Washington Circle. Circle right to 23rd St and turn right to find the Metro a block down. This is also where the free shuttle departs for Kennedy Center.

MORE JAUNTS

Embassy Row

- *Distance*: 1.3 to 2.7-mile loop, allow 1 to 2 hours
- *Start/Finish*: Central fountain at Dupont Circle.
- *Nearest Metro*: Dupont Circle

Points of Interest: **Dupont Circle • Embassy Row • Gandhi statue • Anderson House • Cosmos Club • Sheridan Circle • General Philip Sheridan • Dumbarton Bridge • Massachusetts Avenue Bridge • Winston Churchill • Nelson Mandela • Woodrow Wilson House • Mitchell Park • Spanish Steps • Phillips Collection Gallery**

As one might expect, countless nations have located their foreign embassies in Washington, D.C., with a good number of them lining Massachusetts Ave and nearby streets, especially to the north and west of Dupont Circle. Prior to the Great Depression, most of these classy buildings were private mansions. This one to two-hour loop swings by more than 30 of them, some charming and relatively spartan, others palatial and among the more architecturally exquisite old buildings to be found in the District.

Rather than point out every embassy here, we'll leave it to the reader to seek out the national flags, heroic sculptures and small bronze plaques identifying their respective homelands. Note that attachés (embassy support staff), consulates (often serving travelers and their own citizens), and official residences may also be in the mix. Things do change, so the embassies listed here can vary a bit.

The Embassy Row Loop begins at the fountain in the center of **Dupont Circle** (where the Chinatown-Dupont Circle walk ends; *see p. 137*) [Mile 0.0]. Check out the verse emblazoned around the pool and find the words "in recognition" beneath one of the female forms. Now, with your back to those two words, aim for the walkway leading away from the fountain toward the circular drive and a crosswalk. Cross to the tiny traffic island amid Massachusetts Ave. The traffic pattern is a little

Embassy Row

In May, many embassies open their doors to the roving public as part of *Passport DC* and the *European Union Open House.* Saturday events are attended by thousands—a veritable lovefest of cultural togetherness. Wouldn't it be nice if all the neighboring countries of the world got along as well as they seem to here at Embassy Row. You can catch lectures, films, cultural performances and tours at various embassies throughout the year (see the *dcembassyevents* page at www.facebook.com). To visit an embassy at other times, check their website to see if and when they accept visitors.

odd here, so wait for the walk sign and watch for cars on the right. Jog left on another crosswalk, then right to follow the left side of **Massachusetts Ave**.

You'll pass a small, brick building and plaza on your left before crossing 20th St. A substantial **farmers' market** bustles here every Sunday morning year-round. Following Massachusetts Ave, the **embassies** for Portugal and Indonesia are just ahead. After 21st St there's a humbling statue of **Gandhi** (2000) on the right with the Indian Embassy behind it.

Next is the **Anderson House** (1905) on the left, which hosts the *Society of the Cincinnati*, established after the

Revolutionary War. A free museum is open most days 10:00-4:00. Opposite that is the historic **Cosmos Club** (1901), founded in 1878 by the famed explorer/geographer John Wesley Powell. Cross Q St to stay on Massachusetts Ave. Estonia's Embassy is prominent on a skinny corner to the north.

After 22nd St, you'll pass the embassies to Luxembourg, Togo, Sudan, The Bahamas, Turkmenistan and Greece, then Ireland and Romania at the corner of 23rd St, opposite **Sheridan Circle** [MILE 0.4]. The statue at the center memorializes **Union General Philip Sheridan** (1908). An inconspicuous

Mahatma Gandhi.

Cosmos Club.

MORE JAUNTS

marker near the Romanian Embassy commemorates the place where Chilean diplomat Orlando Letelier and associate Ronni Moffitt were murdered in 1976.

The EMBASSY ROW LOOP continues around Sheridan Circle (clockwise) passing embassies for Latvia and the Republic of (South) Korea. The Kenya and Vietnam embassies are north of the Circle (several others are a little farther east along R St).

Stay on Massachusetts Ave to pass the embassies to Burkina Fasso, the Kyrgyz Republic, Croatia, Madagascar, Paraguay, United Arab Emirates, Malawi and the Ivory Coast, across from the intersection of S St. The loop now turns sharply right on S St [MILE 0.6] and up a longish hill (not wheelchair friendly). For an easier

To Georgetown:

If desired, one could hike to Georgetown from Sheridan Circle by heading left on 23rd St to Q St, then turning right to cross the Dumbarton Bridge (1915) spanning Rock Creek and the namesake trail and parkway below. Bison guard the abutments. From the bridge, another 0.2 mile stroll to 27th St would intercept the Georgetown Loop (see p. 117).

Bison at Dumbarton Bridge.

Embassy Row, Massachusetts Ave.

outing, just return to Dupont Circle via Massachusetts Ave. To see more embassies along Massachusetts Ave, read on. Or to continue the loop, start up S St and skip the next two paragraphs.

One could extend the walk up Massachusetts Ave another 0.7 mile to see at least a dozen more embassies (Zambia, Marshall Islands, Venezuela, Lesotho, Japan, India, Turkey, Belize, Iran, Brazil, Bolivia, South Africa and Great Britain), as well as statues of **Winston Churchill** (1966) and **Nelson Mandela** (2013) in front of the British and South African embassies. The Massachusetts Ave Bridge crosses over Rock Creek, offering good views along the way.

Just past the British Embassy is the **U.S. Naval Observatory** (1893), the official keeper of the clock in America. Once based on the stars, the timekeeping is now done with lasers and atoms to provide the accuracy needed—down to a thousandth of a nanosecond—to guide Navy ships and keep the GPS apps working on our smartphones. A digital display for the mother of all clocks off the seconds near the main gate, though maybe not quite worth the extra hike unless you're a true clockster. Access inside is restricted to infrequent evening tours (recommended); reserve online well in advance at www.usno.navy.mil/usno.

Now back to the loop. Walking east up S St, pass the Chad Embassy and cross 24th St to find the **Woodrow Wilson House** (1915) on the next block. This was the former president's home after he left office in 1921. One-hour tours are available for a modest fee (*10:00-4:00 Wed-Sun*). The neighborhood here is known as **Kalorama**, Greek for "nice view."

Next, pass the Netherlands, Pakistan and Mauritania Embassies (left) and Myanmar (Burma) and Laos (right), as well as **Mitchell Park** on the left [MILE 0.8]. The park offers a perfect greenspace for a snack break or some lazin' in the sun or shade. If you like, take the steps up from mid-block and turn right for a cozy sitting area. Outdoor movies are shown on the lawn in summer. (Note that the hike to Adams Morgan splits off near the park; *see p. 123*.)

Continuing on S St to the far end of Mitchell Park, turn right onto 22nd St and descend the ornate **Spanish Steps** (1911). Watch for the commerative plaque, then a local history sign on the

Spanish Steps.

left near the Dominican Republic Embassy. Continue to R St and the embassies to Bulgaria and Tanzania, and hang a left. Keep an eye peeled for a small sign denoting the former home of **Franklin and Eleanor Roosevelt** across R St from the Mali Embassy.

Cross Florida Ave and make a right at 21st St [MILE 1.1]. Then mosey left on Hillyer Pl across from the **Philips**

Woodrow Wilson House.

Collection gallery (bigger than it looks), where you can view the work of the masters (modest admission fee). The Morrocan Embassy, incidentally, is at the next corner.

Follow Hillyer Pl to Connecticut Ave and head right on 20th St to pass some inviting eateries. Just ahead at Q St is the north escalator for the Dupont Circle Metro. Or continue south on Connecticut Ave to reach your start at the fountain [MILE 1.3]. If you walked the extra 0.7 mile out Massachusetts Ave, the total walk would be about 2.7 miles.

20th St NW near Hillyer Pl.

National Zoo

SEE P. 133

Park Rd NW

Lamont St

19th St

18th St NW

Kenyon St NW

Mount Pleasant St NW

Irving St NW

Rock Creek

SEE P. 126

MI 1.3

Beach Dr

Adams Mill Rd

Harvard St

Rabaut Park

Connecticut Ave

Woodley

Cathedral Ave

Gates

Tunnel

Ontario Pl NW

Lanier Pl NW

Columbia Rd NW

16th St NW

M MI 0.0
MI 2.2

Calvert St NW

Euclid St NW

Ontario Rd

17th St NW

Kalorama Rd

Rock Creek & Potomac Pkwy

Biltmore St NW

18th St NW

Belmont Rd

Kalorama Park

Adams Morgan

MI 1.2

Meridian Hill Park

MI 2.5

Kalorama Rd NW

V St NW

24th St NW

23rd St NW

19th St NW

U St NW

New Hampshire Ave

15th St NW

California St NW

Florida Ave

T St NW

Phelps Pl

Mitchell Park

Connecticut Ave

Swann St NW

MI 4.1

Map continued on p. 135

S St NW

20th St NW

Riggs Pl

S Street Dog Park

House of the Temple

Sheridan Circle

22nd St NW

R St NW

Rock Cr-Potomac Pkwy

Hillyer Pl

Q St NW

18th St NW

17th St NW

16th St NW

Massachusetts Ave

M

P St NW

MI 0.0

Dupont Circle

Rock Creek

O St NW

M

Dupont Circle to Adams Morgan

▶ *Distance*: 2.2 miles, allow 1.5 to 2 hours

▶ *Start*: Central fountain at Dupont Circle (*green route on map*)

▶ *Nearest Metro*: Dupont Circle

Points of Interest: **Dupont Circle • Embassy Row • Spanish Steps • Mitchell Park • Kalorama Park • Adams Morgan • Duke Ellington Memorial Bridge**

Fountain at Dupont Circle.

Mitchell Park.

Here's another cool jaunt that traverses several historic neighborhoods, including a chunk of Embassy Row, Kalorama Heights and, of course, Adams Morgan. It features architectural styles that span the gamut, from stately and elegant to quotidian and artsy-funky. A lunch stop or refresher beckons at numerous sidewalk cafes along the way.

The walk climbs a few hills, but is a good way to extend the EMBASSY ROW LOOP (*p. 119*) or the CHINATOWN-DUPONT CIRCLE hike (*p. 137*). The finish takes you briefly beyond Adams Morgan to the Woodley Park Metro Station. For a more ambitious circuit, follow it up with the National Zoo-Dupont Circle trek (*p. 133*) to form a seven-mile loop.

From near the central fountain (1921) at **Dupont Circle [MILE 0.0]** head northwest on **Massachusetts Ave** to 22nd St—see EMBASSY ROW on p. 118 for specific directions to this point, if needed. You'll pass a number of **foreign embassies** and other historic sites of interest, as described in the EMBASSY ROW walk. Turn right at 22nd St, which leads uphill just left of Florida Ave. Walk three blocks north to reach, and ascend, the **Spanish Steps** (1911). Just beyond, at S St, turn left. (Wheelchair hikers would face a tough hill climb up Florida Ave and Phelps St to reach S St.)

Saunter past **Mitchell Park [MILE 0.5]** and turn right on 23rd St, or walk through this attractive park and make your way past the cute, yellow community building to 23rd St. Follow 23rd St north through **Kalorama Heights** for several blocks to Kalorama Rd and turn right.

MORE JAUNTS

Or meander left a little to explore a quiet niche of elegant old homes.

Follow Kalorama Rd to Connecticut Ave, which, by the way, provides a good return route to Dupont Circle. The big bridge over Rock Creek, a/k/a the **William Howard Taft Bridge** (1907), is just around the bend to the left, suggesting a minor detour there and back for the view (or catch it later from the other end). Next, cross Connecticut Ave and continue two more blocks on Kalorama Rd to 19th St. **Kalorama Park** is on the

Kalorama Park

left, good for a nap in the grass on a warm day [MILE 1.2]. Walk the obvious path up through the park and exit right of the patio and recreation center to cross Columbia Rd to Belmont Rd.

Follow Belmont to 18th St in the heart of **Adams Morgan** and turn left. Adams Morgan was once two highly

segregated, black and white neighborhoods, intentionally brought together as one over 50 years ago. Blocks of proud and playful, 1800s Victorian buildings suggest some extra inspiration on the part of the architects back in the day. Today, an eclectic amalgamation of shops, ethnic diners and hopping imbiberies line the busier streets, luring unwitting customers to (gasp!) abandon their jaunts.

As you reach the north end of 18th St at Columbia Rd, cross left at the light to a small **plaza**. Jog left again to the crosswalk leading to Biltmore St. Follow Biltmore St west about three blocks and round a curve to Calvert St. This puts you at the east end of the **Duke Ellington Memorial Bridge** (1935) [MILE 1.9]. Note the **presidential mural** across the street. Head left across the scenic bridge, with Rock Creek Pkwy abuzz below.

Continue to the traffic light at Connecticut Ave. The 900-foot-long Taft Bridge you might have seen earlier is now to the left (south). Via Connecticut Ave, it's a 1.1-mile glide back to Dupont Circle. To reach the Woodley Park Metro Station [MILE 2.2], cross both streets here and head north a half block on Connecticut Ave. Or keep on truckin' a few blocks more to reach the main entrance to the zoo.

18th St in Adams Morgan.

Rock Creek Park

Rock Creek Park (1890) is D.C.'s largest, a nearly 3,000-acre national park and urban wilderness of forested hills, glens, the stony creek, picnic areas, a nature center, well preserved historic features and 30+ miles of trails. A paved hiker-biker path runs through much of the park, often near the creek. The oft-hiked WEST RIDGE TRAIL passes near the Rock Creek Nature Center and links the historic Peirce Mill to the north end at Boundary Bridge. Closer to the creek is the unpaved VALLEY TRAIL. Both run the length of the park.

Other trails connect to Silver Spring (p. 189), CAPITAL CRESCENT TRAIL (p. 181), Glover Archbold Park (p. 182), C&O CANAL TOWPATH (p. 182), Dumbarton Oaks (p. 116), the National Zoo's OLMSTED WALK (p. 126), the National Mall, tributary greenways and surrounding neighborhoods. Find a trail map at the nature center near Military Rd, on the park's website (www.nps.gov/rocr); or posted at many access points.

The park is a popular place almost year-round, although you can nearly always find a few miles of lonely trails away from the hubbub. Rock Creek Park and its connecting trails span the entire District from the Potomac River to Chevy Chase, Maryland, although the bulk of the park lies north of the zoo.

It's even possible to pick up the ROCK CREEK HIKER-BIKER TRAIL outside Rockville, Maryland, and follow it all the way to the National Mall—quite a haul, of course, and more efficiently done as a bike ride. A big plus is that much of Beach Dr is closed to cars on the weekend, making this scenic stretch popular with cyclists all year long. To get off the beaten track, lash your bike to a hitching post along the way and wander up a trail—with your trusty map, of course. Most of the unpaved trails, by the way, are closed to bikes. If you choose to drive, a number of trailheads with parking are shown on the park map.

Rock Creek Park is also easily reached on foot from any number of bus stops in all directions and from a few Metro stations, including Woodley Park and Cleveland Park on the west (recommended) and Silver Spring to the north. If you're new to the park, several short to moderate loop options are described below to help get you acquainted with the layout and better known features.

The main entrance to the zoo is on Connecticut Ave midway between those first two Metro stations and makes an easy add-on to your walk. Begin at Woodley Park to hike paved paths to the ROCK CREEK TRAIL (next page) and lower east entrance of the zoo, returning via the zoo's OLMSTED WALK. Note the zoo closes at 7:00 pm (5:00 pm, October to mid-March).

For a more ambitious outing on more primitive trails in wilder terrain, consider the two loops on p. 129-134. Note that the creek is closed to swimming due to water quality issues. If you step off the trail, also beware that poison ivy is very common in the woods. Both the leaves and hairy vines can be toxic. ("Leaves of three, let it be!")

Rock Creek Hiker-Biker Trail

▶ *Distance*: 2.7-mile loop, allow 1.5 to 2 hours

▶ *Start*: Woodley Park Metro Station (*map, p. 122*)

▶ *Nearest Metro*: Woodley Park

Points of Interest: **Duke Ellington Bridge** • **Taft Bridge** • **National Zoo** • **Olmsted Walk**

For an easy stroll to the ROCK CREEK HIKER-BIKER TRAIL, exit the Woodley Park Metro [MILE 0.0] and walk south on **Connecticut Ave** (downhill) to the traffic light; cross Calvert St. The walk heads right—or make a quick detour left to a good view from the **Duke Ellington Bridge** (1935) or straight ahead for a look off the **Taft Bridge** (1907). Both bridges stand 125 feet above Rock Creek.

Return to the intersection and follow Calvert St a block west to 24th St. Cross and turn left on the paved path leading down to a crosswalk on the left just above Rock Creek Pkwy. This is loosely referred to as the ROCK CREEK TRAIL. Follow it across the road—caution! (A right here would take you to Georgetown and the National Mall.) Pass under the massive Taft Bridge, and Duke Ellington Bridge just beyond.

After a narrow sidewalk and small bridge near a parkway **tunnel** [MILE 0.6], go left along Rock Creek around a long horseshoe bend in the creek. This section is gated and closed at night, as is the zoo. If it's closed during the day (rarely the case), it's possible, but not much fun, to walk the skinny sidewalk through the tunnel and pick up the trail at the other gate, bypassing the big bend (*see map on p. 122*).

Near the tip of the horseshoe bend, cross a zoo service road. Stay on the ROCK CREEK TRAIL to the other end of the parkway tunnel, and soon reach a road bridge. Cross to find the lower entrance to the **zoo** and the lower end of OLMSTED WALK [MILE 1.4]. Hike up through the zoo for a mile to the main entrance at Connecticut Ave. Head left there to return to the Woodley Park Metro Station [MILE 2.7].

Connecticut Ave (or Taft) Bridge. Both Rock Creek Pkwy and the trail go under the arches.

Marine mammal habitat along the zoo's American Trail.

Peirce Mill–Boulder Bridge Loop

▶ *Distance*: 4.0 to 6.0-mile loop, allow 2 to 4 hours

▶ *Start*: Mel C. Hazen Trail at Connecticut Ave (*map, next page*)

▶ *Nearest Metro*: Cleveland Park

Points of Interest: **Melvin C. Hazen Trail • Western Ridge Trail • Peirce Mill • Theodore Roosevelt Trail • Pulpit Rock • Boulder Bridge • Valley Trail • Rapids Bridge**

Peirce Mill. Park rangers crank up the gristmill for demonstrations twice a month, April-October (2nd and 4th Saturdays, 11:00-2:00).

Boulder Bridge in Rock Creek Park.

KRIS WILCOX photo

Unlike the other, more civilized urban walks included in this guide, the hike described here takes you into some of the wilder parts of Rock Creek Park. It's not so wild you need to worry about lions and tigers and bears (oh my), though all those critters do happen to be hanging out at the zoo nearby. Instead, you're more likely be met by fearsome deer, squirrels, birds and the occasional red fox, not to mention lots of other folks out enjoying a hike in the park.

The PEIRCE MILL-BOULDER BRIDGE LOOP offers hikers a nice introduction to Rock Creek Park, staying mostly near the creek, while taking in a few historical features and scenic bridges. Trails can be rough and rocky in places and trail signing isn't perfect, so carry a map and keep track of your progress. The route described here is straight-forward, but if you get turned around, a fellow trailster can help get you back on track.

The Cleveland Park Metro Station is a convenient starting point [MILE 0.0]. Exit the station to the east side of **Connecticut Ave** and walk north 0.2 mile to the MELVIN C. HAZEN TRAIL on the right. Descend several switchbacks to the scenic creek. The trail soon crosses the creek bed, normally an easy rock-hop.

Follow the yellow-blazed trail through quiet forest to a big lawn and picnic area near **Rock Creek** [MILE 0.5]. A trail on the right crosses the smaller creek on a footbridge, but ignore that one and walk across the lawn to the paved hiker-biker trail close by; turn left. This is actually part of the WESTERN RIDGE TRAIL.

MORE JAUNTS

127

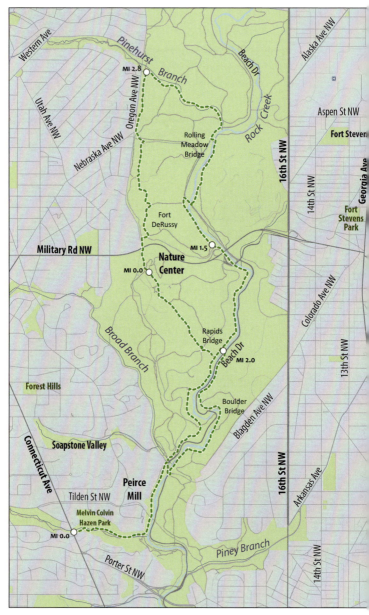

Rock Creek. To help improve and protect the park, visit www.rockcreekconservancy.org.

(Right leads 1.3 miles to the zoo and the bottom end of OLMSTED WALK.)

Following the paved path leftward, pass beneath Tilden St to find the old **Peirce Mill** (1829) just beyond. The carriage barn is up the hill and a matching **stone distillery** is across the street, but has no public access. A 1903 **dam** on Rock Creek looks like a relic from the milling days, but was apparently built to create a scenic waterfall. A fish ladder ascends the opposite side.

Continue along the bike path (or the parallel gravel path) to an intersection with Broad Branch Rd. You'll return to this point later. Cross and turn right to also cross Beach Dr. Then follow the sidewalk over the bridge above Rock Creek. At the far end of the bridge, turn left on the THEODORE ROOSEVELT TRAIL, a favorite saunter of the late president [MILE 1.0]. The hillside trail is narrow and rough, but easy enough. In 0.2 mile, reach the VALLEY TRAIL and turn left. **Pulpit Rock** is on the left near the junction.

Follow the blue-blazed VALLEY TRAIL past a few places where you could access the creek for a break among tons of sitting rocks. Be cautious in stormy weather, due to the risk of flash flooding. Soon round a big bend in the creek to spot the graceful arch of **Boulder Bridge**—a great photo op [MILE 1.6]. Just ahead, a spur on the left leads to the bridge, although the hike continues straight along the VALLEY TRAIL.

The path climbs briefly before easing off again for the next scenic stretch along the creek. Noisy rapids form here during times of high runoff. Take the next spur on the left leading to **Rapids Bridge** [MILE 2.0]. This is roughly the mid-point of the hike. If a restroom stop is calling, you could feasibly stay on the VALLEY TRAIL for another 0.2 mile and turn right to tennis courts with restrooms, then return to Rapids Bridge

(a half-mile round trip). Note that the next hike also passes this footbridge on the hike down from the Rock Creek Nature Center.

Cross to a wide, unpaved trail on the other side and turn left for the downstream return hike to Peirce Mill. Just below Rapids Bridge, two paths ascend the hillside to the right. The second climbs to Ross Drive and the nature center; the PEIRCE-BOULDER LOOP continues straight ahead. The trail soon leaves the creek, rounds a bend and climbs a hill to a junction [MILE 2.4]; stay left. After cresting a ridge, the path descends to Broad Branch Dr and the crosswalk you negotiated earlier [MILE 3.0].

Continue straight to pass the low dam near the mill. From the Peirce Mill walk up to Tilden St and turn right to reach the first street on left, below the old distillery. Take this access road into a **picnic area** with a small restroom building (decent enough). Skirt the right side and continue across the grass to the MELVIN C. HAZEN TRAIL you hiked at the start [MILE 3.5]. Take it back up to Connecticut Ave [MILE 4.0]. Alternatively, you could stay on the paved path to cross Rock Creek and walk the extra 1.3 miles to the zoo (keeping left on a trail bridge beneath the Porter-Klingle overpass). Then ascend to Connecticut Ave via OLMSTED WALK.

Rapids Bridge–Rolling Meadow Bridge Loop

▶ *Distance*: 2.2 to 4.2-mile loop, allow 1.5 to 2.5 hours
▶ *Start*: Rock Creek Park Nature Center (*map, p. 128*)
▶ *Nearest Metro*: None; convenient bus access from Friendship Heights Metro

Points of Interest: **Rock Creek Nature Center** • **Rapids Bridge** • **Miller Cabin** • **Milkhouse Ford** • **Valley Trail** • **Rolling Meadow Bridge** • **Western Ridge Trail** • **Fort DeRussy**

Rolling Meadow Bridge in winter.

This scenic, 4.2-mile hike covers some interesting ground with a few surprises, including a beauteous stretch of boulder-strewn Rock Creek. It offers a tad more of a workout with more ups and downs than the previous loop, but nothing too grueling. We are, after all, still in the big city, though you'd hardly know it once you're two minutes down the trail. The hike catches a good chunk of the WESTERN RIDGE TRAIL, VALLEY TRAIL, other connecting trails near Rock Creek and several historic sites and bridges. Or knock off two miles with a shortcut option.

Begin at the **Rock Creek Nature Center**, reached by car or via a nearby bus stop on Military Rd. If bussing over from the west (Friendship Heights or Chevy Chase), hop off at the first stop inside **Rock Creek Park** at Glover Rd. Tell the driver you're headed for the nature center and s/he will likely know the stop. An obvious paved path leads south from the corner at Glover Rd and climbs into the woods to reach the nature center in about 250 yards.

Valley Trail near Boulder Bridge.

The center provides an excellent introduction to local wildlife and common plants in Rock Creek Park. Exhibits inside include preserved creatures behind glass, habitat info and other displays. There's also a small planetarium and creative space for kids, plus ranger-led activities. The info desk has trail maps, while a small gift shop and restrooms round out the amenities inside. Nature trails and interpretive signs await some exploring outside.

For the loop hike, walk left as you exit the

center's main entrance. Go to the far end of the upper parking lot, then left down the hill past the horse center. Take the obvious trail at the end of the lot [MILE 0.0]. In under a hundred yards, stay right at a fork. This winding path descends into a little valley before reaching a T-intersection; turn left [MILE 0.2].

In another 0.1 mile look for a less obvious path on the right leading a few yards to a remarkable **cache of stone rubble**. At least a thousand heavy chunks of carved sandstone are piled in rows and heaps like the spoils of an archaeological dig. This was once the East Portico and steps of the U.S. Capitol building, stored here following a major rebuild around 1960. The same reconstruction project produced the columns displayed at the National Arboretum (*see p. 179*). Look, but leave it as is.

Return to the main trail and head right for a downslope glide to Ross Dr. Pass beneath the bridge and soon reach an unmarked junction at Rock Creek; turn left [MILE 0.7]. **Rapids Bridge** is just a short hop upstream. (The footbridge marks the north end of the previous hike up from Peirce Mill.) But don't cross yet. Instead, continue up the creek on the prettier west (left) side. For about a mile, above and below the Rapids Bridge, impressive whitewater forms here

Remnants of the U.S. Capitol's 1960 rebuild.

during periods of high runoff. Countless **large boulders** hint at the watery chaos grinding away at the creek bed.

When you reach the end of a road bridge [MILE 1.3], cross the road (but not the bridge) to a paved path that continues left along the creek. Pass beneath Military Rd just ahead, then after the path rounds a bend to the left, turn right on an unpaved trail [MILE 1.5] and go right again in a few yards more. (To shorten the loop by two miles, you could stay left here to reach **Fort DeRussy** in 0.4 mile and the WESTERN RIDGE TRAIL just beyond that, then skip to the last paragraph for the finish.)

From the junction (saving DeRussy for later), the loop heads right for a pleasant stretch traversing steeper slopes above the creek. The historic

MORE JAUNTS

Rock Creek below Rapids Bridge.

Western Ridge Trail junction.

Miller Cabin is visible across the creek. Not far beyond is **Milkhouse Ford**. An interpretive sign explains the old crossing.

At the next road bridge, cross over Rock Creek [MILE 1.9]. At the end of the bridge, hang a sharp left on a good trail that continues upstream, now on the east side of the creek. (Or check out the Miller Cabin first, if desired, with restrooms close by.) Back on the trail, you'll soon intercept the VALLEY TRAIL. Stay left and continue upstream to the next footbridge, a slender concrete arch over the creek. This is the **Rolling Meadow Bridge** [MILE 2.3].

Cross the footbridge, briefly head right along Beach Dr, taking the next left on the PINEHURST BRANCH TRAIL. Leaving Rock Creek behind, stay right at the first major fork, ignore any narrow offshoots, then continue straight at a signed four-way junction. Ascend the meandering valley to the green-blazed WESTERN RIDGE TRAIL [MILE 2.8]. Turn left and

follow this all the way back to the nature center, though it's easier said than done. Signing is not always clear and, in 2016, the green blazes were not entirely consistent with the park map.

Ignore a couple of trails left and right before meeting a paved path near Bingham Dr [MILE 3.2]. Turn left here, stay right at a fork (also paved) and follow this around the bend to cross Bingham Dr and head back up into the woods. When you reach another road, walk left 40 yards, cross the road and walk toward the woods. The trail seems to disappear briefly, but just head across the grass outside the horse corral—the **Park Police horse stables**. You should easily spot the trail sign and green markers near the fence.

The unpaved path leads around the fence and into the woods again. Ignore the next left and reach a T-intersection [MILE 3.9]. The loop goes right briefly, then left on the paved trail that leads down to the traffic light on Military Rd. However, it's worth making a quick side trip left from the T-intersection.

Barely 100 yards up the trail is the earthen remains of Fort DeRussy, an important Civil War site (0.4 mile via the shortcut before Miller Cabin). Head back to the traffic light to cross Military Rd to the bus stop noted earlier and the paved path leading up to the nature center [MILE 4.2].

Gravity won this one in Rock Creek Park.

Site of Fort DeRussy.

National Zoo to Dupont Circle

▶ *Distance*: 3.3 to 4.8 miles, allow 1.5 to 3.0 hours

▶ *Start*: Connecticut Ave zoo entrance (*maps, p. 122, 135*)

▶ *Nearest Metro*: Woodley Park or Cleveland Park

Points of Interest: **National Zoo • Olmsted Walk • Rock Creek • Rabaut Park • Meridian Hill/Malcolm X Park • Joan of Arc • Dante & James Buchanan statues • U Street Neighborhood • African American Civil War Memorial & Museum • House of the Temple • Dupont Circle**

Uncle Beazley.

Nice kitty.

Doddering around the Smithsonian's National Zoo, of course, makes a great daytrip by itself. But it can also serve as a unique first leg of a longer trek through some other interesting parts of the city. Even if you've already toured the zoo, a relaxed two-hour stroll over to Dupont Circle—with an admission-free zoological send-off—is all the more enjoyable. There are some longer hills and stairs on the route, so this is not the best choice for wheelchair hikers. (The zoo sometimes offers courtesy shuttles; ask at the Visitor Center as you enter the zoo.)

For this hike, start at the zoo's main gate (open at 8:00 am) on the east side of Connecticut Ave, roughly midway between the Woodley Park and Cleveland Park Metro Stations. It's about a ten-minute walk from either station to the zoo gate [MILE 0.4]. If you need to bypass the zoo for some reason, start at Woodley Park and follow the directions for the ROCK CREEK HIKER-BIKER TRAIL (*p. 126*) to the bottom end of the zoo's OLMSTED WALK, where you can intercept the balance of the route to Dupont Circle.

As you enter the **National Zoo** (1889) from Connecticut Ave, you are at the top of OLMSTED WALK, the broad pedestrian thoroughfare to which all the habitat sidepaths connect. Indeed, it was named for

133

Frederick Law Olmsted, the renowned landscape architect and principal designer of the zoo grounds (and the U.S. Capitol grounds).

A fun route to consider if you're only passing through the zoo is to take OLMSTED WALK as far as **Uncle Beazley**, the big, burly triceratops, and turn right there. Then follow the **American Trail** to its end near the red barn and the bottom end of OLMSTED WALK.

Exit the zoo's east gate [MILE 1.3] via Olmsted Walk, then walk left along the black fence to the Harvard St Bridge—not the lower bridge straight ahead (*see map p. 122, blue route*). Cross **Rock Creek** to the traffic light and continue ahead to cross Adams Mill Rd. Hang a left to cross Harvard St and follow it up the hill to **Mount Pleasant** and **Rabaut Park**, a half-mile trudge from the bottom of OLMSTED WALK [MILE 1.8].

Walk through Rabaut Park to where you can see **three old churches**, one tall and cylindrical, and the others with high steeples. The intersection here is rather convoluted, but the plan is to head right (south) on 16th St by walking left of the church on the right (less confusing than it sounds). A couple of crosswalks will

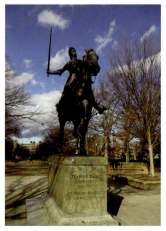
Joan of Arc, Meridian Hill/Malcolm X Park.

get you there. Look for the street signs to confirm you're on 16th St.

Follow 16th St past several **foreign embassies** (Poland, Cuba and Lithuania) to Euclid St. Cross both streets at the light. Continue a few more steps down 16th St, then hang a left into **Meridian Hill Park** (1940), also known locally as **Malcolm X Park**. Take a quick right on the curvy paved path or climb a few steps and turn right to walk south along the central lawn. Note that the park is managed by the National Park Service and is closed overnight. Elaborate paths, stairs and memorials make it an interesting place to explore.

Make your way to the south end of the central lawn area and a nice overlook of North America's largest **cascading fountain** (except in winter when the water is off). A memorial to **Joan of Arc**, astride a horse and waving her sword, is close by. A legendary **drum circle** has gathered here every Sunday afternoon for the last 50 years, since the death of Malcolm X. Newbies are welcome, if you can muster the vibe.

Church at Mount Pleasant.

The game plan is to work your way down to the far southeast corner of the park at W St and 15th St NW. The suggested route is to head left at the overlook, descending stairs and paths to the fountain. (Or you can backtrack a little to find a steepish, stairless path leading down to the same area.) When you reach the base of the long staircase, follow the curvy path ahead with a few steps downward to a bold statue of 13th century master poet, **Dante** (1921). Either continue down the curvy way to a

modest monument to **James Buchanan** (1930), our 15th president, or wander right for a closer look at the cascade. Descend to the walkway above W St and head left to 15th St NW [MILE 2.5].

Cross W St and New Hampshire Ave and walk a block down 15th St to the ornate **stone church**, St. Augustine (1893), on the left. Here, at V St, the route turns left to take a wide swing through the popular U Street neighborhood. (If you need to speed things up, you can save

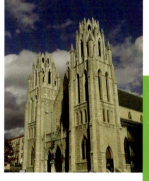
Stone church.

13th century Italian poet, Dante.

Map continued on p. 122

MORE JAUNTS

a mile of walking by continuing down 15th St to U St directly. From there, you would turn right on U St, then go left on New Hampshire Ave a couple of blocks to Swann St to intercept the route in the last paragraph below.)

For the longer, more interesting route, turn left at the stone church onto V St, continue to 14th St NW and turn right. In a block, turn left on happenin' **U St** and stroll eastward to 10th St. You'll pass the U St Metro and a herd of eateries, imbiberies and coffee shops. The nighttime music scene is a big draw at many area venues.

At 10th St, cross a plaza leading to a second U St Metro entrance and the inspiring **African American Civil War Memorial** (1998) [MILE 3.2]. Across Vermont Ave is the associated **museum** honoring the service of more than 200,000 African Americans who served in defense of the Union (open most days 10:00-4:00; www.afroamcivilwar.org).

Continue south along Vermont Ave to the next corner and turn right on T St.

African American Civil War Memorial.

Walk this back to 14th St, admiring the old architecture of endless brick townhouses. Cross 14th St, turn left and walk a short block to Swann St [MILE 3.6]. Turn right and follow Swann to 16th St. Turn left and walk a block south on 16th to find the rather monumental **Masonic**

House of the Temple (1915) on the left. The Temple was designed by John Russel Pope, the same architect behind both the National Archives building and Jefferson Memorial.

Turn right on S St and take this to 17th St. Cross to the wag-happy **S Street Dog Park**, then go right (north) along 17th St to the next corner. Cross New Hampshire Ave, turn left, then right to get back on Swann St [MILE 4.1]. (The shortcut from V St leads to this point.)

Follow Swann St a long block to 18th and turn left there to pass several restaurants with outside seating. In two blocks more, turn right on quiet Riggs St with the artful gables, then go left on 19th St and right on R St near the Sierra Leone Embassy. Connecticut Ave is just ahead; walk left two blocks to reach **Dupont Circle** [MILE 4.8].

Architectural eye candy, U St area.

◎ Chinatown to Dupont Circle

▶ *Distance*: 1.7 miles, allow 1 to 1.5 hours

▶ *Start*: Friendship Archway, H St at 7th St NW (*map, next page*)

▶ *Nearest Metro*: Gallery Place-Chinatown

Points of Interest: **Friendship Archway • Mount Vernon Square • Carnegie Library •
Kiplinger Gallery • Washington Convention Center • Samuel Gompers Memorial Park
• Thomas Circle • Mary McLeod Bethune Museum • Logan Circle • General George
Henry Thomas • Samuel Hahnemann • Scott Circle • General Winfield Scott Memorial
• Foreign embassies • Daniel Webster • John Witherspoon statue • Dupont Circle**

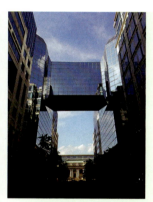

8th St NW, looking north.

Inside the old Carnegie Library are
the Historical Society's Kiplinger
Gallery (early maps and images of
Washington), various collections and
a research library (10:00-4:00 Tues-Fri).

This little foray through downtown D.C. samples a collection of lesser known memorials and architectural gems that add to the tangible richness of the national city. The walk also traverses a few urban circles and squares—European-inspired intersections of streets and avenues envisioned as major focal points and memorial sites in Pierre L'Enfant's original design for the city.

Start at the iconic **Friendship Archway** (1986) at 7th and H Sts, outside the Gallery Place-Chinatown Metro Station [MILE 0.0]. Cross 7th St and keep walking west on H St to the Calvary Baptist Church at 8th St NW; turn right. Head north past the conspicuous, **stone bell towers** of another Baptist church and original home of the Washington Hebrew Congregation (1898). President McKinley helped lay the cornerstone.

Keep walking up 8th St beneath a glassed-in skybridge to K St across from **Mount Vernon Square**, then amble left to cross K St at the light. The stately old **Carnegie Library** (1902) looming in the Square once served as D.C.'s main public library. It now houses the **Historical Society of D.C.** If desired, mosey right to visit the Historical Society. The signed public entrance is via the ramp below and right of the main steps.

Continue north on 9th St to the next corner at Mount Vernon Pl [MILE 0.3]. Note the sprawling **Walter E. Washington Convention**

137

Center just ahead. Go left across 9th St to begin a 0.8-mile trek along Massachusetts Ave. Close by is an unusual architectural contrast: a restored United Methodist Church (1917) juxtaposed with a modern office building.

At 10th St, cross Massachusetts Ave and continue west to Samuel Gompers Memorial Park (1933), a substantial tribute to the founder of the American Federation of Labor. At the next corner, jog right and left on crosswalks to keep following Massachusetts Ave. After 12th St, dally past the sky-tickling Church of the Ascension and St. Agnes (1874).

Walk two blocks more to Thomas Circle [MILE 0.8], staying to the right side. Across

the Circle, towering skyward, is another classic church building, the National City Christian Church (1930). President Lyndon Johnson's state funeral was held here in 1973. A little to the north between 14th St and Vermont Ave is the Luther Place Memorial Church (1873), another tall and eye-catching stone edifice.

(For extra credit, you could follow Vermont Ave past Luther Place and the Mary McLeod Bethune Museum on the next block to Logan Circle for another generous helping of Victorian architecture, several historical markers

Samuel Gompers Memorial.

St. Agnes Church, designed like it came from a storybook.

Fifty thousand people attended the dedication of the General Thomas Memorial in 1879.

the statue of Massachusetts **Senator Daniel Webster** (1900) donning a caped overcoat [MILE 1.2]. Webster's D.C. home was nearby. Walk around the statue till you're back-to-back with Mr. Webster and looking straight down **N St**. Follow N St, which becomes a delightfully restive nook of a street, largely occupied by foreign embassies, nongovernmental organizations, boutique hotels and a few cozy professional offices. (At 17th St you could wander two blocks left to the **National Geographic Museum**; modest admission fee.)

At Connecticut Ave, note the statue of New Jersey statesman and signer of the Declaration of Independence, **John**

and, at the center of the Circle, the mustachioed Civil War general, and later Illinois senator, John Logan, on his fine horse. Then retrace your steps to Massachusetts Ave. Allow 20 minutes or so for this half-mile side trip.)

Now head toward the center of Thomas Circle and the memorial to **Union General George Henry Thomas** astride his stately steed. Leave the Circle to the General's right, aiming for the left side of Massachusetts Ave, across from National City Church. In a nearby pocket park, left of the bike rental station, a **bronze elk** is browsing in the trees.

At 15th St, recross Massachusetts Ave and continue past the Tunisian Embassy, then a robust monument to the founder of homeopathy, **Samuel Hahnemann** (1900). Short sidewalks and crosswalks lead counterclockwise around **Scott Circle** and the memorial to **General Winfield Scott** (1874). Early critics complained the artist made him too old and fat and his horse too meek, given his long and illustrious Army career.

Stay left of the Australian Embassy and keep circling the Circle till you reach

Daniel Webster.

Witherspoon. Turn right on Connecticut (the White House is left). Follow this major thoroughfare and hopping night strip a long block to **Dupont Circle**. The Metro station is semi-hidden on the left near the Circle. The **marble fountain** (1921) in the center of the Circle [MILE 1.7] is dedicated to Civil War Admiral Samuel Dupont. (For more sauntering, try the EMBASSY ROW LOOP (*p. 118*) or a trek to Adams-Morgan; *p. 123*).

139

Old Downtown–Chinatown Loop

▶ *Distance*: 2.0-mile loop, allow 1 to 2 hours

▶ *Start*: Navy Memorial (*map, p. 144*)

▶ *Nearest Metro*: Archives–Navy Memorial

Points of Interest: **U.S. Navy Memorial** • **General Winfield Scott Hancock Memorial** • **Temperance Fountain** • **Grand Army of the Republic** • **Newseum** • **Canadian Embassy** • **John Marshall Park & statue** • **Abraham Lincoln Statue** • **Darlington Memorial** • **National Law Enforcement Officers Memorial** • **Judiciary Square** • **National Building Museum** • **Chinatown** • **German-American Heritage Museum** • **Chinatown Friendship Archway** • **Pepco Edison Place Gallery** • **Smithsonian American Art Museum & National Portrait Gallery** • **Martin Luther King, Jr. Memorial Library** • **St. Patrick's Church** • **Ford's Theater** • **Petersen House** • **Penn Quarter**

This little spin around downtown Washington ranks right up there with the JAUNT and is one of the more interesting urban treks you'll find near the National Mall. It's a nice reprieve from the Mall if the museums are crowded, and a good stroll among the old architecture, public spaces and urban art that help define downtown Washington. It's also a good excursion for newcomers looking to get better acquainted with the city's complex geography and historic urban core.

The main focus is what's vaguely known as Old Downtown, more commonly regarded as Penn Quarter and Chinatown. There are fine places to linger and copious cool things to see along the way, including a peek inside the National Building Museum, American Art Museum and Portrait Gallery, and Ford's Theatre.

As with the JAUNT, begin this downtown loop at the Archives–Navy Memorial Metro Station (*see also p. 39; map, p. 144*). But this time we'll head east along **Pennsylvania Ave** (toward the Capitol). From the **Navy Memorial** [MILE 0.0], pass behind the **General Winfield Scott Hancock Memorial** (1896) near the top of the escalators, then cross 7th St NW at the crosswalk. Notice the **Temperance Fountain** (1884) with the heron on top, inspired to favor water over whiskey as a more proper thirst quencher.

Penn Quarter plaza on 7th St NW.

Heron atop Temperance Fountain.

To the right is a larger **memorial to the Grand Army of the Republic** (1909), honoring Civil War Veterans of the Union Army. The plaza here is photogenic, surrounded by unique, historic buildings.

Heading up Pennsylvania, cross 6th St NW to the popular (but not free) **Newseum** (2008) where you can browse (from the sidewalk) the daily front pages of newspapers from every state. Just beyond is the robust and beflagged **Canadian embassy** with an interesting native sculpture atop the steps. Immediately past that is **John Marshall Park**. The recommended route makes a swing through the park. But you have a choice to consider here also, so read on before leaving Pennsylvania Ave.

If you don't mind stairs and it's daytime, head left through John Marshall Park (two blocks long). If it's late, or if you're a wheelchair hiker, you can backtrack a little and head up 6th St NW from the Newseum. This avoids the flight of stairs (two dozen steps) at the upper end of John Marshall Park. John Marshall Park can be deserted in the evening, so 6th St offers a good alternate. If you do choose 6th St, head up to Indiana Ave and turn right to ascend a short, steep block to 5th St NW. Cross Indiana Ave and aim for the red brick pathway at the opposite corner that leads to a bright, golden statue. You'll intersect the John Marshall route here.

Otherwise, you can skip the 6th St alternate and amble through Chief Justice John Marshall's pretty big park. If you walk up the right side, you'll pass a couple of studious fellows who became so engrossed in their **chess game**, somebody had them bronzed. (Apparently, some bonehead made off with the bronze chessboard a couple of years ago, a serious federal crime). Seated above is a statue of **Justice Marshall** (1884) [MILE 0.4], pretending not to

Justice John Marshall; a chess game.

notice the little chess game going on in his court. Marshall, in fact, was an avid chess fan.

Beyond Justice Marshall, cross C St and continue ahead to reach a broad set of steps. Climb these and cross D St, followed by another set of steps to a marble pose of **Abraham Lincoln** (1868) in front of the **D.C. Court of Appeals** (former City Hall). Turn left and follow the walkway near the

Abraham Lincoln. The sculptor, Lot Flannery, happened to be at the play at Ford's Theatre the night Lincoln was shot. About 20,000 people attended the dedication.

building to the brilliant, golden girl and deer statue known as the **Darlington Memorial** (1923). (Intercept the 6th St alternate route here.)

From the delicate golden girl, angle toward 5th St and continue north a half-block to E St; turn right. The stately, red brick **National Building Museum** (1887) soon comes into view. Cross E St and walk through the **National Law Enforcement Officers Memorial** (1991) honoring the many thousands of officers in the U.S. who have died in the line of duty. The lion figures at either end of the memorial evoke courage and strength. (Nearby, construction of a new, largely underground, **National Law Enforcement Museum** began in 2016.) At the north end, a cross-walk leads to the main entrance to the National Building Museum [MILE 0.8]. The Judiciary Square Metro escalator is close by. (*For a good walking route to this point from Union Station, see p. 185.*)

The loop leads around the left (west) end of the building, but you might take a closer look first, both inside and out. The National Building Museum occupies an impressive building of its own. Built in the 1880s, the 15-million brick structure is famous for an elaborate Civil War frieze that extends for nearly a quarter-mile around the exterior of the building. Widows of Civil War veterans came here to collect their pensions, once paid in cash.

To continue the walk to Chinatown, briefly head west on F St (right as you exit the museum) to the far corner of

Darlington Memorial.

National Building Museum

Inside the National Building Museum are some of the largest indoor columns in the world, plus an indoor fountain, hundreds of busts and a clever cooling system, not to mention all the exhibits about, you guessed it, buildings (some require a fee). Scheduled tours are available and donations are appreciated.

National Law Enforcement Officers Memorial.

Exterior frieze, Building Museum.

Friendship Archway, Chinatown.

Chinatown

Though much diminished from just 20 to 30 years ago, with many families forced out by rising rents, Chinatown retains just enough heritage, Chinese script and Oriental decor to affirm you're in a special cultural place. In some ways it feels like the center of the city, although with all the redevelopment in the downtown core in recent years, it's hard to say precisely where the city's center truly is. Clusters of new buildings have sprung up in almost every direction, luring people this way and that and tugging at the center. Yet the resilient, 30-year-old Friendship Archway seems to rise above it all, at least metaphorically.

Beauteous inside and out, the building housing the American Art Museum dates to 1867, as the former home of the U.S. Patent Office. Today;s galleries of comtemporary art, American celebrities, sculptures and presidential portraits warrant extended browsing. Be sure to check out the upper floors.

the building. Turn right on a brick walkway that leads through lawns (with good photo ops of the frieze), before angling left slightly to reach the intersection of 5th St and G St. Cross both and saunter north on 5th St to H St. Turn left to enter the heart of **Chinatown**.

At 6th St there are a couple of short diversions to ponder. One could walk left a half-block to the **German-American Heritage Museum**, which highlights immigration and contributions to American education and conservation (*11:00-5:00, closed Sun-Mon*). Or a block right is the **Sixth and Eye** historic synagogue, a popular events venue in an intimate setting. On H St, walk to 7th St and the elegant **Friendship Archway** (1986) in front of the Gallery Place–Chinatown Metro escalators [MILE 1.1].

From the Friendship Archway, cross 7th St NW and continue west on H St to 8th St NW. Turn left, but notice to the right the looming **bell towers** of the Greater New Hope Baptist Church (a good walk to Dupont Circle heads that way; *see p. 137*). As you round the corner onto 8th St (left), the towering red brick building above you is the Calvary Baptist Church (1862). Next, look for the **Edison Place Gallery** on the right before reaching G St and the Smithsonian's **American Art Museum and Portrait Gallery** (since 1968).

Turn right on G St, cross 9th St NW and pass by the city's **Martin Luther King, Jr. Library**. Continue west on G St another block, then turn left on 10th St NW. St. Patrick's Catholic Church (1884) calls for a photo stop. Peasants to presidents have attended services here since 1794, just after the founding of the

MORE JAUNTS

St. Patrick's Church.

You can still catch a play at Ford's Theatre—a very nice venue.

Federal City.

Walk down 10th St to F St and note the **wax museum** on the right. Notice the painted iron works in the building across F St. Turn left to continue the loop [MILE 1.7]. However, you should first stroll another half-block south on 10th St to visit **Ford's Theatre** (1863), the place where President Lincoln was shot in 1865. The **Petersen House** (1849) where he took his last breath is right across the street. Free tickets are required and lines can form in the busy season, but excellent exhibits and the view inside the lovely old theater are worth the wait (www.nps.gov/foth).

If returning to F St from the theater, turn right and walk east to 9th St, passing many historic buildings. Across 9th St is the nonprofit **International Spy Museum**, in office buildings once filled with, not surprisingly, patent attorneys. A little beyond, on the left, is the American Art Museum and Portrait Gallery's south entrance.

Continue east to 7th St and turn right. The Monaco Hotel at the corner was once the **General Post Office** (1839). Street performances often occur outside the Metro escalators nearby. Cross F St and watch for a marker on the right commemorating **Samuel Morse** and the nation's **first telegraph office** (1845).

From afternoon to evening, the home stretch down **Penn Quarter's 7th St** to Pennsylvania Ave becomes quite a lively scene in good weather, so allot some time to loiter and soak up the buzz. You'll find plenty of places to chow down or wet your whistle, although on Friday and Saturday nights many will fill up around the dinner hour.

After crossing E St, notice the **Shakespeare Theatre** on the right. One block left is the National Academy of Sciences' **Marian Koshland Science Museum** (*10:00-6:00 daily, closed Tuesday, nominal fee*). March on to cross D St (a left here would take you to the **Woolley Mammoth Theatre**, another local favorite).

Your starting point at the **Navy Memorial** and Archives Metro Station is coming right up on the right [MILE 2.0]. If your timing is good, you can often catch a free summer concert in the plaza where the U.S. Navy Band frequently performs (*7:30 pm Tuesdays; see p. 39 for more about the Navy Memorial*).

Capitol Hill–Eastern Market Loop

▶ *Distance*: 2.8 mile-loop, allow 1.5 to 2 hours

▶ *Start*: Pennsylvania Ave. SE at 2nd St SE (*map, next page*)

▶ *Nearest Metro*: Capitol South (walk north to Independence Ave, east to 2nd St SE)

Points of Interest: **Capitol Hill neighborhood • Seward Square • Marion Park • John Phillip Sousa home • Marine Barracks • Barracks Row • Market Park • Eastern Market • Lincoln Park • Abraham Lincoln Emancipation Memorial • Mary McLeod Bethune Memorial • East Capitol Street • Frederick Douglas Museum**

Impressive architecture on E. Capitol St.

7th St NE off Pennsylvania Ave.

Marion Park.

This 2.8-mile loop through the historic Capitol Hill neighborhood branches off the NATIONAL JAUNT a couple of blocks east of the U.S. Capitol (*see Section 6, p. 84*). The Capitol Hill trek leads a little deeper into the neighborhood and delivers a pleasing buffet of history, architecture, village hub-bub and relative quietude. Among the more noteworthy stops are Barracks Row, Eastern Market, Lincoln Park and an old church attended by late presidents. You'll find plenty of quaint and stylish eateries enroute.

Make your way to 2nd St NE and Pennsylvania Ave behind the **Library of Congress**, then cross to the southeast corner of the intersection [MILE 0.0]. Follow **Pennsylvania Ave** east-ish (away from the Library of Congress) for a couple of blocks to 4th St, passing several pubs and restaurants popular with Congressional staffers and local denizens. Turn right on 4th just before **Seward Square**. Walk south about three blocks, crossing North Carolina Ave and D St. At E St SE, cross to **Marion Park** and head left, working your way to the far southeast corner of the park at 6th and E St SE [MILE 0.6]. Note that E St spans both sides of park. From the park, continue south on 6th St to G St (there is no F St here).

Turn left at G St. In a block, pass the old Christ Church on Capitol Hill (1807). John Quincy Adams, James Madison and James Monroe were among the presidential parishioners.

MORE JAUNTS

The virtuous Adams attended services twice on Sundays. A few doors down on the left (636 G St) is a private residence and boyhood home (1805) of the renowned and prolific march composer **John Phillip Sousa**—think *Stars and Stripes Forever* and *Semper Fidelis*. One can imagine the boy twirling his baton and leading imaginary marching bands around the neighborhood in the 1860s. This was serious stuff for young Sousa. By age 13, he was playing violin with the United States Marine Band headquartered just up the street.

Follow G St east to 8th St and turn left. Across 8th St and to the right is the guarded entrance to the **Marine Barracks**. This is where Sousa, in his mid-twenties, would ultimately lead and transform the **U.S. Marine Band** into what is still the U.S. president's official ensemble. You can catch a free performance here on Friday evenings, May through August (reservations rec-

Barracks Row

Businesses sprang up here two centuries ago to serve the Washington Navy Yard to the south, as well as the Marine Barracks. Riots in 1968, following the assassination of Martin Luther King, Jr., reduced some buildings to charred ruin, and things deteriorated from there. Beginning in the 1990s, however, new stars aligned and the area has since been charmingly restored.

ommended; www.barracks.marines.mil/Parades/EveningParade).

Next, head north on 8th St. The commercial strip here is called **Barracks Row** and is one of D.C.'s oldest historic business districts. Continue north to D St, cross and angle left into the **Market Park** square, ambling toward the obvious Eastern Market Metro escalators [MILE 1.1]. At the corner just beyond, cross both Pennsylvania Ave and 7th St. Walk north on 7th St, passing more quaint cafes, shops and such, to reach the actual **Eastern Market** (1873) on the left. Be sure to walk on through. A

Browsing inside Eastern Market.

popular street fair and flea market fill the street outside on weekends.

Just past the market, at North Carolina Ave, turn right, keeping to the sidewalk to cross 8th St. Hang a left here to cross Independence Ave, then jog a little right between a garden patch and an **extraordinary mosaic**. Continue right along North Carolina Ave another three blocks to **Lincoln Park** [MILE 1.6].

Savor the sculptures near the center of the park, including one of the earliest memorials to Abraham Lincoln placed after his death, known as the **Emancipation Memorial** (1876). Frederick Douglass was the lead speaker at the dedication. Nearby is a

memorial to **Mary McLeod Bethune**, a tireless teacher, friend of the Roosevelts and a leading advocate for African American causes. When the memorial to Ms. Bethune was dedicated in 1974, nearly 20,000 people came.

Circle back to the west end of Lincoln Park to East Capitol St (in the direction Ms. Bethune is facing). Cross 11th St and follow **East Capitol St**, a delectable D.C. residential avenue replete with stoic architecture and whimsical detail, for seven scenic blocks (11th St to 4th St). At 4th St [MILE 2.4], turn right, then steal a left on A St NE. Pass the **Frederick Douglass Museum** just ahead (open only for events). Douglass, the famed statesman and former slave, lived here with his family for a time in the 1870s before moving to the Cedar Hill estate in Anacostia (where tours are available).

In two blocks more, reach 2nd St to rejoin Section 6 of the NATIONAL JAUNT [MILE 2.6]. Massachusetts Ave is three blocks to the right; turn left there for Union Station. Or, to complete the CAPITOL HILL LOOP and return to the starting point, head left on 2nd St for three blocks to Pennsylvania Ave [MILE 2.8].

Ms. Bethune's likeness was crafted by sculptor Robert Berks, whose creations include the Einstein Memorial on Constitution Ave and the JFK bust at the Kennedy Center.

MORE JAUNTS

Anacostia Riverwalk

▶ *Distance*: 2.7 to 3.5-mile loop, allow 1.5 to 2.5 hours

▶ *Start*: Navy Yard Metro Station

▶ *Nearest Metro*: Navy Yard and Waterfront stations

Points of Interest: **Yards Park • Anacostia Riverwalk • Washington Navy Yard • National Museum of the U.S. Navy • Nationals Stadium • Fort McNair • Titanic Memorial • Washington Channel • Arena Stage • Maine Avenue Fish Market • Kenilworth Aquatic Gardens • Bladensburg Waterfront Park**

The ANACOSTIA RIVERWALK has developed nicely over the past few years, with nearly 20 of 28 planned miles completed. The mostly paved trail system extends along both sides of the Anacostia River and along the Southwest Waterfront, almost uninterrupted, from the National Mall to Bladensburg Waterfront Park (two miles northeast of the National Arboretum). As described below, two sections are particularly inviting to hikers.

The first is easily accessed from the Navy Yard and Waterfront Metro Stations and is centered on Yards Park and the Nationals' baseball stadium. The second, a brand new section near Kenilworth Gardens, opened in the fall of 2016 and is a few miles farther up the river, but still accessible by Metro, bike, bus or car. Some other areas tend to be of more interest to cyclists. Note also that the RIVERWALK links to another 40 miles of paved paths in the upper Anacostia watershed (*see p. 179-180*).

The first section to explore is along the north side of the Anacostia River from Yards Park and the Navy Yard, around Nationals Stadium and possibly over to Fort McNair, the Titanic Memorial and the Southwest Waterfront. A major redevelopment project is underway on the Southwest Waterfront, so it may be 2017 or later before there's a good waterfront walk to be had all the way through to the National Mall. Note that many areas can become deserted by nightfall, so plan to complete your walk during the day.

Water play at Yards Park.

The tubular bridge.

For now, begin at the Navy Yard Metro Station [MILE 0.0]. Exit to New Jersey Ave and M St, cross both streets and walk east along M St for one block to a **pedestrian corridor** opposite 3rd St SE; turn right. Walk this south to Tingey St and turn left, then go right at 4th St. The old building with the smokestacks was part of a massive **Naval Gun Factory**, at one time the largest in the world.

Follow 4th St to its end at **Yards Park** and the ANACOSTIA RIVERWALK just ahead [MILE 0.5]. The walk to the Titanic Memorial heads right, but first wander left to explore the shore adjacent to the park and the historic **Washington Navy Yard** (1799), the oldest operating Navy

installation in the U.S. The **National Museum of the U.S. Navy** is in the large white building inside the security fence. Navy buffs and curiosity seekers might want to check it out, along with the old cannons and artifacts on display outside (hours and details at www.history.navy.mil). For access, you'll need to keep walking along the river to the gate at 11th St SE [MILE 1.0]. Turn left there and follow the path a block up the hill to the visitors gate (photo ID required). Inside the museum, ask for a walking tour map.

If you're not visiting the museum, turn back at the 11th St gate or at the Vietnam-era **Swift Boat** on display outside the fence, then retrace your steps

The old Naval Gun Factory.

Navy Swift Boat.

MORE JAUNTS

to Yards Park. (The USS Barry, a 400-foot, 1956 destroyer, was also docked here for decades, but was towed away to Philly in May 2016.) Continue west across a splendidly **tubular bridge** near a kids' **water play area** [MILE 1.6], a popular cooling-off zone in the warmer months. Stay left to follow an over-water section of the RIVERWALK that leads toward **Nationals Park** (2008), the first-ever LEED-certified major league stadium [MILE 2.0].

For the shorter outing, retrace your steps to the wading pool at Yards Park, walk up its left side to the upper fountain, then follow 3rd St SE north to M St. The Navy Yard Metro Station will be a block to the left. The total mileage for this option is about 2.7 miles.

Or, to continue the hike over to the **Southwest Waterfront**, keep left of the stadium, following Potomac Ave to S. Capitol St. Cross both streets and head north a block to P St; turn left [MILE 2.3]. In two blocks, reach 2nd St SW and **Fort McNair** on the left.

Continuing west on P St, you'll meet a treed walkway where the road turns right to become 4th St SW. But follow

Titanic Memorial.

the walkway straight to the waterfront and the striking **Titanic Memorial** in a small plaza [MILE 2.8]. Dedicated in 1931 at a site near the river at Foggy Bottom, the memorial was relocated here in 1968 to make way for the Kennedy Center.

Amble north along **Washington Channel**, passing the harbor police and fire stations. Near the yacht club, angle right past an elevated **plaza** (sometimes with outdoor music) to Maine Ave, or see below for the fish market. To finish the walk, cross to the prominent **Arena Stage** [MILE 3.3] and head right along the big, curvy building. Notice a curious feature inside, visible through the windows. Cross 6th St SW at the light. Maine Ave becomes M St here, which you can follow one long block to the Waterfront Metro Station [MILE 3.5].

Depending on construction activity, one might also be able to continue northwest from the yacht club, along the waterfront or Maine Ave, for about a half-mile to reach the historic **Maine Avenue Fish Market** (1805). This is the oldest operating fish market in the U.S. You can keep walking up Maine Ave beneath several overpasses to reach the

Fort McNair

Nestled at the confluence of the Anacostia and Potomac Rivers, this strategic site for defending against invaders was included in Pierre L'Enfant's 1791 plan for the city. It remains an active Army post today. It is also the place where the aiders and abetters of Lincoln's assassin were tried and hung in 1865. One Saturday each season, the courtroom can be viewed during an open house. At other times, a quick self-guided tour of the grounds may be feasible, but you'll need a photo ID at a minimum. You can walk a block down 2nd St to the visitors gate to inquire about access.

National Mall in 0.3 mile, at the east end of the Tidal Basin.

One other hot tip: the Smithsonian Metro Station is about a half-mile north of the fish market. At the end of the boat harbor, just before passing under a railroad bridge across Maine Ave, take the steps on the left to a pedestrian overpass that leads to a large hotel. Follow the long walkway rightward around the building to some wide steps leading up to a circle at the end of Maryland Ave. Take Maryland Ave one block and turn left on 12th St. In two blocks more, the Smithsonian Metro Station will be on the left.

* * *

The second ramble on the RIVERWALK is an excellent four-mile jaunt from **Kenilworth Aquatic Gardens to Bladensburg Waterfront Park**. The trail opened in October 2016, just as this book went to press. The artist renditions looked great and the reality is equally impressive. You can be among the first to enjoy it via boots or wheels. The park and especially the gardens are also worth a visit in case you're in the market for a shorter walk (*see also p. 179*).

The new trail section links to Benning Rd. NE, although better access for footsters may be at Kenilworth Gardens or Bladensburg Park. The project includes some elevated boardwalk and five bridges (thus the $22 million price tag). A new 400-foot-long trail bridge across the river to the National Arboretum is also planned for the near future.

Completing this missing link connects the RIVERWALK to Maryland's portion of the upper watershed, reaching as far as Silver Spring, College Park and beyond. The more extensive trail system, however, is perhaps best enjoyed by bike.

Some areas are a little isolated

Kenilworth Gardens boardwalk.

from the rest of D.C., so if you're new to exploring remote sections of the trail system, go with a group or with someone who knows their way around. New bridge construction closer to Anacostia, including a major new overwater park (*see p. 191*), will also improve the walking environment in the near-term.

An added bonus is seasonal kayak rentals at Bladensburg Waterfront Park.

Great blue heron at Kenilworth Gardens.

Potomac Heritage Trail

▶ *Distance*: 3.6 to 9.0 miles, allow 2 to 6 hours

▶ *Start*: Theodore Roosevelt Island or Key Bridge

▶ *Nearest Metro*: Rosslyn

Points of Interest: **Potomac Heritage National Scenic Trail • Mount Vernon Trail • Theodore Roosevelt Island • Key Bridge • Spout Run • Potomac River • Windy Run Falls • Thrifton Hills Park • Custis Trail • Donaldson Run • Potomac Overlook Park & Nature Center • Gulf Branch Park & Nature Center • Chain Bridge • Fort Marcy**

Crossing Spout Run.

While the C&O CANAL TOWPATH gets much of the attention for a stroll up the Potomac River (it's wide, level and convenient to Georgetown), the POTOMAC HERITAGE TRAIL on the Virginia side of the river offers an actual hike on a boot-sized trail. If you're good with a more primitive path, you can enjoy a winding, scenic saunter for a couple of hours, or an eight-mile trudge (one way) to Turkey Run, or a loop back to Georgetown via Chain Bridge and the C&O Canal. Multiple access points offer a range of trip choices.

Muddy spots, rough tread and rocky clambering in some areas may not be everyone's cup of tea, but that shouldn't be a big deal for most experienced hikers—if the river isn't running high. If it's been stormy, or about to be, consider postponing for drier weather. Improvements are gradually being made and the trail seems destined to become a D.C. favorite.

Locally, a good, carless hike starts at the PHT's south end near Theodore Roosevelt Island, where it splits off from the MOUNT VERNON TRAIL (a short walk from Key Bridge or the Rosslyn Metro Station). An out-and-back hike to the small, picturesque falls at Windy Run (except when it's dry) is an easy trek for most mortals (1.8 miles each way), although traffic noise on G.W. Pkwy detracts for the first mile.

For **Windy Run**, find the signed junction [MILE 0.0] on the MOUNT VERNON TRAIL just north of the **Theodore Roosevelt Island** parking area. The trail doesn't look like much at the

On the Potomac Heritage Trail.

beginning and can get a little muddy in damp weather, but things should quickly improve as you head upriver. The trail passes under **Key Bridge** [MILE 0.3] and hugs the **G.W. Pkwy** in a few places before reaching a footbridge over **Spout Run** [MILE 1.0]. You'll pass good views of the **Potomac River** on the way to the falls at Windy Run [MILE 1.8]. Barely a trickle in drier times, the 30-foot **waterfall-cascade** can impress after a rain. In winter, following a few days of frigid weather, large icicles can form here (and elsewhere), so be cautious of slick surfaces and falling ice.

Left of the falls, an old trail steeply climbs a few stone steps and ledges into Windy Run's gradual valley above. Signs warn of the risk of a fall and advise visitors not to use the trail. I won't advise you to either, especially if it's snowy or icy. At other times, the stony steps are commonly hiked by those coming down to the river from **Windy Run Park** and vice-versa. Experienced hikers will likely find the steps easier to clamber up than the short scramble at Gulf Branch Falls (described below) and perhaps wonder what the fuss is about. But don't chance

Potomac Heritage Trail

The Potomac Heritage Trail is actually a part of the much larger Potomac Heritage National Scenic Trail, a major corridor running from the Allegheny Highlands of southwestern Pennsylvania to the mouth of the Potomac River at Chesapeake Bay. The system consists of more than 700 miles of existing trails, including, in the D.C. area, the C&O Canal Towpath, Mount Vernon Trail and this ten-mile chunk referred to simply as the Potomac Heritage Trail (PHT). Another 100 miles of planned new trails will help tie it all together (see www.nps.gov/pohe).

it if you're unsure of your ability, or have younger kids in tow.

If you do head up, it's possible to complete a 4.4-mile loop back to Rosslyn and Key Bridge via neighborhood streets and the CUSTIS TRAIL. The WINDY RUN TRAIL leads through the park, with some easy rock-hopping across the creek, to the end of Kenmore St. One could take the sidewalk up to Lorcom Ln, go left three blocks to Edgewood St, then cross to the paved path descending into **Thrifton Hills Park**. This path leads 200 yards to the I-66 overpass. Pass beneath it and immediately turn right to reach the CUSTIS TRAIL, 1.1 miles from the PHT. A sharp right atop the ramp takes you to Key Bridge in another 1.5 miles. CUSTIS

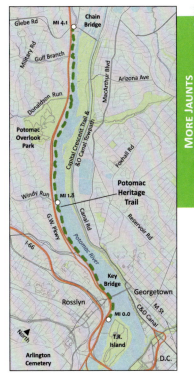

makes a better bike ride than a walk, but will do for a hike in a pinch (just walk to the right so bikes can pass).

Back at Windy Run, if you continue up the PHT, you'll quickly reach the rusted relics of an **old steam boiler** that ran equipment associated with a rock quarry here over a century ago. Some of the stone was used in the construction of Healy Hall, the gothic building with the spiky towers at Georgetown University (prominent from near Key Bridge). If you keep on trucking upriver on the PHT 1.3 miles past Windy Run you'll come to **Donaldson Run**. About 0.1 mile farther is a nice rocky point good for a lunch break [MILE **3.2**].

At Donaldson Run, you'll notice another steep path climbs an easy rocky ledge left of the creek, followed by a steep set of stone steps. If you head up, expect a few rock hops across the creek—generally easy unless the water is high. You'll pass the crumbling remains of an old dam on the left side. Then turn left at a signed junction to hike upslope into **Potomac Overlook Park**. The former overlook is long gone, but it's still a pretty nice park. When you reach a junction just before the top of the ridge, turn right on the WHITE TRAIL. This winds around the hillside to a small wood building just past a house. Aim for the little wood building for a fun **raptor surprise**. Then walk the paved park road right to the **nature center** for some excellent exhibits on the region's natural history (0.8 mile from the PHT).

Either return to the river the way you came, or keep following the park road for a two-mile neighborhood route back to CUSTIS TRAIL (left on Military Rd, left on Nellie Custis Dr and left on Lorcom Ln to merge with the Windy Run loop above). The PHT-Donaldson-Custis loop is about 7.3 miles.

Back on the PHT, the trail beyond

Donaldson Run becomes much more rugged, with a lot more clambering. Some sections may be very close to the river at higher flows, so due caution is in order. Strong currents and undertows should be adequate warning for not getting too close to the water's edge.

Near **Gulf Branch**, the trail may be impassable if the river is running much above 30,000 cubic feet per second (to check the current flow, search online for "USGS Little Falls gage"). If the trail isn't clear, turn back. Mucking around the brush and rocks increases the risk of encountering poison ivy or even the occasional copperhead snake—our only venomous snake close to D.C.

For a good look at a copperhead snake, stop by the Potomac Overlook Park Nature Center. Copperheads are shy critters and generally not agressive, Nevertheless, it's always good practice in the woods and rocks to watch where you put your hands and feet. Bites are rarely fatal, but if you're bitten, call 911 or seek immediate medical attention.

Barred owl at Potomac Overlook Park.

Gulf Branch Falls.

Across Gulf Branch, **steep stone steps** and generally easy scrambling (with a handrail) lead past the small, pretty **falls** to a choice between hiking along the creek for 0.7 mile to the **Gulf Branch Nature Center** (a local bus stops close by on weekdays), or switchbacking up the hillside on the PHT. If you choose the latter, the hike upriver is on much better tread and climbs high for great views, before descending to the **Chain Bridge** across the Potomac River. Head down a stone stairway to pass under the bridge [MILE 4.1]. Go left for the bridge walkway or right for **Fort Marcy**, about 0.6 mile up **Pimmit Run** (well signed). For points beyond, visit www.nps.gov/pohe. As you might have guessed, the PHT on the Virginia side doesn't connect all the way through to Great Falls, ending instead at Scott's Run (see p. 194).

If you walk across Chain Bridge to the Maryland side you'll find a ramp at the other end that links to the C&O CANAL TOWPATH (see p. 182), where you can enjoy a more leisurely, four-mile walk back to **Georgetown** and Key Bridge. Figure a nine-mile loop back to your starting point, or 8.2 miles if you end your hike at Georgetown. If doing the PHT–C&O Canal loop, start with the PHT to get the more challenging part out of the way before the easy glide back to Georgetown.

You could shorten the return by three miles by working up to MacArthur Blvd to catch a bus back to Georgetown. Here's how: from Chain Bridge walk south on the C&O CANAL TOWPATH 0.5 mile and climb the steps to the CAPITAL CRESCENT TRAIL bridge at Arizona Ave. Cross the bridge to a path on the right which starts easy but steepens on the short haul up to Potomac Ave. Follow Potomac Ave two blocks to Cathedral Ave, turn right and walk three pleasant blocks to MacArthur Blvd. The bus stop is a few yards to the right.

Great Falls, by the way, is still another ten miles upriver from Chain Bridge via the C&O.

Trail signs help with wayfinding.

MORE JAUNTS

Four Mile–Bluemont–Lubber Run

▶ *Distance*: 3.7 to 5.5 miles, allow 1.5 to 3.5 hours

▶ *Start*: East Falls Church or Ballston Metro Station

▶ *Nearest Metro*: East Falls Church, Ballston

Points of Interest: **East Falls Church • Four Mile, W&OD, Bluemont Junction & Lubber Run Trails • Ballston • The Ellipse • Welburn Square • Bluemont Park • Glencarlyn Park • Lubber Run Amphitheater**

When the mood strikes to saunter some miles on easy paved paths, the trek from the East Falls Church Metro Station to Ballston might satisfy the urge. The shorter 3.7-mile option catches parts of the FOUR MILE, WASHINGTON AND OLD DOMINION (W&OD) and BLUEMONT JUNCTION TRAILS. Or add a couple miles to include peaceful Lubber Run. A 5.5-mile loop option begins and ends at Ballston and skips the extra leg from East Falls Church to Bluemont Junction. (Wheelchair hikers: both routes have short hills.) For the Ballston start, skip the next four paragraphs. To begin at East Falls Church, read on.

Hop off the Metro at **East Falls Church**, exiting the station beneath an overpass [MILE 0.0]; turn right. This is Sycamore St. Walk to the traffic light at 19th St and cross both streets. In a couple steps more, turn left on the obvious paved path skirting the lawn. Cross a bridge and head left to a quiet street, then left once more to find the W&OD TRAIL just ahead (well signed). Turn right to follow the W&OD along the I-66 sound wall.

At a fork [MILE 0.4], keep right on the FOUR MILE TRAIL (the fork is about 100 yards before a pedestrian overpass visible ahead). If there aren't many bikes out, you could also stay left on the W&OD all the way to Bluemont Junction, but the FOUR MILE is usually less busy and a little farther away from the traffic noise.

The FOUR MILE TRAIL crosses a low bridge then continues 0.2 mile to Ohio St. Cross at a crosswalk (when safe) to a short, steep walk-

BLUEMONT JUNCTION TRAIL. Expect similar pa~~ trails along the FOUR MILE, W&OD and LUBBER RUN TRAILS.

Sun going down at Lubber Run Park..

Visit www.walkarlington.com for more good sauntering around greater Arlington.

way leading down to a col-de-sac. Follow this little street three short blocks to pick up the FOUR MILE TRAIL again at a bend [MILE 1.0]. Reach another col-de-sac in 0.3 mile, but this time zag left then right to continue on the W&OD TRAIL.

Just before the next overpass (Wilson Blvd), keep left at a fork to pass under the bridge. Beyond the bridge is another fork [MILE 1.7]. Keep right to continue on the FOUR MILE TRAIL past tennis courts and ballfields. Notice the **caboose** across the creek (at a place where steam trains met a century ago), then a bridge leading left to the BLUEMONT JUNCTION TRAIL [MILE 1.9]. For the longer loop via Glencarlin Park and Lubber Run, continue straight ahead (south) and skip the next three paragraphs.

For the easier hike to Ballston, take the BLUEMONT JUNCTION TRAIL across the W&OD, up the long, gentle hill and on to **Ballston**. When you reach the traffic light at Wilson Blvd [MILE 2.8] and George Mason Dr, cross both streets to continue on the BLUEMONT. At a

Bluemont Junction caboose (interpretive site).

T-intersection near Fairfax Dr, head right about two blocks to Glebe Rd and cross [MILE 3.3].

The Ballston Metro Station is four blocks ahead on Fairfax Ave. But for a more interesting finish, go south (right) on Glebe Rd to the end of the first building, then angle left to a trellis-covered walkway leading past a hotel to a plaza called **The Ellipse**. At the far end, cross Taylor St and jog a little left to amble through **Welburn Square**. Then go left on Stuart St a half block to the Metro station at Fairfax Dr [MILE 3.7].

MORE JAUNTS

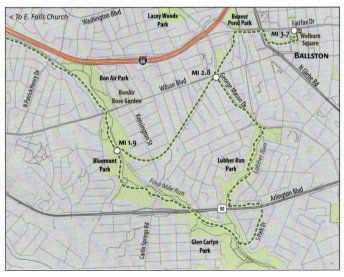

157

If beginning your walk at Ballston, you could head west on Fairfax Dr four blocks to Glebe Rd, cross, then continue two blocks more to pick up the BLUEMONT JUNCTION TRAIL behind a sound wall. Turn left in 50 yards and follow the BLUEMONT JUNCTION TRAIL a bit over a mile to the W&OD TRAIL. Cross it and the bridge ahead to meet the FOUR MILE TRAIL at the ballfields. Turn left to carry on with the loop or to finish the longer 5.5-mile hike from East Falls Church.

Now heading south from the **Four Mile/Bluemont junction**, you'll pass through **Bluemont Park**. The trail might get a little confusing, but just stay on the paved path running between restrooms and a play area to continue along Four Mile Run. Soon after passing under Carlin Springs Rd, you'll be forced back onto the W&OD TRAIL. Right after passing below Arlington Blvd, the FOUR MILE TRAIL rematerializes at a fork, but now stay left on the W&OD TRAIL through what's called **Glencarlyn Park**.

Cross the creek on three bridges in the next quarter-mile. Sixty yards past the third, turn left on a paved path directly opposite a play area* with restrooms (about a mile from Bluemont Junction). The path climbs briefly to the neighborhood above and the end of Park Dr. Follow the left side of Park Dr to Arlington Blvd and cross the latter at the traffic light. Take an immediate left on another paved path and continue along the street ahead, crossing Columbus St. Walk a half-block more to the signed LUBBER RUN TRAIL on the right (1.6 mile from Bluemont Junction).

The attractive LUBBER RUN TRAIL leads

*The FOUR MILE TRAIL passes the play area and continues another five miles to the MOUNT VERNON TRAIL (see p. 169). From the play area, the next half-mile is quite pleasant. Watch for a small, pretty waterfall-cascade just downstream of the first bridge.

along the creek to a quaint **amphitheater** in the forest, where you can often catch free, live performances on summer nights. After 0.6 mile, the trail reaches George Mason Dr. Turn left at the sidewalk, then in 60 yards cross a ramp at the crosswalk to continue walking along George Mason Dr beneath an overpass. Keep to the sidewalk (and crosswalks) until you reach Wilson Blvd, about 0.5 mile from the LUBBER RUN TRAIL. The BLUEMONT JUNCTION TRAIL will be on your left.

As described earlier for the Bluemont route to Ballston, cross both streets to pick up the trail again on the other side of the intersection. Then scroll above to review the directions for the last mile to the Ballston Metro station.

Lubber Run Trail.

Lots of new buildings in Ballston.

Old Town Alexandria

Just across the river and a few heron flaps south of D.C., lies Old Town Alexandria—close enough to make the cut for the National Nearby, but far enough away to feel like a new place. Or should we say, a new *old* place. Old Town is one of the oldest and largest historic districts in the U.S., with hundreds of historic buildings clustered around a highly walkable urban core.

The city traces its roots to 1749, shortly after Lawrence Washington, a colonial legislator, sent his little brother George out to survey the shore along Captain Alexander's estate on the Potomac River. It was eyed by some as a possible townsite and tobacco shipping port. The Captain wasn't too keen about having a new town amid his 500 acres of paradise, but negotiations ensued. When the beer steins were empty and the politicking was over, the new town was declared.

To smooth things over with the Captain, the town-makers promised to name the city after the Alexander family, an idea the captain apparently liked so much that he donated most of the land for the new town. The local citizenry, however, ignored all this and instead called their little town Bell Haven. It would take a few more years (and beers) before the official name finally stuck.

Today's Alexandria sprawls considerably beyond that early vision of a bustling tobacco port. Yet, amazingly, the city's historic core and renowned, authentic charm remain largely intact.

With a clowder of land use tigers ever nipping at the shins of city planners, we can only hope the charm holds for another hundred years.

The old city is centered on a mile-long, quite jauntable stretch of King St, between the Potomac River and the King Street Metro. Diverse shops, used bookstores, posh and humble eateries, funky pubs and coffee shops, fine art and performance venues and the indispensible dispensaries of ice cream occupy dozens of quaint, old buildings, some from the 1700s and early 1800s. City Hall, nearby churches and the 333-foot tall George Washington Masonic Memorial point their gables and spires to the clouds, while back down on Earth, brick walks, street trees, urban art and a few street musicians enrich the ambience.

Though King St and the riverfront are main attractions, the Old Town Historic District extends across many more blocks. Historic sites abound, many of them pivotal in the stories of American Independence and the Civil War.

One could easily enjoy an aimless stroll along King St without a map or a guide. But to add some depth and breadth to your adventure, consider one or both of the short loops suggested below. The first begins at the King Street Metro Station in a newer part of downtown Alexandria and eases into the old city. The second begins at the riverfront in the heart of Old Town. From D.C., you can quickly reach King St via the Yellow Line (under 20 minutes from L'Enfant Station), or via the Blue Line by way of Rosslyn. Or snag a foot ferry to or from D.C. or National Harbor.

Alexandria: New Town/Old Town Loop

▶ *Distance*: 2.5-mile loop, allow 1.5 to 2 hours

▶ *Start*: King Street Metro Station

▶ *Nearest Metro*: King Street

Points of Interest: **John Carlyle Square • U.S. Patent & Trade Office • National Inventors Hall of Fame • African American Heritage Park • Alexandria National Cemetery • Shiloh Baptist Church • 19th century slave pens • Freedom House Museum • Friendship Firehouse • King Street • Old Town • Washington Masonic Memorial • D.C. boundary markers**

The relatively new parts of Alexandria south of King St, also known as Carlyle, offer an interesting introduction to the modern city, although the loop outlined here quickly leaves the slicker parts behind in favor of the quaint old streets that lured most of us here to begin with. It's almost like visiting two cities in one walk. Allow an hour or more to complete this easy stroll.

From the King Street Metro Station [MILE 0.0], exit near the station manager's kiosk and walk right (southwest) along the building past the bus shelters to a stop sign at the end of the drive. Continue ahead to the semi-hidden **pedestrian tunnel** under Duke St. Historical maps and artwork decorate the inside walls of the lighted tunnel (closed at night). When you emerge at the other end, walk across the small, brick plaza and continue rightward along Dulany St to Jamieson Ave.

Cross Jamieson and stroll a half-block more to the next crosswalk. Cross to **Carlyle Square**, the plaza lined with glass-block pillars [MILE 0.3]. Head right toward a small geodesic globe for a nice photo op. The big daddy of glass pillars looms dead ahead, which, along with most of the surrounding buildings, comprise the **U.S. Patent and Trade Office** (2005). The big building also houses a small gift shop, several displays and a wall of inventors in the **National Inventors Hall of Fame** (*10:00-5:00 Mon-Fri, 11:00-3:00 Sat.; free*). To find it, enter the high

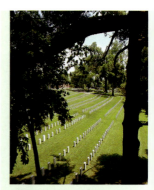

Alexandria National Cemetery, established during the Civil War. Several of those who went after John Wilkes Boothe, Lincoln's assassin, are also buried here.

Geodesic globe near the U.S. Patent and Trade Office and Inventors Hall of Fame.

atrium and hang a right just inside.

The walk turns left (east) at Ballenger Ave near the globe, so explore the park and Hall of Fame as desired, then head east a block on Ballenger to John Carlyle St. Cross and turn right, but notice to the left another downtown park with an outdoor stage for summer events. After walking a block down John Carlyle St and passing a few local eateries, turn left on Emerson Ave. Reach Holland Ln in another block [MILE 0.6].

Many will cross Holland Ln here to the wheelchair ramp and red brick path on the opposite side, then go left into the city's **African American Heritage Park**. Oddly, Holland Ln lacks a crosswalk here, so the safer bet might be to walk right a block to the nearest set of crosswalks leading to the same red brick path, then amble left to the park.

You have a couple of options here. For the direct route, walk past a sculpture of bronze trees to the roofless **gazebo** at the corner. Or, for an extra 0.2-mile mosey (recommended), turn right down a set of stone steps and go right on the gravel path. Follow this

African American Heritage Park.

short, scenic loop through forest and wetlands, crossing a curved wooden footbridge where the serene path swings back around to the north. Across Hooff Run (the creek) is the **Alexandria National Cemetery** (1862). Tragically filled to capacity just two years into the Civil War, it was the predecessor to Arlington National Cemetery. (Access is from the east off Wilkes St.)

The gravel path soon reaches a sitting area and walkway leading up toward the gazebo noted above [MILE 1.0]. Ascend the easy ramp or steps and turn right on the curving brick path above. Go right a short block to a crosswalk that leads across Jamie-

Historic Shiloh Baptist Church.

son Ave to a wide creekside path next to **Hooff Run**. After a few steps, look back at the inconspicuous **stone bridge** (1856) you just crossed. Originally built for Alexandria's first railroad, it's now the city's oldest surviving bridge.

When the path reaches Duke St, zag right (east) to the traffic light at S. Peyton St. Cross Duke St here, but keep going east along Duke another block to the **Shiloh Baptist Church** (1893) [MILE 1.3], where you begin to leave newer Alexandria behind and enter the Old.

The Shiloh congregation was formed in the early 1860s by former slaves. The unassuming church stands adjacent to the notorious **slave pens** of what was, in the 1830s, one of the two largest slave trading operations in the U.S. (the other was in New Orleans). When Virginia seceded from the Union in 1861, Union troops took control of the city and slaves were granted relative freedom, despite continued horrid living conditions.

Duke St can be a noisy-busy arterial, but tough it out just a tad more. On the next block, you'll find the building (1812) that housed in the 1830s the principal slave-trading company, **Franklin and Armfield**, and later, Price, Birch and Co.,

the last bastion of Alexandria's once-legal slave trade. Thousands of slaves were bought, sold and "penned" in and around this building.

James Birch sold into slavery Soloman Northup, the kidnapped free man from New York, whose heart-gripping story is told in the award-winning film, *12 Years a Slave*. The building now houses the excellent **Freedom House Museum** with moving exhibits about the slave trade and slave pens (*10:00-4:00 Mon-Fri*).

At the next corner, turn left on Payne St. In a block, turn right on Prince St. Follow this four blocks east to Alfred St, passing the colorful, inviting facades of historic townhouses. At Alfred St, scoot left a half block to view some ancient firefighting equipment at the historic **Friendship Firehouse** (1855), open weekends only (*1:00-4:00*). Continue a few steps more to King St [MILE 1.8].

To further immerse yourself in lower **Old Town**, you can walk about nine blocks all the way down lovely old **King Street** to Union St [MILE 2.3], just short of the river. The OLD TOWN LOWER LOOP starts at the waterfront plaza fronting the boat harbor nearby.

Or complete the UPPER LOOP by walking left (west) up King St 0.7 mile to the Metro station. The **George Washington Masonic National Memorial** (1932) towers above and behind the station.

Friendship Firehouse.

City of Alexandria, with King Street (left), Amtrak station (center) and the Potomac River in the distance.

George Washington Masonic National Memorial

Built by the Masons in a decade and dedicated in 1932 to honor one of their own—our first U.S. president—this 333-foot tall monolith is perhaps Alexandria's most recognizable landmark. With its sheer scale, imposing front steps, fascinating interior and unique history, the Washington Masonic Memorial ranks among the grander monuments in the D.C. area. For a modest admission fee, a tour guide takes you up the elevator, with much to see on several floors. The view from the observation deck is awesome (*9:00-5:00 daily*).

To reach the memorial from the King Street Metro, exit the station and walk left (northeast) along the front of the station to the King St underpass below the trains. Turn left and pass through to the traffic light just ahead at the intersection with Callahan Dr and Russel Rd.

Before making your way up to the memorial, look across King St and a few yards up Russel Rd. On the right-hand side between the sidewalk and the street is a small fenced off block of stone. This is one of the original boundary markers (1791) for the District of Columbia (*see p. 15*). Then aim for the path and steps to the main entrance to the memorial.

Alexandria: Old Town Lower Loop

▶ *Distance*: 1.4-mile loop, allow 1 to 1.5 hours

▶ *Start*: Old Town riverfront plaza (Torpedo Factory)

▶ *Nearest Metro*: King Street

Points of Interest: **King Street • Torpedo Factory • Riverfront plaza • Alexandria Seaport Foundation • Founders Park • Carlyle House & Garden • Wise Tavern • Alexandria City Hall • Gadsby's Tavern • Market Square • Ramsay House • Stabler-Leadbeater Apothecary Museum • Appomattox statue • Lyceum • Alexandria History Museum • historic Elks Lodge • Athenaeum • Captains Row • Waterfront Park**

Alexandria City Hall.

Another sunny day at Market Square..

You'll find plenty of good walking along Old Town Alexandria's main drag, King St, as well as nearly every cross-street for blocks around. It's a treat to ramble along some of the same side streets George Washington, Thomas Jefferson and other presidents and statesmen trod over two centuries ago. One of their favorite watering holes, Gadsby's Tavern, is still there at the corner of Union and Cameron Sts, though minus the suds.

To add a little structure to your rambling, the following loop will take you to some of the more interesting sites and perhaps broaden your sense of what a great ol' town this truly is. The loop is also wheelchair-friendly, despite a few minor hills.

King Street is really at the heart of what brings people to **Old Town** (locals and tourists alike), so be sure to hike a few blocks' worth before or after your more ambitious wandering. Stray at will when something catches your eye—a straight-up street grid makes it easy to find your way back to the start. Or just ask for directions. You'll find most Alexandrians to be a quite amicable bunch.

Begin the loop at King St near the riverfront plaza or in front of the **Torpedo Factory** (1918) north of King St [MILE 0.0]. Yes, the Navy once made torpedoes here, though production stopped soon after WWII. The building has housed an elaborate complex of art studios for more than forty years. You can easily burn an hour or more browsing three floors of working artists and their eye-catching bounty.

There are several ways to reach the plaza fronting the Torpedo Factory. From the King Street Metro Station, you could saunter all the way down King St (1.2 miles), allowing 30 minutes or more for leisurely walking. Or walk down from Alfred St from where the NEW TOWN/OLD TOWN upper loop meets King St (p. 162). Or, save your feet for later and take the free trolley bus from the Metro station to the waterfront. One could also bike here from the MOUNT VERNON TRAIL, or MVT (see p. 168). Finally, several foot ferries connect Old Town to Washington, D.C. and National Harbor.

If you came down King St, at the last cross-street, Union St, which is also where the trolley stops, angle left up the steps and into the covered pedestrian walk that quickly leads to the Torpedo Factory and riverfront plaza (wheelchair access is a few more yards down King St). Street musicians and artists often perform in and around the plaza.

Looking at the river, head left to follow the boardwalk along the water and out

Riverfront plaza, Old Town Alexandria.

around a restaurant. You'll soon reach a small boatbuilding workshop operated by the **Alexandria Seaport Foundation**, then a fork at **Founders Park** just beyond. If you have a hankering, explore the park and points farther upriver via Alexandria's WATERFRONT WALK (see also the MVT on p. 169). Otherwise, go straight and hop on over to the corner of Union St and Queen St [MILE 0.2].

Cross Union St to follow Queen St west one block to Lee St; turn left. Take Lee St to Cameron St and cross both streets to the fenced **Carlyle Garden** on the corner. You can access

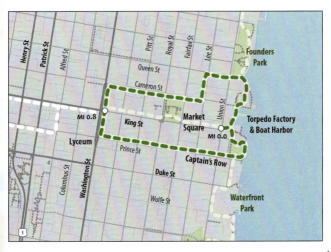

the garden from a small parking lot on Cameron St imediately uphill. From the garden, take a narrow red-brick path uphill to another gate and the main entrance to **Carlyle House** (1753), one of the oldest buildings in Alexandria [MILE 0.4]. Evening footsters and wheelchairs may need to take the sidewalk up to Fairfax St to see it.

Carlyle House, on Fairfax St, is open for tours most days (10:00-4:00, closed Monday). The original owner, Scotsman John Carlyle, was a founder of Alexandria. Calling on the Carlyles at their posh abode were some of the nation's Founding Fathers (George Mason and Benjamin Franklin, to name a couple).

From Carlyle House, jog right on Fairfax St to return to Cameron St. On the corner next to Carlyle House is the original **Bank of Alexandria** (1792). The cream yellow building on the corner to the north (across Cameron) is the **Wise Tavern** (1788), which has a rather special place in American history, as explained on a plaque near the corner. Continue up Cameron adjacent to **Alexandria City Hall** (1871). When you're half-way up the block, you might duck inside for a display of historic photos.

Continuing along Cameron St, cross Royal St to the famed **Gadsby's Tavern** (1785). Well preserved Gadsby's, though no longer a pub, was one of George Washington's more favored hangouts in Alexandria. Outside on the corner is the old underground ice house.

Keep chugging up the left side of Cameron and cross Pitt St. On the next block, keep an eye out for a plaque on the left identifying the location of **George Washington's townhouse** (white with two dormers). The house is a 1960 replica of the original and remains a private residence with no public access.

At the end of the block on the opposite side is the lesser known, great Leaning Tower of P (the parking lot kiosk). In another block, reach Washington St, Alexandria's chunk of the **George Washington Memorial Parkway**. The walk turns left here, but note the church and grounds across Washington St. This is **Christ Church** (1773), another major Old Town landmark—George Washington and Robert E. Lee were regular patrons, Washington with his own family pew. In 1942, Franklin Roosevelt brought

The Marquis de Lafayette, George and at least three other presidents dined and savored the suds at Gadsby's Tavern: Thomas Jefferson, John Adams and James Madison. The brief tour, for a modest fee, is highly recommended (1:00-5:00 Sun-Mon, 10:00-5:00 Tue-Sat). The City Hotel (1790) next door still hosts a classy restaurant and period events in the ballroom.

Winston Churchill here for a service.

Follow Washington St left a block to reach King St [MILE 0.8], where you have a choice to make. The loop continues straight on Washington St (recommended, see the next paragraph). Or bail out here and head left down King St for the easy 0.4-mile stroll back to the Torpedo Factory. Half-way to the river, pass **Market Square** and City Hall. The Saturday morning farmer's market here is alleged to be the oldest, continuous market in the nation (since 1753).

On the corner across Fairfax St is the oldest house in Alexandria, the **Ramsay House** (1724), built at another location and moved here by the city's first mayor. And if you cross King St you'll find the **Stabler-Leadbeater Apothecary Museum** (1805), a remarkably intact historic pharmacy, a few doors down on Fairfax St.

To continue the LOWER LOOP (just two blocks longer), cross King St and walk south on Washington St another block to Prince St. In the middle of the intersection is the **Appomattox statue**, a memorial to Alexandria's Confederate casualties (1889), both an expression of humility and a call for post-war unity.

Before turning left on Prince St, notice the columned building on the opposite corner. This is the **Lyceum** (1839), once a science and lecture hall, then a hospital during the Civil War, and now **Alexandria's History Museum** and worth browsing (*10:00-5:00*).

Heading left on Prince St, follow it six blocks to Union St. On the way, at Pitt St, look to the right a half-block for the St. Paul's Episcopal Church (1817). The church was designed by the prolific British architect, Benjamin Latrobe, one of the principal architects of the U.S. Capitol. Just after crossing Royal St, keep an eye peeled for the old **Elks Lodge** (1909), with a distinguished bronze elk hanging outside a second-story window.

At Lee St, on the left, is the Greek neo-classical **Athenaeum** (1852) [MILE 1.2]. Originally a bank, then a church, the building now houses an art gallery and venue for special events. The large white house next door (uphill) dates to the 1780s. Ahead, you'll enter an area known as **Captains Row** with beautiful old brick townhomes also dating to the 1780s. The cobblestone street preserves the original sense of place here for posterity—notwithstanding the late model cars lining the curbstones. You might need more than a boatman's salary to snag one of these places today.

At Union St, walk left a block to the starting point of the loop [MILE 1.4], passing the **Fitzgerald Warehouse** (1797) on the southeast corner at King St, built to withstand frequent flooding of the river. As an alternative, you could continue to the end of Prince St at **Waterfront Park** and wander left along the water's edge for a good look at the mighty Potomac and the almost as mighty Woodrow Wilson Bridge (Capital Beltway). **National Harbor** is just beyond it. The park path leads you back to Strand St, where a right takes you to King St and the Torpedo Factory just ahead.

To explore more of Alexandria's pedestrian-friendly, historically rich waterfront, see p. 173 for the WATERFRONT WALK and MOUNT VERNON TRAIL from Old Town to Dyke Marsh.

see p. 173

The Lyceum (Alexandria History Museum).

MORE JAUNTS

Mount Vernon Trail

On the Virginia side of the Potomac River, the MOUNT VERNON TRAIL (MVT) is one of the more popular trails inside the Beltway. Joggers and cyclists especially gravitate here all year long. But the trail's 18-mile length is plenty walkable too, and easily completed over several outings. The MVT is paved throughout, except for a few pleasant boardwalk sections. And despite some short hills, it's generally wheelchair-friendly.

Due to the high volume of bikes on nice weekends, you may find things more relaxed early or late in the day, on weekdays, or when the weather is less than perfect. A few areas also tend to be more congested than others, like the MVT's north end at Rosslyn, the Theodore Roosevelt Island parking lot, Gravelly Point Park near the airport, the Old Town Alexandria waterfront and at the Mount Vernon estate where the trail technically begins at Mile Zero. Traffic noise can be annoying at times, and some sections are certainly more interesting than others, as noted in the descriptions below. But don't let all that deter you from enjoying a good walk along the Potomac.

Always walk to the right so bikes can squirt past. Cyclists are supposed to yield to pedestrians, but keep an eye out for the less courteous rider. To enhance the experience for hikers within such an exceptional greenway corridor, the National Park Service really ought to add some skinnier foot trails in strategic locations to provide at least an occasional reprieve from heavier bike traffic. Volunteers could help make it happen.

There are many places to access the trail from D.C. and Northern Virginia, and several segments are convenient to Metro stations (Rosslyn, Arlington Cemetery, Crystal City and King Street). The RIVER LOOP (p. 105) travels the north 1.5 miles of the MOUNT VERNON TRAIL, from Key Bridge to Memorial Bridge.

Below is a brief account of the three-mile section from Memorial Bridge downriver to Crystal City, and the four-mile section from Crystal City to King St in Old Town. Through most of Old Town, the MVT bike route follows Union St.

One of several bridges along the Mount Vernon Trail, this one near Reagan National Airport.

However, there's a great pedestrian-only route along much of the Alexandria riverfront known as the WATERFRONT WALK. It rejoins the MVT 0.4 mile north of Jones Point (a mile south of King St). This is followed by a 1.8-mile section from the lighthouse to the DYKE MARSH TRAIL near Bellhaven Marina.

To hike the rest of the trail to Mount Vernon, it may be more practical to drive, bike or bus to a closer starting point (as noted on p. 175).

MVT: Memorial Bridge–Crystal City–Old Town

▶ *Distance*: 3.3 to 6.7 miles one way, allow 1.5 to 3.5 hours

▶ *Start*: Arlington National Cemetery Metro Station (south side) or Memorial Bridge

▶ *Nearest Metro*: Arlington National Cemetery, Crystal City

Points of Interest: **Arlington National Cemetery • George Washington Memorial Parkway • Lady Bird Johnson Park • Merchant Marine Memorial • Lyndon Johnson Memorial • Boundary Channel • Gravelly Point Park • National Airport • Crystal City • Abingdon Plantation • Four Mile Run Trail • Dangerfield Island • Alexandria waterfront • Tidelock Park • Rivergate Park • Orinoco Bay Park • Founders Park • Torpedo Factory • Old Town**

On the MVT near the Navy–Merchant Marine Memorial, crossing over Boundary Channel and the trail to the Lyndon Johnson Memorial. Washington Monument is conspicuous across the Potomac River.

Water park at Crystal City.

The 6.7-mile trek along the MOUNT VERNON TRAIL (MVT) from Memorial Bridge or Arlington National Cemetery to Old Town Alexandria can easily be split into two shorter walks by starting or ending at Crystal City, roughly halfway to Old Town. Some parts are more appealing than others, but both segments have enough interesting stuff to make them worth putting up with a few dull minutes here or there. The recommended start is at the Arlington Cemetery Metro Station [MILE 0.0]. Scroll down a few paragraphs if you prefer to start at Crystal City. (*To visit the cemetery, see p. 190.*)

For the northerly segment (3.3 miles), the easiest access to the MVT near Memorial Bridge is to walk there from Lincoln Memorial (*see RIVER LOOP, p. 105*), or exit the Arlington National Cemetery Metro Station (south side), turn right at the top of the escalator, and follow the sidewalk and paved path to the far side of a large traffic circle. Cross two lanes of traffic at a crosswalk (generally not difficult) and turn right at the signed trail junction just beyond (left leads to the bridge).

Cross a one-lane ramp, then stay left at a fork. Finally, cross the two north-bound lanes of **George Washington Memorial Pkwy** at a crosswalk (there's usually just a very brief wait for a break in traffic). Immediately ahead is a T-intersection with the MVT [MILE 0.5]; turn

MORE JAUNTS

169

right (left would take you to Theodore Roosevelt Island and Rosslyn).

The trail is well signed to Alexandria. The first bit of greenspace is called **Lady Bird Johnson Park**, a great place for tulips and daffodils in spring. A memorial to her husband and our 36th President, **Lyndon Johnson**, is reached by staying left at the next fork [MILE 1.1], near the curiously captivating **Navy-Merchant Marine Memorial**; however, the MVT stays right here to cross the bridge over **Boundary Channel**.

Navy-Merchant Marine Memorial.

Continuing south on the MVT, you'll pass beneath I-395, U.S. 1, a railroad overpass and Metrorail bridge, before strolling into **Gravelly Point Park** [MILE 2.2], a popular place to watch airliners take off and land at **Reagan National Airport**. As the MVT passes the airport (this is the dull part), you'll cross three more trail bridges. Just after the second is a junction [MILE 3.0]; the right fork circles around to Crystal City, passing through a tunnel to reach Crystal Dr and a nice urban park on the right (0.3 mile from the junction). Free outdoor concerts are often held here on summer evenings, usually on Friday. For the Metro station, walk left a few yards, then head up 18th St one longish block. If you're starting your walk at Crystal City, the same route in reverse, of course, will take you to the MVT, where you would turn right for Old Town Alexandria.

Back at the Crystal City fork, continue south on the MVT across the next bridge and soon find a path to the airport on the left [MILE 3.3]. This path, an optional side trip, provides access to the terminal, the **Abingdon Plantation** historic site and the airport Metro station. Getting to the Metro here is somewhat circuitous (Crystal City is easier).

Following the MVT to the south end of the airport, you'll find a junction with the FOUR MILE RUN TRAIL on the left

LBJ Memorial

For the LBJ Memorial, follow the left fork near the Navy-Merchant Marine Memorial and stroll beneath the bridge to a parking lot and boat harbor. Walk to the shore of Boundary Channel and head right on a lumpy path. The Pentagon is across the channel, which also marks the D.C.-Virginia boundary. Walk to the north end of the parking lot where signs point to the memorial, 0.5 mile from the MVT. Explore the loop, small plaza and a monolithic stone marker. A scenic footbridge crosses the channel to another parking lot. Retrace your steps to the MVT.

Abingdon Plantation

For the ruins of this 18th century to-bacco plantation, preserved in a surreal setting between airport parking garages, take the short airport path off the MVT, a little south of Crystal City. The path rounds a curve and leads down a concrete ramp to a short tunnel and back up another ramp that spits you out on the other side of a road. Aim for the obvious entrance to the parking garage and climb the steps one level up. Then walk east across the width of the garage to a boldly painted black and white walkway; turn right. Follow this to its end near a sidewalk and a grassy hill. Another pathway leads up the grassy hill to the Abingdon ruins. Excellent interpretive signs will fill you in on the story of this intriguing and historically important place. Return to the MVT by the same route.

[MILE 4.1]. This portion of the FOUR MILE RUN TRAIL is generally of more interest to cyclists (a better chunk to walk is north of Columbia Pike; *see p. 156*). Staying right, you'll pass **Dangerfield Island** and sailboat marina [MILE 4.9], where you can chow down or rent a bike or boat (in season). In a quarter-mile more, reach a slithering **boardwalk** section through a large wetland. Just beyond this, keep left to find another boardwalk and the river's edge at the start of the Alexandria waterfront [MILE 5.5].

Walk through a caged boardwalk to find a junction at **Tidelock Park**. Go left (bikes stay right) and follow the squiggly path to the waterfront. This begins Alexandria's **Waterfront Walk**, which leads to Old Town. You'll swing around a couple of office buildings to a large plaza with steps and curious **sculptures**, including a miniature version of the Washington Monument [MILE 5.8].

Walk along the river through **Rivergate** and **Orinoco Bay Parks**, before running out of trail at Pendleton St. Walk left and around the corner to follow Union St one block to pick up the waterfront trail again at **Founders Park** [MILE 6.3]. Again, just follow the river to the main **plaza** and **Torpedo Factory** on the **Old Town** waterfront. A covered walkway leads to **King St**, the main drag in Old Town [MILE 6.7]. If you started at the Crystal City Metro, it's a four-mile walk to this point.

MVT, a slithering boardwalk north of Old Town Alexandria.

MORE JAUNTS

Potomac River from the MVT.

MVT: Memorial Bridge to Crystal City & Old Town Alexandria

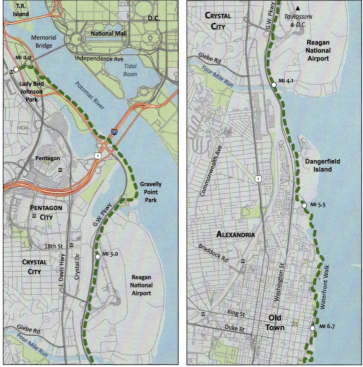

MVT: Old Town–Jones Point–Dyke Marsh

▶ *Distance*: 2.8 to 7.8 miles round trip, allow 1.5 to 4 hours

▶ *Start*: Old Town riverfront plaza (Torpedo Factory)

▶ *Nearest Metro*: King Street

Points of Interest: **Torpedo Factory** • **King Street** • **Waterfront Park** • **Captains Row** • **Shipyard Park** • **Fords Landing** • **Jones Point Park & Lighthouse** • **Woodrow Wilson Bridge** • **George Washington Memorial Parkway** • **Cameron Run** • **Belle Haven Marina** • **Dyke Marsh**

Waterfront Walk, Shipyard Park.

Torpedo Factory, Alexandria.

Alexandria's foot-friendly waterfront offers some enjoyable urban carousing along the Potomac River, with good views, much history, almost no hills (wheel-chair-friendly) and something new around every bend. An interconnecting pedestrian route, called the WATERFRONT WALK, snakes around developed areas to link nine riverfront parks. The MOUNT VERNON TRAIL (MVT) follows Union St through Old Town (the cycling route). The WATERFRONT WALK rejoins the MVT near Jones Point.

The previous trail description covers the area north of King St as part of a longer hike from Crystal City. Heading south from King St is just as entertaining, and quieter traffic-wise. Figure three miles round trip to the Jones Point Lighthouse, or a longish 7.8 miles to the Dyke Marsh overlook and back. For King St and greater Old Town see p. 164.

Begin at the **riverfront plaza** in front of the **Torpedo Factory** (*see p. 165 for directions*) [MILE 0.0]. Walk south between buildings to the corner of King Street and Strand St and follow the latter a block to **Waterfront Park** on the left. Take the path around the park, which hosts a cannon and a modest monument to shipbuilders. After the path turns away from the river, continue a block up Prince St to Union St and turn left. Notice the cobblestone street above, a block known as **Captains Row** lined with old homes dating to the late 1700s.

Walk south along Union St for two blocks

MORE JAUNTS

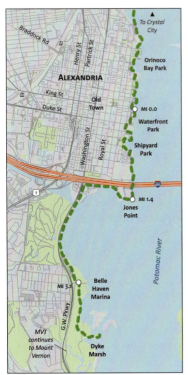

MVT: Old Town Alexandria to Jones Point & Dyke Marsh

Jones Point Lighthouse..

and turn left on Wolfe St. This takes you back to the river at **Shipyard Park** [MILE 0.5]. A nice gravel path leads around condominiums and back to Union St. Walk one more block south to pick up the path again (a new connecting path is planned here). Broad walkways take you around another large development. This park is called **Fords Landing**, named for a Ford car parts assembly plant that once jutted into the river here. Note that railings are absent, so keep the kids close. Interpretive signs share some of the area's history. Rest benches and, if you're lucky, an onshore summer breeze make this a good place to sit and imagine how things might have looked a century or two ago. Once around this development, you'll intersect the **MVT** at a sharp bend [MILE 1.0]; turn left.

The route now enters **Jones Point Park**. At the end of a black metal fence, jog a little left to read an interpretive sign about the old shipyard that once occupied the riverfront here. Continue on the gravel path along the river's edge to where it meets pavement again. But rather than rejoining the MVT there, continue straight ahead, walking along the water and under the massive **Woodrow Wilson Bridge**, a part of the Capital Beltway. Stay left on another gravel path in trees along the river. Follow this around a bend to the **Jones Point Lighthouse** (1855) [MILE 1.4]. The first **cornerstone** of the District of Columbia was laid here in 1791. Stone markers line the old boundaries (*see also p. 14*).

When you leave the lighthouse, generally stay left to walk past more interpretive signs to the MVT, which runs left along the base of the big bridge. Head left when you reach it and continue up the hill to the **G.W. Pkwy** [MILE 2.0]. The MVT turns left here and leaves Alexandria behind.

For a short side trip to a nice view of

the river and Alexandria waterfront, turn right instead, then right again in a few yards on the wide path adjacent to the west-bound lanes of the Woodrow Wilson Bridge. Reach the first of two signed **overlooks** about 0.6 mile from the point you left the MVT, making this a 1.2-mile side trip—or more. You could also walk another two miles to National Harbor, perhaps returning to Old Town by foot ferry.

Back on the MVT, the next pleasant section crosses **Cameron Run**, once known as Great Hunting Creek, on an attractive stone-faced bridge. The path runs close to the river before reaching a picnic area with prime spots along the water, plus restrooms. Just ahead is the road into **Belle Haven Marina** [MILE 3.1], an optional stroll to the left (kayak and sailboat rentals available). Close by is the trailhead for **Dyke Marsh**. A large sign tells you about the marsh and its wildlife. A 0.8-mile trail follows an old road bed and boardwalk to a scenic **overlook** on the river. Return to Alexandria by the same route. (Or walk another half-mile south on the MVT to a lengthy boardwalk across more of Dyke Marsh.)

From the Belle Haven access road, the MVT continues another seven miles to **Mount Vernon**. Busses run from there back to the Huntington Metro Station, but not via G.W. Pkwy. So bus access in between Alexandria and Mount Vernon is not terribly convenient to the MVT. That makes for a long one-way hike if you choose to continue on. It's a scenic slog nonetheless. Diehards might prefer to catch the Huntington bus to Mount Vernon and begin a northward trek more ceremoniously at **Mile Zero**.

Major kudos if you hike it all. That ought to be worth some serious celebrating!

MVT below Woodrow Wilson Bridge.

Prothonotary Warbler. Dyke Marsh is a local favorite for birding.

Dyke Marsh, south of Belle Haven Marina.

MORE JAUNTS

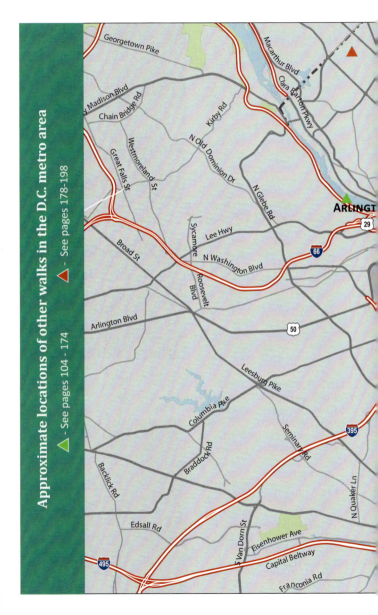

Approximate locations of other walks in the D.C. metro area

▲ - See pages 178-198

▲ - See pages 104 - 174

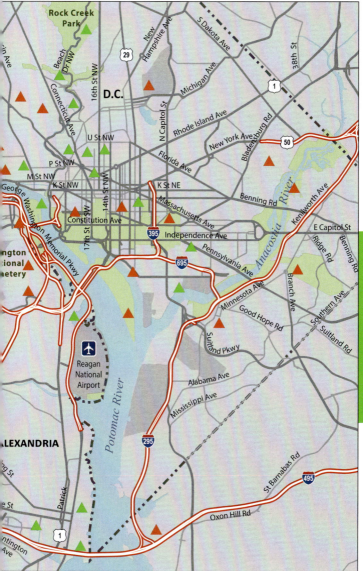

Rock Creek Park

D.C.

U St NW

P St NW

M St NW

K St NW

Constitution Ave

Arlington National Cemetery

ALEXANDRIA

Reagan National Airport

Potomac River

Anacostia River

New Hampshire Ave

S Dakota Ave

38th St

Michigan Ave

Rhode Island Ave

New York Ave

Bladensburg Rd

Florida Ave

K St NE

Massachusetts Ave

Independence Ave

Pennsylvania Ave

Benning Rd

Kenilworth Ave

E Capitol St

Ridge Rd

Benning Rd

Minnesota Ave

Good Hope Rd

Branch Ave

Southern Ave

Suitland Rd

Suitland Pkwy

Alabama Ave

Mississippi Ave

St Barnabas Rd

Oxon Hill Rd

George Washington Memorial Pkwy

Beach Dr NW

Connecticut Ave

16th St NW

N Capitol St

14th St NW

17th St SW

MORE JAUNTS

177

OTHER WALKS & HIKES AROUND D.C.

For more good strolls and hikes around Washington, D.C., check out the suggestions below. Space doesn't allow for detailed maps and descriptions, but the routes are typically straight-forward. Basic navigation skills and a good D.C. map should suffice, or research the details online. Hiking guides for the region also cover some of these places well. Most are inside the Capital Beltway, accessible by Metro, bus or bike, and are organized thusly:

▶ PARKS & NATURAL AREAS

National Arboretum
Kenilworth Aquatic Gardens
Lake Artemesia & College Park
Greenbelt Park
Sligo Creek
Capital Crescent
C&O Canal Towpath
Glover Archbold Trail
Tregaron Estate
Hains Point
Oxon Hill Farm & National Harbor
Fort Dupont & Fort Circle

▶ URBAN SAUNTERS

Union Station to Judiciary Square & Chinatown
Chinatown to Farragut Square
Farragut Square to Foggy Bottom
Simón Bolívar to Albert Einstein
Southwest Waterfront
D.C. Historic Neighborhood Loops
Downtown Bethesda, MD
Downtown Silver Spring, MD

▶ MORE D.C. SIGHTS ON FOOT

U.S. Marines/Iwo Jima Memorial & Netherlands Carillon
Arlington National Cemetery
9/11 Pentagon Memorial & Air Force Memorial
Cedar Hill & Anacostia Community Museum
National Cathedral & Bishops Garden
Basilica of Immaculate Conception

▶ BEYOND THE BELTWAY

Great Falls
Along the Potomac River
Other Regional Favorites

Parks & Natural Areas

There are a number of larger parks and natural areas inside the Beltway with good hiking and easy sauntering. Check out the following gems in the D.C. area's big outside.

National Arboretum

Expect miles of paths and much to ogle at the **National Arboretum** (1927), a little east of downtown Washington.
There's no Metro station nearby, but it's easy enough to take the Metrobus (B2) to the entrance off Bladensburg Rd NE. The B2 runs often, so one idea is to catch the snazzy new H St Streetcar on the north side of Union Station (follow the signs inside the station), then after a dozen blocks, transfer to the northbound B2 at 15th St NE/Bladensburg Rd. It's a one-mile bus ride from there to the arboretum. Step off the bus near R St and follow it two blocks east to the gate (well signed).

Highlights include Fern Valley, the Asian Gardens, Dwarf Conifer Forest, Capitol Columns, flowering tree and shrub collections, and botanical research facilities on nearly 500 acres of rolling meadow and forest managed by the **U.S. Department of Agriculture**. Something is always blooming from early spring through late fall, though winter walks are pretty nice too. (*Open 8:00-5:00 every day but Christmas; free admission; info: www.usna.usda.gov.*) A planned trail bridge across the Anacostia River will eventually connect the arboretum to Kenilworth Aquatic Gardens (*below*) and the RIVERWALK (*p. 148*), which will enhance bike and foot access immensely.

Kenilworth Aquatic Gardens

Soft paths meander through a cluster of historic, excavated ponds harboring waterfowl, lilies and other plants from around the world. More trails and boardwalks explore native woods and wetlands, and a small national park visitor center helps explain the goings on.

A major new link in the ANACOSTIA RIVERWALK opened in the fall of 2016 and passes by the gardens, including over-water sections. That and a planned new trail bridge to the **National Arboretum** should give communities on both sides of the river all the more reason to don our walking (or biking) shoes to explore the Anacostia River corridor (*see p. 148*). The parking lot and main entrance to the gardens are off Anacostia Ave, a half-mile northwest of the Deanwood Metro Station. Browse the website for further details and directions, www.nps.gov/keaq.

College Park & Lake Artemesia

An extensive system of paved trails offers good walking in and around the city of **College Park** and the **University of Maryland**, about eight miles northeast of D.C. The College Park Metro Station provides convenient access for hikers and bikers, including a family friendly, two to three-mile tour of **Lake Artemesia**, also good for picnicking and birding. You can fill out the adventure with a visit to the university grounds or the historic **College Park Aviation Museum** located at the world's oldest operating airport (10-minute walk from the Metro station). Wilbur Wright was a flight instructor here. The museum is open most days of the year (*9:00-5:00, nominal admission fee*). To reach it, walk out the east side of the Metro station (not the tunnel), turn right on Paint Branch Pkwy, then make the first left on Corporal Frank Scott Dr and follow the museum signs.

Trail-wise, a good option is to leave the Metro, head left on Paint Branch Pkwy and scoot through an underpass to a crosswalk beyond that leads to the trail system. Cross when safe and stay right at the next two trail junctions to reach the loop around Lake Artemesia (or keep left twice for the university and more paved paths). If a longer bike ride beckons, the NORTHEAST BRANCH ANACOSTIA TRAIL south to Bladensburg or beyond is a good choice (*see also p. 148*). Anacostia River trail maps are recommended and easy to come by online.

Greenbelt Park

This lesser known national park, located about seven miles northeast of D.C., spans more than a thousand acres of rolling forest and includes a large, pleasant campground and miles of nature trails. Find the entrance at the north end of the park off Greenbelt Rd, not far from the junction of the Capital Beltway and Baltimore-Washington

Pkwy. Budget travelers could feasibly walk or bike to the park and campground from the College Park Metro Station via Paint Branch Pkwy and Good Luck Rd (under two miles). Open year round. A small visitor center and park brochure can get you oriented. See also www.nps.gov/gree.

Sligo Creek

This pleasant, mostly paved, nine-mile hiker-biker trail runs between Wheaton and Hyattsville, generally along the relatively quiet Sligo Creek Pkwy. It's a well used branch of the greater ANACOSTIA TRIBUTARY TRAIL system. With a meandering creekside greenway and more than two dozen bridges along the way, any part of the trail makes an interesting walk, particularly in the more extensive natural areas. Multiple parks and picnic areas offer access and parking, with potential Metro access immediately southwest of the West Hyattsville station (more appealing to cyclists). There's also reasonable access from the Silver Spring and Forest Glen stations if you have a good map or GPS.

For a decent, Metro-to-Metro, five-mile hiking loop (not quite a loop), exit the Forest Glen station and cross to the east side of Georgia Ave. Walk the north side of Forest Glen one block to Woodland Dr and turn left. In a few blocks, turn right on Belvedere Blvd at **General Getty Park**, or first make a quick tour of the loop around the park. Follow Belvedere to its end at Dameron Dr and turn right. In two blocks head left through a small park area (opposite Sanford Rd) to finally reach the SLIGO CREEK TRAIL, a mile from the Forest Glen Metro. There's a very nice one-mile stretch to the left (*or keep walking north to Wheaton Regional Park in 2.6 miles; see p. 196*). However, for the trek to Silver Spring head right (south).

Stay on the main path as it wanders back and forth across the creek, beneath the Capital Beltway and across several roads. At Wayne Ave (3.0 miles), continue along Sligo Creek Pkwy past a small parking area and over a bridge. At the next small parking area, a quarter-mile past Wayne Ave, turn right to leave the trail (*it's about five miles from here to the West Hyattsville Metro Station*).

Now cross Dale Dr and walk up Hartford Ave, but take the first right on Denver Rd, which leads to **Nolte Park**. Take the path around the ballfields and descend a few steps to Easley St; turn left. Follow Easley around the bend to the **Bullis Park** ballfield and take the paved path on the right. It leads past a play area to Houston St. Jog right, then go left on Hankin St and left on Bonifant St. In two blocks more, turn right on Fenton St. Follow that three blocks through downtown **Silver Spring** to Colesville Rd and turn left to reach the Metro station in another three blocks (*see also the downtown loop on p. 189*).

Capital Crescent

A kind of bicycle beltway, the CAPITAL CRESCENT TRAIL, a/k/a GEORGETOWN BRANCH TRAIL, links communities, parks and other major trails on the north side of the metro area. For an ambitious three-hour trek, the 7.5-mile chunk from **Bethesda** to **Georgetown** passes

Sligo Creek.

through Little Falls Park and an impressive tunnel under MacArthur Blvd en route. Or walk from Georgetown as far as **Fletcher's Cove** (2.3 miles) and return via the C&O CANAL TOWPATH, where the two trails run parallel. Bethesda to the ROCK CREEK HIKER-BIKER TRAIL (2.3 miles) is another possibility. A two-mile paved loop at **Little Falls** (and a shortcut midway) makes a nice family outing on foot or by bike (navigate to Westmoreland Park by car for easiest access). Whatever your choice, expect some company on this popular trail almost any day of the year. (*See also www.cctrail.org*).

For the longer hike to Georgetown, exit the Bethesda Metro Station to the west side of Wisconsin Ave and walk south about three blocks to Bethesda Ave; turn right. The CAPITAL CRESCENT TRAIL is just ahead cutting diagonally through the intersection with Woodmont Ave. Turn left for Little Falls (2.2 miles from Bethesda Metro), the tunnel (3.3 miles) and Georgetown. Or go right for Rock Creek or to check out Bethesda's people-friendly downtown (*see p. 189*).

From Georgetown, you might start at the fountain in **Waterfront Park**. Walk upriver past the **Labyrinth** to the end of the park, keep under the viaduct and **Key Bridge** (feels uninviting here) to a little beyond the kayak and wake board rental place to pick up the paved path. Near the **Arizona Ave Bridge** (3.2 miles), it's possible to cut through the neighborhood and catch a bus back to Georgetown (*see p. 155*).

OTHER WALKS & HIKES

C&O Canal Towpath

The GEORGE-TOWN and RIVER LOOPS (*p.105 and 113*) touch on the C&O Canal's story and include short sections of the TOWPATH running parallel to M St. Upriver from Georgetown's **Key Bridge**, the trail takes you to **Fletcher's Landing** (picnicking, boat rentals) in 2.3 miles. The CAPITAL CRESCENT TRAIL (*p. 181*) runs parallel to the C&O and offers a slight change of scenery for the return walk. See the POTOMAC HERITAGE TRAIL for a longer loop via **Chain Bridge** (*p. 152*).

Another popular, scenic stretch is at **Great Falls** on the Maryland side of the Potomac River (*see p.193*), between the museum/visitor center and Widewater/Old Angler's Inn, two miles to the south. Watch for turtles. Canal barge rides are available on weekends, April-October.

Find the main entrance to the national park off MacArthur Blvd about four miles northwest of the Beltway. If you're headed to Great Falls, maybe also check out the beauteous, historic carousel at **Glen Echo**, adjacent to the **Clara Barton House** and one-time headquarters of the American Red Cross (undergoing res-toration in 2016). Above Great Falls, the possibilities are boundless for the next 170 miles. For maps and details, visit www.nps.gov/choh.

Glover Archbold Trail

Like a mini Rock Creek Park (not all that mini), this 220-acre NPS green-way reaches almost from **Tenleytown** to **Georgetown**, a four-mile trek overall. A good three-mile trail (unpaved) runs the length of the park and is often used by nearby residents, maybe less so by other D.C. denizens. It was named for its two principal 1924 land donors, and fortunately escaped being turned into a four-lane highway in the late-1940s.

To walk it all, exit the Tenleytown Metro Station to the west side of Wisconsin Ave and walk south about two blocks to the traffic circle. Continue several more blocks to Van Ness St (or nab a bus to this point). Turn right here to find the unpaved trail on the left just ahead, where it cuts through a big lawn area (a half-mile from the Metro station).

Stay on the main path throughout, often close to the creek, **Foundry Run**,

or explore various spur trails to neighborhoods. Signs are usually posted at major junctions and street crossings. You might need to walk a little left or right from crosswalks to locate the continu-ing path (at Reservoir Rd, a grassy slope leads down to the path).

The GLOVER ARCHBOLD TRAIL ends at Canal Rd, not far from Georgetown University. Walk left about 70 yards along the sidewalk, then at the end of a guardrail, hang a left on a steep walkway leading down to a curious **tunnel** beneath Canal Rd. At its other end you'll find the CAPITAL CRESCENT TRAIL (*p. 181*) and some steps on the left leading up to the C&O CANAL TOWPATH. Either of those will take you a half-mile downriver to **Key Bridge** in Georgetown.

Tregaron Estate

Gardiner Greene Hubbard, co-founder and first president of the National Geographic Society, purchased a prime parcel in Cleveland Park in the 1880s and built a mansion there called **Twin Oaks**, which must have impressed inventor Alexander Graham Bell, who'd already married Hubbard's daughter. But time does fly and years later, half the estate, including the mansion, would be acquired by Taiwan for its embassy, while the other half was purchased by Joseph Davies, a former ambassador to Russia, and his wife **Marjorie Merriweather Post**, the heir to Post cereals and, for a time, the richest woman in America. They named their little paradise **Tregaron**, after a Davies family town in Wales.

Two decades ago, the estate was nearly lost to a housing development. But thanks to the work of the **Tregaron Conservancy**, another kind of wealth— Tregaron's natural and human history— was ultimately preserved across 13 acres for all to enjoy.

For a two-mile loop, you can walk to the estate from the Cleveland Park Metro Station. Exit to the east side of Connecticut Ave and walk south past a good selection of neighborhood shops and eateries. Immediately after crossing a bridge, turn right at a crosswalk and head west along Devonshire Pl NW. Keep left at the fork on Cortland Pl NW and follow this to its end at Klingle Rd. The entrance to Tregaron's trails is directly across the street (0.7 mile to here).

The path bends left to a **small pond** with rest benches. If desired, walk around the left side and climb a few stone steps. At the landing above, turn right and descend another set of steps back to the pond. Before a little arched bridge, turn left to walk downstream under a stone arch bridge; stay left at the fork. When you reach a large lawn area, you can choose between the short-and-easy, or the somewhat longer, hillier route. The easier option heads along the length of the hillside lawn and curves left past a bench before meeting a paved drive; turn right there.

For the longer option (recommended), don't hike the big lawn and instead amble a few yards to the right and take the short boot trail connecting to another wide path close by and go left. Soon reach a junction with the GRAND STAIRCASE TRAIL and turn right (straight is easier and both routes reconnect not far down the trail). Descend dozens of stone steps to the creek and curve left to head up-valley, negotiating a few more steps as you regain the elevation you lost.

Just after the two paths reconnect, zag right on a less obvious path at the corner of a black fence. This path climbs gradually, makes a big turn at a pretty stone staircase and reaches a junction near the paved drive mentioned earlier. Turn right to follow it down to the north gate at Macomb St (1.6 miles). To carry on with a short hike to the **National Cathedral**, head left and see p. 192. Or, for an easy return to the Cleveland Park Metro, turn right on Macomb St, then left on Connecticut Ave.

Hains Point

A four-mile spin around Hains Point and the public golf course is an easy escape from the crowds on the Mall. The less traveled road is popular with bikes and joggers, who generally go clockwise with the traffic. The loop is also a good, family-friendly bike ride. On foot, either direction works. High water has messed up the sidewalk in a few other spots, but they're easily bypassed.

You can get there from the National Mall at the **George Mason Memorial** (*see p. 62*). If you were standing at the entrance to the memorial looking at pensive George, head right on the sidewalk adjacent to Ohio Dr SW. Pass beneath the I-395 overpass, take the crosswalk over to the west walkway next to the **Potomac River** and go left. Note that portions of the walkway have subsided and may be under water during higher tides, forcing you to walk along the road or lawn, generally no big deal.

For a much shorter loop, watch for Buckeye Dr which crosses to the east side of the peninsula north of the golf course and meets the loop road and walkway 1.5 miles north of Hains Point. Tennis courts are close by. A nice miniature golf course is a short putt south.

The peninsula was named for Army General Peter Hains, a veteran of the Civil War, Spanish-American War and WWI. Across **Washington Channel** is D.C.'s **Southwest Waterfront**,. Farther south is historic **Fort McNair**. From the tennis courts, Ohio Dr leads north to the **Tidal Basin**.

On the way, you can extend the walk to the Southwest Waterfront (*see p.*

188) by turning left on a walkway adjacent to the I-395 bridge, just past the tennis courts. Atop the ramp, go right to cross over the channel. Traffic noise is annoying, but there are good views of the harbor and historic fish market. Follow a zigzag wheelchair ramp to **Benjamin Banneker Overlook** (left goes to the Mall and Smithsonian Castle). Circle right and take the obvious path down to Maine Ave. Cross and turn right for the fish market. Then continue along Maine Ave to reach the Tidal Basin. This option adds a mile to the Hains Point walk.

Oxon Hill Farm & National Harbor

It's most efficient to drive to **Oxon Hill Farm**, on the east side of the Potomac River, just north of the Beltway. You'll find about two miles of family-friendly walking trails to mosey, among farm animals, historic outbuildings, a small visitor center, veggie gardens, native woods and the riverfront at **Oxon Cove** (*8:00-4:30 daily*).

National Harbor is nearby, but on the south side of the Beltway (no Metro stations). Good paths lead along the river north and south (wheelchair and stroller-friendly). The Harbor is basically a resort area with an interesting beach and some unexpected quirkiness, like the half-buried sculpture called *The Awakening*. Also bike and kayak rentals, the Capital Wheel, a Chesapeake Bay mosaic and plenty of eats and shops.

You can make a bit more of an adventure of it by taking the foot ferry from Old Town (*see p. xx*) or biking over the noisy, but scenic, **Woodrow Wilson Memorial Bridge** from **Jones Point Park** in Alexandria (*see p. 174*). The trek to

National Harbor beach.

National Harbor is 3.2 miles each way (or 4.6 from King St). The path from the bridge to the Harbor is nicely designed, a pleasant walk. Midway, a tunnel leads to a pond and a semi-dull hiking or biking route to Oxon Hill Farm, 1.4 miles from the tunnel. This paved path climbs a long hill past the new casino to Oxon Hill Rd (go left) and Bald Eagle Rd (left again) to reach the farm.

Fort Circle/Fort Dupont

Fort Marcy.

Almost since its inception, Washington, D.C. has been defended by military forts along the Potomac and Anacostia Rivers and elsewhere. A "circle of forts" nearly enclosed the city during the Civil War and many are now parks with maintained trails. At **Fort Dupont,** south of the Anacostia River, you can learn about other old forts, summer concerts and the FORT CIRCLE HIKER-BIKER TRAIL (some isolated areas, so go with a group; www.nps.gov/cwdw).

Farther south, the sprawling lawns, munching deer herds, visitor center and massive brick and stone works at **Fort Washington** overlook the Potomac River, inviting another foray. Cannons, big doors and a drawbridge at Washington's oldest fort have kept the bad guys at bay for decades. The **waterfront path** is mildly interesting, but not well connected to other trails or amenities within the park (*see* www.nps.gov/fowa).

Urban Saunters

This guide describes many miles of worthwhile saunters around the greater metro area. If you're hungry for more, here are some candidates for further exploration. Some are short, pleasant walks between Metro stations. Others you might need to do a little homework to set your own course.

Union Station to Judiciary Square & Chinatown

For a fine stroll a little off the beaten path, try this route from Union Station to the National Building Museum and Chinatown. Or add a mile or two by continuing on to Farragut Square (*next page*) or Dupont Circle (*p. 137*). As an aside, the eight-mile Metropolitan Branch Trail (east end of Union Station) will eventually connect to Silver Spring, via several Metro stations (*details:* www.metbranchtrail.com).

From **Union Station**, head west toward the **National Postal Museum**, worth a stop even if you're not a seasoned philatelist (stamp collector). The Postal Museum (1993) shares a building with D.C.'s old city post office (1914). Expanded to two floors in 2013, the museum contains excellent displays on stamps, printing, the history of the mail and collecting.

Jog around the corner at 1st St NE and take the Massachusetts Ave sidewalk down to the next traffic light. Cross North Capitol St to the **National Guard Memorial and Museum**. The museum offers galleries, artifacts, exhibits, video and compelling stories detailing the history of the Guard, including the colonial and U.S. militias that preceded it. Press the intercom button for access (*9:00-4:00*) and check in briefly at the desk.

Cross Massachusetts Ave to the new **Holodomor Memorial** (2015) honoring the Ukrainian victims of that horrific 1930s genocide. Just behind the memorial, turn right on F St.

After a long block away from some of the noisier downtown hubbub, cross New Jersey Ave and a sliver of 1st St NW. On your left, the unusual glass tower shaped like a vertical wing houses a business association. But keep walking straight ahead, passing through the trim greenspace of **Georgetown University's Law Center** to 2nd St NW, where a massive construction project rises above I-395 hidden below. Head left one block to E St and turn right. (If needed, one could walk past the glass tower to E St and turn right there instead.) E St takes you to 3rd St NW; turn right again and follow this two quieter blocks to G St.

On the way to G St, pass the Holy Rosary Catholic Church (1923) with a humble statue of **Christopher Columbus** outside, then the **Casa Italiana** (1981), an Italian language school and Holy Rosary cultural center, adorned with statues of four greats from Italian society and the arts. Beyond is the oldest synagogue in D.C., now the **Lillian and Albert Small Jewish Museum** (1876). An interesting historical display is at the corner (*see* www.jhsgw.org).

Turn left at G St to reach the red brick **National Building Museum**

Floor tile, National Building Museum.

looming ahead. The building's decorative bas-relief is highly conspicuous. The main F St entrance is on the left (south) side, across from the Judiciary Square Metro and **memorial to fallen officers**. Or pass along the right side of the museum to continue on to 5th St NW and H St, **Chinatown** and the **Friendship Archway** at 7th and H Sts (*see also p. 143 for the finish*).

Chinatown to Farragut Square

This little slice of downtown Washington picks up a few more sites of interest among blocks of mostly modern architecture, but with several historic buildings of note, a museum, a couple of plazas and three park-like squares. Mostly, though, it's an easy 1.2-mile stroll to get better acquainted with the heart of the city. To add some distance, start at Union Station (above) or continue with the next walk over to Foggy Bottom.

Begin at the **Friendship Archway** at H and 7th Sts NW in front of the Chinatown-Gallery Place Metro Station. Cross 7th St and continue west on H St to 8th St and a little past 9th. Look for a digital video passageway on the right (called *The Gateway*). Pass through to a broad plaza, then hang a quick left on **Palmer Alley** to amble a stretch of upscale retail. When the pedestrian way ends at 11th St, turn right, then go left at the next corner to follow New York Ave. Just before 13th St, you'll pass a gift shop and entrance to the 1987 **National Museum of Women in the Arts** (*10:00-5:00 most days, modest admission fee*).

Next, head right on 13th St to I St and cross to **Franklin Square**, named for the illustrious Benjamin. Walk through or around the square (best during daylight hours) to the far corner at 14th St NW and K St. Continue west a block on K St to **McPherson Square**, then make a diagonal through the square past Union Army **General James McPherson**'s proud statue (1876), before heading right on I St. A Metro station and the **U.S. Department of Veterans Affairs** are close by. As you cross 16th St NW, notice the **White House** in plain view to the south. At 17th St, turn right to saunter through **Farragut Square**, popular with the lunch crowd. Civil War **Admiral David Farragut** (1881) in the center is remembered for the line, "Damn the torpedoes, full speed ahead!" Metro stations are at both ends of the square.

You may have noticed that much of the old architecture in downtown Washington is still intact, though in many cases just a few walls or facades above the street are original, with modern structures nestled behind. Uniquely absent are the 40-storey skyscrapers common to other major American cities. To maintain a somewhat European feel to a city juxtaposed with so much grandeur, building heights have been restricted in downtown D.C. since 1899. Rarely does a building exceed twelve stories, a reality that contributes much to the city's human scale of development. There are no dark canyons of overwhelming hotel and office towers impeding the flow of light and air. While the mega-developers would love to cash in on greater height and density, the city has so far resisted.

Farragut Square to Foggy Bottom

This lazy one- mile stroll catches a bit of downtown D.C. near the White House before ambling through the George Washington University (GWU) campus to the Foggy Bottom Metro. For a longer trek, begin with one of the prior two walks, or maybe continue on to Georgetown or Rosslyn (*see last paragraph*).

From the Farragut North Metro station, exit to K St, which you'll find at the top of the escalator. Cross and mosey toward the center of **Farragut Square** (1881) and a statue of its namesake **Admiral David Farragut**. Angle slightly right to reach the corner of 17th and I Sts (there is no J St) and cross the latter. Follow 17th St two blocks south to Pennsylvania Ave and turn right. The **Renwick Gallery** and **White House** are to the left (*see SECTION 2 of the JAUNT, p. 46*).

Walk west along Pennsylvania Ave to just past 18th St and make a soft left on H St. The **World Bank** is on your left and unassuming **Edward R. Murrow Park** is that patch of green on the north side of Pennsylvania. Staying on H St, cross 19th, swagger past the **IMF** (while pondering the age-old question, *What could I do with a billion dollars?*), then cross 20th St to the campus of **George Washington University**.

The next two blocks invite some meandering to check out the grounds and buildings, including the **Textile Museum** with much to see at 21st and G Sts (*open daily except Tues, hours vary, modest admission fee*; www.museum.gwu.edu). Or just continue west on H St to 22nd and turn right there. In a block, turn left on I St to find the Foggy Bottom Metro in one block more. To continue to **Georgetown**, turn right (north) on 23rd St, cross **Washington Circle** and look to

the left for Pennsylvania Ave, which will take you over the Rock Creek bridge and into Georgetown at M St.

Simón Bolívar to Albert Einstein

This short jaunt snags a few sights of interest that are a little off the beaten track, but still fairly close to the Mall. Begin at the corner of 17th St NW and Constitution Ave and follow the AMERICAS MINI-LOOP described on p. 52. When you reach the statue of **Simón Bolívar** (opposite the **Art Museum of the Americas**), continue past the small reflecting pond to cross Virginia Ave. Immediately cross 19th St NW to a walkway cutting through a lawn area, then turn left on 20th St NW (notice the fountain to the right). Note that if you continued west on C St for another block, you would reach the **U.S. State Department** (1941), where a worthwhile tour of the Diplomatic Reception Rooms is available (must reserve in advance).

At Constitution Ave, head right to pass the stout **Federal Reserve** building (1937). Cross 21st St and keep slogging past the **National Academy of Sciences** (1924). Visitors can enter this building on weekdays to view the ornate ceilings, interior decor, exhibits, portraits and science-based artwork. (*Open Mon-Fri 9:00-5:00*, www.cpnas.org. *To learn more about the science of science, also visit the Marian Koshland Museum downtown at 6th and E Sts; 10:00-6:00, closed Tues; nominal admission fee*).

Fittingly, outside the National Academy of Sciences, near the corner at 22nd St NW, sits a larger-than-life bronze statue of the renowned physicist **Albert Einstein** (1979), pondering his equations. The memorial was dedicated in 1979 to honor his 100th birthday. The sculptor, Robert Berks, also crafted the famed JFK bust at the Kennedy Center. Perhaps stroll over to the **Lincoln Memorial** and D.C. Circulator stop from there. The nearest Metro station, Foggy Bottom, is a slog up the hill on 23rd St NW, 0.6 mile from Dr. Einstein. To reach Einstein from the Lincoln Memorial or Vietnam Veterans Memorial on the Mall, walk north along Henry Bacon Dr to Constitution Ave and cross both streets.

Southwest Waterfront

A massive redevelopment project that is reinventing the Southwest Waterfront has temporarily dampened the area's appeal for a lazy, waterfront stroll. Determined footsters can still enjoy the less disturbed portion to the south, including a good walk to the **Titanic Memorial**. Things should improve noticeably by 2017, although additional phases are planned. The developers promise to provide much public outdoor space, including piers, parks and promenades.

From the Waterfront Metro Station, walk two blocks west on M St to 6th St SW. Turn left, round a bend and make your way toward the waterfront close by. Walk left (south) 0.3 mile to the rather sobering Titanic Memorial.

To connect to the ANACOSTIA RIVERWALK, head east from the Titanic to P St and follow it a few blocks more to S. Capitol St SW. Turn right, then go left on Potomac Ave to find the RIVERWALK on the other side of **Nationals Park** (baseball stadium). See p. 148 for more on the RIVERWALK. The historic **fish market** is on the northern end of the **Southwest Waterfront**, sure to be a more enjoyable stroll once the construction mess ends.

D.C. Neighborhood Heritage Trails

This guide highlights quite a number of historical sites, though in a magnificent old city like Washington, there are, of course, far more places worth visiting than could possibly be listed here. Various guidebooks, and even guided walking tours, are available to help you sleuth them out.

Thanks also to the good work of Cultural Tourism DC, there are at least 18 Neighborhood Heritage Trails around the city. You may have noticed a few of the eye-catching signs on various street corners. They not only identify and describe countless historical sites and structures, but also share some of the great stories of people and communities that have made a difference here over the last thee centuries. Each walk can be easily completed in an hour or two and are highly recommended. For maps and details, an app and more, check out the website at www.culturaltourismdc.org.

Downtown Bethesda, MD

Downtown Bethesda offers enjoyable rambling, easily accessed from the Bethesda Metro Station or CAPITAL CRESCENT TRAIL. Shops and eateries abound throughout. Exit the Metro station to the west side of Wisconsin Ave, walk around a cascading water feature and left past the big yellow sculpture to a circular fountain beyond. The plaza narrows, but amble ahead and left to pass

another waterfall, before descending a herd of short stairways to Montgomery Lane. Turn right, then turn left at the traffic light (Woodmont Ave).

In two short blocks, go right on Elm St. Just before reaching the next corner (a long block), notice an inviting pedestrian thoroughfare to the left called Bethesda Lane. Head there next by first crossing at the crosswalk just ahead. (Caroline Freeland Park is across the street in case you need a shady break or play area for the kids; the Bethesda Library is next door.) Walk through the archways of Bethesda Lane to Bethesda Ave and turn left.

Near Woodmont Ave, notice the CAPITAL CRESCENT TRAIL (CCT) on the right. Aim for it (optional, keep reading). Follow the paved path 100 yards to a wide, curvy walkway on the left. (A few yards beyond is a sitting area with an information sign and map of the CCT.) Take the curvy walkway to Woodmont Ave. Turn left to find Bethesda Ave (again) at the next corner; turn right. Or skip this loop-de-loop and just head east to Wisconsin Ave. The Bethesda Metro Station is three blocks to the left. For extra credit, you could cross Wisconsin Ave to Willow Ln or Elm St which both lead one block to Elm Street Park for some more shady lazin'.

Downtown Silver Spring, MD

Silver Spring's contemporary downtown is worth a spin around the block, or several, really. A classy old theater, a plaza that converts to a winter ice rink, tons of shops and eateries and interesting urban design are entertaining enough for casual footsters.

From the Silver Spring Metro Station, one idea for a one-mile loop is to exit the station to Colesville Rd and squiggle right and up the grassy hill to Wayne Ave. Cross to the north side to follow the GREEN TRAIL east to Georgia Ave. Walk a few steps north on Georgia to Ellsworth Dr; turn right. Then go left on Fenton St and left on Colesville, Silver Spring's main drag, to return to the Metro station. For a longer hike that ends downtown, see SLIGO CREEK (*p. 180*). Or find Rock Creek Park's trails a mile to the west (carry a map).

- - - - - - - - - - - - - - - - - -

More D.C. Sights on Foot

Here's another handful of major D.C. sights to visit on foot, though they're more like saunters than jaunts.

U.S. Marines/Iwo Jima Memorial & Netherlands Carillon

North of **Arlington National Cemetery** near Rosslyn is the larger-than-life sculpture of U.S. Marines raising the American flag at **Iwo Jima** near the end of WWII, based on the famous photo from that event. Perhaps the best way to reach it on foot is via the Arlington Cemetery Metro Station. Walk west on Memorial Ave and north on Schley Dr to **Custis Walk**, which crosses the road a little right of the **Memorial to Women in Military Service** (1997).

Where you leave the Cemetery grounds, notice a paved bike path on the right—it will take you the half-mile back to the Metro if the Cemetery is closed when you return. Walk to the towering **Carillon** donated to the U.S. by The

Netherlands in 1954. The bells toll at noon and 6:00 pm daily. Follow the path north and stay right at the fork for Iwo Jima (a mile from the Metro station).

Arlington National Cemetery

This renowned resting place for American veterans and leaders, dating back to the Civil War, is a humbling place to explore—a stunning reality check on the real cost of war. For additional background on the **Arlington National Cemetery** (1864), see the RIVER LOOP on p. 105, or visit www.arlingtoncemetery.mil for details on where and when to go and what to see (*open 8:00am-7:00pm, 5:00pm October-March*).

You can get there easily from the Arlington Cemetery Metro Station (*the station closes at 10:00 pm April-September, 7:00 pm October-March*). Or walk across **Memorial Bridge** from Lincoln Memorial and the Mall, a 20-minute hike.

If you need a tip for a good walking tour of the Cemetery, follow the winding path away from the **visitor center** (pick up a map there) to Roosevelt Dr. Follow it up the hill to the **Tomb of the Unknown Soldier** (1921) and **Memorial Amphitheater** (1920). At the Tomb, pause to observe the frequent *Changing of the Guard*. Stroll to several memorials close by, then pick up the **Crook Walk** just north of the Amphitheater. It leads down then up many steps to **Arlington House** (1803) and an excellent view of Washington, D.C. The **Kennedy Gravesite** is just below, but you'll need to make a wide turn on roads to reach the access point (well signed). Then follow **Custis Walk** to Schley Dr and turn right to return to the visitor center. Or continue north on the Custis Walk to visit the U.S. Marines/Iwo Jima Memorial (*above*).

9/11 Pentagon Memorial & Air Force Memorial

This humbling reminder of the tragic events of September 11, 2001, is best reached from the Pentagon Metro Station, less than a half-mile away. As you exit the station, conspicuous signs point the way. Sidewalks lead around the south side of the **Pentagon**, passing between parking lots and entering the **9/11 Memorial** on the southwest side. To make sense of it all, look for a sign noting a phone number you can dial for a recorded audio tour. The Air Force Memorial, described below, is close by. Pentagon tours are available, but must be reserved in advance.

The sky-high **Air Force Memorial** (2006) is a 15-minute walk from the 9/11 Pentagon Memorial and definitely worth a visit. As you exit the Pentagon Memorial, turn right at the corner and walk through the underpass just ahead. Stay on the sidewalk to a traffic light. Cross here and continue leftward and upward along Columbia Pike, below the grassy hill, to a hidden entrance gate left (south) of the memorial.

The shining, curved blades reach 270

feet in height— far more impressive than one might imagine from afar.

Air Force Memorial.

Cedar Hill & Smithsonian Anacostia Community Museum

Cedar Hill and the Anacostia Museum are both worthy of a visit, and though doable on foot, going by car or bus isn't such a bad idea, at least for now. Trails and connectivity across the river are improving (*see the RIVERWALK on p. 148*), and an old bridge across the river at 11th St is about to be converted to a major over-water park, perhaps opening by 2019. All of this should improve the Anacostia trekking experience considerably. After a period of economic stress, those investments, plus a rich history and growing arts focus foretell better days ahead for this 160-year-old D.C. community.

Cedar Hill is where statesman and former slave Frederick Douglass spent the waning years of his life. Scheduled tours of the house are available, along with a small visitor center and short film about this remarkable man. Either drive there (recommended) or bike, bus or walk the 0.7 mile from the Anacostia Metro Station (*details and directions*: www.nps.gov/frdo).

The **Smithsonian Anacostia Community Museum** is a crossroads of art, history and culture established a half-century ago. Exhibits and collections reflect diverse American stories of urban living, with an emphasis on communities "east of the river." View a broad assortment of artwork, crafts, artifacts, documents and films (*10:00-5:00*). The research library contains hundreds of local books and tens of thousands of photographs, plus free Wi-Fi. Artists, speakers and performers often make free public appearances (event

OTHER WALKS & HIKES

schedule at www.anacostia.si.edu).

From the Anacostia Metro Station it's a quick bus ride (recommended), or a hilly, not-too-interesting 1.3-mile walk (or pedal). A free shuttle from the Mall runs on summer weekends. The FORT CIRCLE TRAIL is also close by (*see p. 185*).

National Cathedral & Bishop's Garden

This impressive, dare we say, monumental D.C. landmark, at 301 feet tall, is visible from many areas of the city.

The world's sixth largest **cathedral** is really something to marvel at up close. Completed in 1990, the English-inspired Gothic structure took 83 years to construct. An earthquake in August 2011 busted things up a little and repairs were still underway in 2016.

For a look inside America's best known cathedral, you could attend mass (Episcopalian) or spring for a guided tour for a modest fee, including a view from the heights (*10:00am or later*). Or amble around the inspired **Bishop's Garden** across the drive to the south (via the stone archway opposite the cathedral).

The nearest Metro station is at Tenleytown. Snag a bus or walk south on Wisconsin Ave. 1.3 miles to Woodley Rd. Or from Georgetown, head north on Wisconsin Ave to just beyond Cathedral Ave (under two miles). A parking garage is also available. For a more interesting trek, hike through the Tregaron Estate from the Cleveland Park Metro Station, then from the north gate go west on Macomb (*see p. 183*). Turn left on 34th St, right on Lowell St and left on 36th St. The cathedral looms—you can't miss it.

Basilica of Immaculate Conception

Many may not realize it, but this enormous **Catholic basilica** ranks among the largest churches in the world, with 70 chapels,

great arched halls and a sublime crypt, all fantastically finished in a multitude of colored tiles, stonework, glass and voluminous artwork—enough to rattle even the most ardent agnostic. The basilica (1961) and adjacent campus of **Catholic University** are easily reached from the Brookland Metro Station. Exit to the wide path curving up the hill above a lawn area. Jog right at the street, then take the next left and follow this up the hill through campus to the obvious domed basilica and 329-foot high tower. (*Open 7:00am-7:00pm daily, 6:00pm November-March; tours are available.*)

• •

Beyond the Beltway

▶ **GREAT FALLS**

▶ **ALONG THE POTOMAC RIVER**

▶ **OTHER REGIONAL FAVORITES**

If you're angling to get out of town, there are plenty of good hikes and walks within a one to three-hour drive of the D.C. metro area. A few are highlighted here. But pick up a regional hiking guide at a book store or outdoor shop for the full scoop on most of these and many more. From the mountains to the coast, you'll find ridge rambles to rocky overlooks, treks to scenic waterfalls and wildlife areas, lakeside and seaside walks, and easy strolls among small towns and historic sites.

Some of the best semi-local hikes can be found at Great Falls, along the Potomac River, on Sugarloaf Mountain, Sky Meadows, Bull Run Mountains, Harpers Ferry and Shenandoah National Park, among others. There are a number of regional parks and natural areas with countless miles of trails to trod, including lesser known parks and historic areas managed by the National Park Service.

When hiking in more remote areas, prepare accordingly, be nice to your feet and don't lose the trail. Remember there may be a few venomous snakes around—rattlesnakes and copperheads. Rattlesnakes seem to prefer rocky areas in the mountains, while copperheads are more likely in wooded areas. Though the slithering critters are rarely encountered, it's good practice to stay on the trail and watch where you step or put your hands (*see also p. 154*). Poison ivy (hairy vines and leaves of three) is very common in the forest—another good reason to stick to the trail.

▶ **GREAT FALLS**

While the Potomac's famous falls are, indeed, great and are the main attraction near D.C., the rocky gorge below the falls is also impressive and worth some extra wandering. Expect good trails and multiple overlooks on both the Virginia and Maryland sides of the Potomac. If you had to pick one, the Maryland side may be a slight favorite, since you have to earn the wider view of the falls with a short hike on the boardwalk across **Olmsted Island**. That said, **Great Falls** and **Mather Gorge** are equally stunning from either side.

The Virginia side is officially **Great Falls National Park**, which offers quicker access to view the falls. Expert kayakers occasionally thread their way through the torrent. A good hiking loop leads

south past more overlooks where you might also see rock climbers jamming the cracks below. But take care near the edges (kids especially). You can access this side of Great Falls from Georgetown Pike about 4.3 miles northwest of the Capital Beltway (Exit 44).

The Maryland side is within the **C&O Canal National Historical Park**, where that half-mile stroll on an excellent trail and boardwalk leads to the main viewpoint. (With a setting so dramatic, the Park Service really ought to extend the boardwalk into a loop with some additional vistas.)

The walk south from the **C&O visitor center** along the TOWPATH is also quite scenic (*see p. 182*). One could feasibly bike here from Georgetown via the TOWPATH (15 miles each way). If traveling by car, take MacArthur Blvd and/or Clara Barton Pkwy (they run parallel) 3.9 miles west from the Beltway (Exit 41) and follow the signs.

If a scenic, rocky scramble sounds tantalizing, the BILLY GOAT TRAIL south of the C&O visitor center and Olmsted

Island is a local favorite. Some exposure to heights means it may

Mather Gorge, Great Falls.

Billy Goat Trail near Great Falls, best for experienced hikers (not as hard as it looks).

not be everyone's cup of tea, but most experienced hikers will have no difficulty clambering along. Follow the beaten path and paint marks on the rocks, and turn back if it becomes too much. For details, pick up a regional hiking guide or check at the info desk or the park's websites (www.nps.gov/grfa and www.nps.gov/choh). By all means, stay out of the river, even where it looks calm and inviting—strong currents and undertows have claimed many lives.

▶ ALONG THE POTOMAC RIVER

Parks and preserves along the Potomac River are quite extensive both upstream and downstream of D.C. Below are a few sites that are just a short drive from the city.

Difficult Run

The DIFFICULT RUN TRAIL (not that difficult) is a lengthy trail accounting for 10+ miles of Fairfax County's CROSS COUNTY

TRAIL (40+ miles), which leads across northern Virginia from the Occuquan River to Great Falls (www.fairfaxcounty.gov/parks/cct). The most popular section of DIFFICULT RUN may be the scenic 1.3-mile finish near Great Falls. It's often done as a loop with the RIDGE TRAIL and other connecting routes within the national park.

Most folks start at the Georgetown Pike parking lot on the left just under four miles west of the Beltway. Follow the big creek downstream and under the Pike for great views of slabby cascades and a rocky gorge. At the signed junction for the RIDGE TRAIL, it's definitely worth making the short descent to the wide confluence with the **Potomac River**, before returning to the RIDGE TRAIL for further exploring (carry a trail map). You can also wander upstream from the parking lot for many not-difficult miles of supplemental adventuring.

Scott's Run & Turkey Run

A popular maze of trails (6+ miles) lead through the hilly terrain above **Scott's Run** to the Potomac River and a scenic **waterfall** at the confluence. The POTOMAC HERITAGE TRAIL also passes through the area (*see p. 152*). Trail maps are posted at various locations and at www.fairfaxcounty.gov/parks/scottsrun.

The Scotts Run nature area is on the Virginia side of the river, with two parking lots off Georgetown Pike, just west of the Beltway. Go on a weekday or early on the weekend for less company on the trails. Though rare, a bear was spotted in the park not long ago.

Three miles downriver is **Turkey Run**,

just off the G.W. Pkwy north of Arlington. You'll find short trails, woodsy picnicking and a link down to the POTOMAC HERITAGE TRAIL. (The route to Scott's Run includes a 0.8-mile section of Live Oak Dr.) Or, hike three miles south to **Fort Marcy**, one of the "circle of forts" that safeguarded D.C. during the Civil War. Cannons are perched in a grassy glen and interpretive signs tell the story.

Mount Vernon Estate

George Washington's family estate, **Mount Vernon**, has a long and illustrious history, manifested in well maintained grounds, gardens and historic buildings. The main house has stood since the 1700s. A network of walking paths leads to all the interesting features, so it's easy to knock out a couple of miles of leisurely walking here, albeit for a modest fee. Tours are available and recommended.

The 500-acre estate is located adjacent to the **Potomac River** at the south end of the **G.W. Pkwy** and at **Mile Zero** of the MOUNT VERNON TRAIL (about 15 miles from D.C.). You can drive, bike or bus from the Huntington Metro Station. (*Open daily 9:00-5:00, 4:00 November-March;* www.mountvernon.org).

Pohick Bay & Mason Neck

A few miles south of Mount Vernon are two more sizeable parks with hike-worthy trails, camping, cabins, kayak rentals and the rest. **Pohick Bay Regional**

Park also has a water play area and golf course. **Mason Neck State Park** is a little wilder and adjacent to the **Elizabeth Hartwell Mason Neck National Wildlife Refuge**. Watch for bald eagles. Park details and trail info are easy to find online.

▶ **OTHER REGIONAL FAVORITES**

Across the Mid-Atlantic region are many more parklands, natural areas and historic sites with good trails for rambling. Here are a few more within easy reach of D.C.

Cabin John

On the Maryland side of the river, a nine-mile trail in pleasant forest follows **Cabin John Creek** from MacArthur Blvd near **Glen Echo** to **Cabin John Regional Park** and beyond. This major park has other trails, a nature center and even walk-in campsites. For park access from the I-270 Spur (Exit 1), follow Democracy Blvd west less than a mile to the **Locust Grove Nature Center** parking lot on the right. For a trail map, visit www.montgomeryparks.org/parks-trails/trails.

Rock Creek Regional Park (Rockville, MD)

This isn't the same park as the famous one in D.C., though it is the same creek in a similar landscape good for hiking. It's almost two parks in one, one each at **Frank** and **Needwood Lakes**.

Find picnic and play areas, a nature center and 13 miles of trails, including lake-side loops. The paved, 14.5-mile ROCK CREEK HIKER-BIKER TRAIL now connects all the way to **Rock Creek Park** in D.C., starting at the **visitor center** at the south end of Needwood Lake.

Either bike there from D.C.'s Rock Creek Park, or access one of the park entrances off Avery Rd, one and two miles north of Norbeck Rd, or off Muncaster Mill Rd at the nature center north of Frank Lake. (*See* www.montgomery-parks.org/parks-trails/trails *for maps and details*.) One could feasibly reach the area via paved paths and sidewalks from either the Rockville or Shady Grove Metro Stations (each are two miles from the trail). Montgomery County's Ride On buses will get you there too, but you'll need to sort out the options.

Wheaton Park & Brookside Gardens

Wheaton Regional Park, a few miles north of Silver Spring, has a lot going for it, including the usual amenities for a large park, plus a nature center, horse stables, 11 miles of trails and even a carousel and miniature train ride if your dogs are tired. And there's **Brookside Gardens**, to boot, a 50-acre spread of landscaped walkways, terraces, picturesque ponds, horticultural displays and formal gardens, plus a **conservatory** full of tropical plants. The park and gardens are good for both lazy and ambitious walking. Dogs are okay, but not in the gardens.

Access via Glenallen Ave. a mile east of Georgia Ave and the Glenmont Metro Station. To walk to the park and gardens from the Metro station, exit to the east side of Georgia Ave and go north briefly to Glenallen Ave; turn right. Follow Glenallen via sidewalks and paved path to the gardens entrance at Heurich Rd.

Patuxent Research Refuge

This major wildlife refuge spreads across 20 square miles of diverse habitats supporting dozens of species of mammals, amphibians and reptiles and nearly 250 bird species. The refuge is located midway between Washington and Baltimore, just east of the Baltimore-Washington Pkwy. At least 20 miles of trails and boardwalks access forest, meadows, lakes and wetlands near the **Patuxent and Little Patuxent Rivers**.

A large visitor center is open every day but Thursdays and holidays. A free tram runs seasonally. Hunting occurs in fall and winter, though many trails remain open to hiking. Begin at the **South Tract** (take Exit 22 and drive two miles east on Powder Mill Rd.). For trail maps, directions and details, visit www.fws.gov/refuge/patuxent.

Huntley Meadows

One of the larger wetland conservation areas near D.C. is **Huntley Meadows**, a few miles south of Alexandria. Broad, level trails, boardwalks and a viewing tower bring you up close and personal with a wide variety of birds and other wildlife, including turtles, snakes, rodents, deer, otter and fox. Birders love this place in spring and early summer. A nature center will help you identify what you see, while keeping the kids entertained as well. Easiest access (by car or Fairfax Connector bus from Huntington Metro) is at the corner of Lockheed Blvd and Harrison Ln, west of Richmond Hwy.

Occoquan River

About 20 miles southwest of D.C., near the quaint, historic town of **Occoquan**, is a major corridor of parks and preserves all along the **Occoquan River**. Where it joins the Potomac River, you'll find the **Occoquan Bay National Wildlife Refuge** with miles of walking paths. Above the town are 20 miles of river, reservoir and woodlands spread among several regional parks (**Sandy Run, Fountainhead, Hemlock Overlook and Bull Run**). Hiking and mountain biking trails abound, including the 17-mile BULL RUN OCCOQUAN TRAIL and the 40+ mile CROSS COUNTY TRAIL running north to Great Falls. Maybe try the Fountainhead or Bull Run parks to get acquainted with the area. Access is from north side of the river (*for details, see* www.novaparks.com).

Bull Run Mountains & Sky Meadows

For high-quality mountain hiking less than an hour's drive from D.C., the **Bull Run Mountans Conservancy** protects a 2,500-acre forest with great trails, a rocky high point and pre-Civil War ruins, including

the **Chapman's Gristmill** and cemetery. From I-66 Exit 40, head briefly south then west on the John Marshall Hwy 2.7 miles; turn right, then make a quick left. (*Info:* www.brmconservancy.org.)

About 20 miles farther west (off Hwy 17) is historic Sky Meadows State Park, with high rolling hills, 20+ miles of trails and some of the best views near D.C.

Meadowlark Botanical Gardens

For a pleasant stroll among ornamental and native gardens and ponds, **Meadowlark**'s 95 acres and several miles of paths might be calling. Begin at the **visitor center** off Beulah Rd, south of the Dulles Access Rd and a few miles west of Tysons Corner. Plan on spending at least a couple of hours here. (*Open 10:00am daily, except some major holidays, till 7:00-8:00pm April-September, earlier October- March. Nominal fee. Info*: www.novaparks.com.)

Sugarloaf Mountain

Sugarloaf is the nearest actual mountain to D.C. You'll find a scenic, one-lane mountain loop road and about 15 miles of hiking trails traversing 3,000 acres of privately protected forest land open to the public (donations welcome). The trail network connects picnic areas to rocky overlooks and impressive views from the 1,282-foot summit. Drive there via Comus Rd, west off I-270 about 20 miles north of the Beltway. Open 8:00am daily.

OTHER WALKS & HIKES

197

Shenandoah National Park

This iconic, Mid-Atlantic park, 70 miles from D.C. and 100 miles long, boasts more than 500 miles of trails. Spring brings wildflowers, birds, waterfalls and less crowded trails. Summer offers a welcome reprieve from the lowland heat and humidity, but more traffic and fuller campgrounds on the weekend. Fall means color, milder days and cool nights around the campfire. Winter can get cold and snowy, with frozen waterfalls and lonely trails. Parts of Skyline Dr close in winter. Check the visitor centers and park website at www.nps.gov/shen for park info and current conditions.

Harpers Ferry

Wander this beautiful, historic town at the confluence of the Shenandoah and Potomac Rivers while you eat ice cream or visualize John Brown's War. You can also float the river or take a hike nearby. The C&O CANAL TOWPATH passes through here, as does the APPALACHIAN TRAIL, where you can ponder a 1,000+ mile jaunt to Georgia or Maine. For something a little less ambitious, the view of town from Maryland Heights is worth the steep trudge (4 miles round trip). Or settle for a stroll to Jefferson Rock or across the old railroad bridge. Harpers Ferry is about 65 miles northwest of D.C.

ONLINE RESOURCES

▶ **PARKS & TRAILS INFO**

Federal
National Park Service, National Capital Region (*many sites*): **www.nps.gov/ncro**
National Mall: **www.nps.gov/nama**, **www.nps.gov/nationalmallplan**
Rock Creek Park: **www.nps.gov/rocr**
Great Falls Park: **www.nps.gov/grfa**
C&O Canal National Historical Park: **www.nps.gov/choh**
Potomac Heritage Trail: **www.nps.gov/pohe**
Shenandoah National Park: **www.nps.gov/shen**

Local & Regional
Washington D.C. trails/bikeways info & maps: **www.ddot.dc.gov/trails**
Northern Virginia park & trail info: **www.novaparks.com**
Arlington park & trail info: **parks.arlingtonva.us/off-street-trails**
Arlington Walks (brochure with maps): **www.walkarlington.com**
Alexandria park & trail info: **www.alexandriava.gov/parks**
Fairfax County park & trail info: **www.fairfaxcounty.gov/parks**
Prince George's County park & trail info: **www.pgparks.com/your_parks/trails**
Montgomery County park & trail info: **www.montgomeryparks.org/parks-trails/trails**
Capital Crescent Trail: **www.cctrail.org**

▶ MONUMENTS, MEMORIALS & FEDERAL BUILDINGS

Washington Monument: www.nps.gov/wamo
Lincoln/Jefferson Memorials: www.nps.gov/linc, www.nps.gov/thje
Martin Luther King, Jr. Memorial: www.nps.gov/mlkm
U.S. Capitol tours & info: www.visitthecapitol.gov, www.aoc.gov
White House tours & info: www.nps.gov/whho, www.whitehousehistory.org
National Archives: www.archives.gov/museum
U.S. Supreme Court tours & info: www.supremecourt.gov
Library of Congress tours & info: www.loc.gov/visit
Arlington National Cemetery: www.arlingtoncemetery.mil
Belmont-Paul Women's Equality National Monument: www.nps.gov/bepa

▶ MUSEUMS, GALLERIES & GARDENS

Smithsonian Institution (museums, galleries & National Zoo): www.si.edu
National Gallery of Art & Sculpture Garden: www.nga.gov
National Building Museum: www.nbm.org
U.S. Botanic Garden: www.usbg.gov
National Arboretum: www.usna.usda.gov

▶ GENERAL TRAVEL INFO

Washington D.C. Metro - Metrorail (subway) & Metrobus: www.wmata.com
D.C. Circulator: www.dccirculator.com
Capital Bikeshare: www.capitalbikeshare.com
Foot ferry/water taxi (Mar-Dec): www.potomacriverboatco.com,
   www.dc-watertaxi.com, www.capitolrivercruises.com
Destination D.C.: www.washington.org
*Search online for guided tours on foot or by bike, Segway, amphibious "Duck," or
   hop-on/hop-off bus—all great ways to get introduced to the city.*

▶ HIKING & VOLUNTEER GROUPS

Potomac Appalachian Trail Club: patc.net
Sierra Club/D.C. & Potomac Region: www.dc.sierraclub.org
Capital Hiking Club: www.capitalhikingclub.org
Wanderbirds Hiking Club: www.wanderbirds.org
American Volkssport Association: www.ava.org
Rock Creek Conservancy: www.rockcreekconservancy.org
Many park agencies & conservation groups also support volunteer programs

▶ MISCELLANEOUS

NPS Cherry Blossoms/Bloom Watch: www.nps.gov/cherry
Kennedy Center & Millennium Stage: www.kennedy-center.org
Historical Society of Washington D.C.: www.dchistory.org
Cultural Tourism D.C. & Neighborhood Heritage Trails - www.culturaltourismdc.org
D.C. Metropolitan Police: www.mpdc.dc.gov
Trust for the National Mall: www.nationalmall.org
National Mall Coalition: www.nationalmallcoalition.org
Mount Vernon Estate: www.mountvernon.org
George Washington Masonic National Memorial: www.gwmemorial.org

RESOURCES & MISC.

INDEX

ABOUT THE AUTHOR

When he's not kicking up dust in the mountains or visiting a national park, or some hidden gem or quaint little town somewhere, Ken Wilcox loves hoofing it around Washington D.C. and the greater metro area. This guide is a result of many hundreds of miles of traipsing around this glorious capital city, collecting notes and photos over a two-year period.

Ken has worked as an outdoor recreation planner for many years, nationally and locally (in the Pacific Northwest), and maintains a specialty in trail planning and design. He is the author of three guidebooks to trails in Washington State. Since 2011, Ken, Kris and cat-child Fuji have enjoyed dipping their toes in both oceans (and both Washingtons) and hope to keep it up for some time to come.

RESOURCES & MISC.

D.C. BUCKET LIST

A NATIONAL JAUNT encounters all of the following sites, more or less in the order listed on these two pages. To keep track of your progress, you could check the boxes as you complete each section or loop. (Sites visited on other walks follows.)

A NATIONAL JAUNT

☐ U.S. Navy Memorial
☐ Naval Heritage Center
☐ National Archives
☐ FBI
☐ Old Post Office
☐ Federal Triangle
☐ Environmental Protection Agency
☐ Woodrow Wilson Plaza
☐ Freedom Plaza
☐ General Pulaski Monument
☐ Pershing Park
☐ General Pershing statue
☐ Bald Eagle Memorial
☐ White House Visitor Center
☐ William T. Sherman Monument
☐ U.S. Treasury
☐ Alexander Hamilton statue
☐ The Extra Mile
☐ Marquis de Lafayette statue
☐ White House–North Portico
☐ Lafayette Square
☐ President Andrew Jackson Memorial
☐ St. John's Episcopal Church
☐ General Von Steuben statue
☐ Decatur House
☐ General Jean de Rochambeau statue
☐ Blair House
☐ Renwick Gallery
☐ Eisenhower Executive Office Bldg
☐ Corcoran School of the Arts
☐ First Division Monument
☐ President's Park

☐ White House–South Lawn
☐ National Christmas Tree
☐ Zero Milestone
☐ The Ellipse
☐ Ellipse Visitor Pavilion
☐ Boy Scout Memorial
☐ Enid Haupt Fountains
☐ German-American Friendship Garden
☐ Second Division Memorial
☐ Lockkeeper's House
☐ Organization of American States
☐ Daughters of American Revolution
☐ American Red Cross
☐ Amerigo Vespucci sculpture
☐ U.S. Department of Interior Museum
☐ Art Museum of the Americas
☐ Simón Bolívar Monument
☐ José Artigas statue
☐ Constitution Gardens
☐ Memorial to the Signers of the Declaration of Independence
☐ Vietnam Veterans Memorial
☐ Lincoln Memorial & Reflecting Pool
☐ Korean War Veterans Memorial
☐ John Ericsson Memorial
☐ West Potomac Park
☐ U.S. Park Police Horse Stables
☐ Ash Woods
☐ District of Columbia War Memorial
☐ Martin Luther King, Jr. Memorial
☐ Franklin Delano Roosevelt Memorial
☐ George Mason Memorial
☐ Jefferson Memorial

204

- ☐ Tidal Basin
- ☐ Bureau of Engraving & Printing
- ☐ U.S. Holocaust Museum
- ☐ Floral Library
- ☐ Survey Lodge
- ☐ John Paul Jones Memorial
- ☐ WWII Memorial
- ☐ Sylvan Theater
- ☐ Washington Monument
- ☐ Museum of African American History & Culture
- ☐ Museum of American History
- ☐ U.S. Department of Agriculture
- ☐ Freer Gallery of Art
- ☐ S. Dillon Ripley Center
- ☐ Arthur M. Sackler Gallery
- ☐ Enid A. Haupt Garden
- ☐ Smithsonian Castle
- ☐ Smithsonian Arts & Industries Bldg
- ☐ Voyage Model Solar System
- ☐ Smithsonian Carousel
- ☐ Mary Livingston Ripley Garden
- ☐ Hirshhorn Museum
- ☐ Hirshhorn Sculpture Garden
- ☐ National Air & Space Museum
- ☐ Phoebe Waterman Haas Public Observatory
- ☐ National Museum of American Indian
- ☐ Capitol Reflecting Pool
- ☐ Mid-Atlantic Regional Garden
- ☐ U.S. Botanic Garden & Conservatory
- ☐ Bartholdi Park & Fountain
- ☐ James Garfield Memorial
- ☐ Ulysses S. Grant Memorial
- ☐ Peace Monument
- ☐ Summerhouse
- ☐ U.S. Capitol–West Lawn & West Steps
- ☐ U.S. Capitol–East Plaza
- ☐ Capitol Visitor Center
- ☐ U.S. Supreme Court
- ☐ Court of Neptune Fountain
- ☐ Library of Congress
- ☐ Folger Shakespeare Theatre & Library
- ☐ Belmont-Paul Women's Equality National Monument
- ☐ VFW
- ☐ Stanton Park
- ☐ General Nathanael Greene Statue
- ☐ Federal Judicial Center
- ☐ Union Station
- ☐ Postal Museum
- ☐ National Guard Memorial Museum
- ☐ Holodomor Memorial
- ☐ Freedom Bell
- ☐ Christopher Columbus Fountain
- ☐ Senate Park & Fountain
- ☐ Japanese-American Memorial
- ☐ Robert A. Taft Memorial & Carillon
- ☐ U.S Department of Labor
- ☐ William Blackstone Statue
- ☐ General George Meade Monument
- ☐ John Marshall Park
- ☐ Canadian Embassy
- ☐ Newseum
- ☐ Andrew W. Mellon Memorial Fountain
- ☐ Federal Trade Commission
- ☐ National Gallery of Art East
- ☐ National Gallery of Art West
- ☐ Sculpture Garden & Ice Rink
- ☐ Smithsonian Museum of Natural History
- ☐ Grand Army of the Republic Memorial
- ☐ Temperance Fountain
- ☐ General Winfield Scott Hancock Memorial

D.C. BUCKET LIST (CONT.)—OTHER WALKS & HIKES

- ☐ Memorial Bridge
- ☐ Arlington National Cemetery
- ☐ Theodore Roosevelt Memorial
- ☐ Key Bridge
- ☐ Francis Scott Key Park
- ☐ Old Stone House
- ☐ C&O Canal & Towpath
- ☐ Justice William O. Douglas bust
- ☐ Georgetown Waterfront Park
- ☐ Kennedy Center
- ☐ Peter's Point
- ☐ Car Barn
- ☐ Exorcist Stairs
- ☐ Georgetown University
- ☐ Volta Laboratory
- ☐ Volta Park
- ☐ Book Hill
- ☐ Georgetown Library
- ☐ Duke Ellington School of the Arts
- ☐ Dumbarton Oaks Park
- ☐ Montrose Park
- ☐ Dumbarton Oaks Garden & Museum
- ☐ Oak Hill Cemetery
- ☐ Evermay
- ☐ Dumbarton House
- ☐ Rose Park
- ☐ Dupont Circle
- ☐ Gandhi statue
- ☐ Anderson House
- ☐ Cosmos Club
- ☐ General Philip Sheridan Memorial
- ☐ Dumbarton Bridge
- ☐ Winston Churchill statue
- ☐ Nelson Mandela statue
- ☐ Woodrow Wilson House
- ☐ Mitchell Park
- ☐ Spanish Steps
- ☐ Phillips Collection Gallery

- ☐ Duke Ellington Memorial Bridge
- ☐ National Zoo & Olmsted Walk
- ☐ Peirce Mill
- ☐ Boulder Bridge
- ☐ Rock Creek Nature Center
- ☐ Miller Cabin
- ☐ Milkhouse Ford
- ☐ Fort DeRussy
- ☐ Rabaut Park
- ☐ Meridian Hill/Malcolm X Park
- ☐ Joan of Arc statue
- ☐ Dante statue
- ☐ James Buchanan statue
- ☐ African American Civil War Memorial & Museum
- ☐ House of the Temple
- ☐ Friendship Archway
- ☐ Mount Vernon Square
- ☐ Carnegie Library
- ☐ Kiplinger Gallery
- ☐ Samuel Gompers Memorial Park
- ☐ Mary McLeod Bethune Museum
- ☐ General George Henry Thomas statue
- ☐ Samuel Hahnemann Monument
- ☐ General Winfield Scott Memorial
- ☐ Daniel Webster statue
- ☐ John Witherspoon statue
- ☐ Abraham Lincoln Statue
- ☐ Darlington Memorial
- ☐ National Law Enforcement Officers Memorial
- ☐ National Building Museum
- ☐ German-American Heritage Museum
- ☐ Pepco Edison Place Gallery
- ☐ Smithsonian American Art Museum & National Portrait Gallery
- ☐ Martin Luther King, Jr. Memorial Library
- ☐ St. Patrick's Church
- ☐ Ford's Theater

- ☐ Petersen House
- ☐ Seward Square
- ☐ Marion Park
- ☐ John Phillip Sousa home
- ☐ Marine Barracks
- ☐ Barracks Row
- ☐ Market Park
- ☐ Eastern Market
- ☐ Abraham Lincoln Emancipation Memorial
- ☐ Mary McLeod Bethune Memorial
- ☐ Yards Park
- ☐ National Museum of the U.S. Navy
- ☐ Nationals Stadium
- ☐ Fort McNair
- ☐ Titanic Memorial
- ☐ Maine Avenue Fish Market
- ☐ Kenilworth Aquatic Gardens
- ☐ Bladensburg Waterfront Park
- ☐ Windy Run Falls
- ☐ Thrifton Hills Park
- ☐ Potomac Overlook Park/Nature Center
- ☐ Gulf Branch Park & Nature Center
- ☐ Chain Bridge
- ☐ Fort Marcy
- ☐ The Ellipse (Ballston)
- ☐ Welburn Square
- ☐ Bluemont Park
- ☐ Glencarlyn Park
- ☐ Lubber Run Amphitheater
- ☐ John Carlyle Square (Alexandria)
- ☐ U.S. Patent & Trade Office
- ☐ National Inventors Hall of Fame
- ☐ African American Heritage Park
- ☐ Alexandria National Cemetery
- ☐ Shiloh Baptist Church
- ☐ Freedom House Museum
- ☐ Friendship Firehouse
- ☐ King Street
- ☐ Washington Masonic Memorial

- ☐ D.C. boundary markers
- ☐ Torpedo Factory
- ☐ Alexandria Seaport Foundation
- ☐ Founders Park
- ☐ Carlyle House & Garden
- ☐ Wise Tavern
- ☐ Alexandria City Hall
- ☐ Gadsby's Tavern
- ☐ Market Square
- ☐ Ramsay House
- ☐ Stabler-Leadbeater Apothecary Museum
- ☐ Appomattox statue
- ☐ Lyceum & Alexandria History Museum
- ☐ Athenaeum
- ☐ Captains Row
- ☐ Waterfront Park
- ☐ Lady Bird Johnson Park
- ☐ Merchant Marine Memorial
- ☐ Lyndon Johnson Memorial
- ☐ Gravelly Point Park
- ☐ Abingdon Plantation
- ☐ Dangerfield Island
- ☐ Tidelock Park
- ☐ Rivergate Park
- ☐ Orinoco Bay Park
- ☐ Shipyard Park
- ☐ Fords Landing
- ☐ Jones Point Park & Lighthouse
- ☐ Woodrow Wilson Bridge
- ☐ Belle Haven Marina
- ☐ Dyke Marsh
- ☐ U.S. Marines/Iwo Jima Memorial
- ☐ 9/11 Pentagon Memorial
- ☐ Air Force Memorial
- ☐ National Arbortetum
- ☐ Cedar Hill
- ☐ Anacostia Community Museum
- ☐ National Cathedral & Bishops Garden
- ☐ Basilica of Immaculate Conception